Nomadland

Nomadland

SURVIVING AMERICA IN THE
TWENTY-FIRST CENTURY

JESSICA BRUDER

Swift

SWIFT PRESS

First published in the United States of America
by W. W. Norton & Company 2017

First published in Great Britain by Swift Press 2021

3 5 7 9 10 8 6 4 2

Copyright © Jessica Bruder 2017

Jessica Bruder has asserted her right under the Copyright, Designs and
Patents Act 1988 to be identified as author of this work

Offset by Tetragon, London
Printed in England by CPI Group (UK) Ltd, Croydon, CRO 4YY

A CIP catalogue record for this book is available from the British Library

ISBN: 978-1-80075-030-2
eISBN: 978-1-80075-031-9

Photographs by Jessica Bruder
Photograph page 34 courtesy of Linda May

For Dale

"There's a crack in everything. That's how the light gets in."

—LEONARD COHEN

"The capitalists don't want anyone living off their economic grid."

—ANONYMOUS COMMENTER,
AZDAILYSUN.COM

CONTENTS

Part Three

FOREWORD

AS I WRITE THIS, they are scattered across the country—

In Drayton, North Dakota, a former San Francisco cabdriver, sixty-seven, labors at the annual sugar beet harvest. He works from sunrise until after sunset in temperatures that dip below freezing, helping trucks that roll in from the fields disgorge multi-ton loads of beets. At night he sleeps in the van that has been his home ever since Uber squeezed him out of the taxi industry and making the rent became impossible.

In Campbellsville, Kentucky, a sixty-six-year-old ex–general contractor stows merchandise during the overnight shift at an Amazon warehouse, pushing a wheeled cart for miles along the concrete floor. It's mind-numbing work and she struggles to scan each item accurately, hoping to avoid getting fired. In the morning she returns to her tiny trailer, moored at one of several mobile home parks that contract with Amazon to put up nomadic workers like her.

In New Bern, North Carolina, a woman whose home is a teardrop-style trailer—so small it can be pulled with a motorcycle—is couch-surfing with a friend while hunting for work. Even with a master's degree, the thirty-eight-year-old Nebraska native can't find a job despite filling out hundreds of applications in the past month alone. She knows the sugar beet harvest is hiring, but traveling halfway across the country would require more cash than she has. Losing her job at a non-profit several years ago is one of the reasons she moved into the trailer in the first place. After the funding for her position ran out, she couldn't afford rent on top of paying off student loans.

In San Marcos, California, a thirtysomething couple in a 1975 GMC motorhome is running a roadside pumpkin stand with a children's carnival and petting zoo, which they had five days to set up from scratch on a vacant dirt lot. In a few weeks they'll switch to selling Christmas trees.

In Colorado Springs, Colorado, a seventy-two-year-old vandweller who cracked three ribs doing a campground maintenance job is recuperating while visiting with family.

––––––––––

THERE HAVE ALWAYS BEEN ITINERANTS, drifters, hobos, restless souls. But now, in the third millennium, a new kind of wandering tribe is emerging. People who never imagined being nomads are hitting the road. They're giving up traditional houses and apartments to live in what some call "wheel estate"—vans, secondhand RVs, school buses, pickup campers, travel trailers, and plain old sedans. They are driving away from the impossible choices that face what used to be the middle class. Decisions like:

Would you rather have food or dental work? Pay your mortgage or your electric bill? Make a car payment or buy medicine? Cover rent or student loans? Purchase warm clothes or gas for your commute?

For many the answer seemed radical at first.

You can't give yourself a raise, but what about cutting your biggest expense? Trading a stick-and-brick domicile for life on wheels?

Some call them "homeless." The new nomads reject that label. Equipped with both shelter and transportation, they've adopted a different word. They refer to themselves, quite simply, as "houseless."

From a distance, many of them could be mistaken for carefree retired RVers. On occasions when they treat themselves to a movie or dinner at a restaurant, they blend with the crowd. In mind-set and appearance, they are largely middle class. They wash their clothes at Laundromats and join fitness clubs to use the showers. Many took to the road after their savings were obliterated by the Great Recession. To keep their gas tanks and bellies full, they work long hours at hard, physical jobs. In a time of flat wages and rising housing costs, they have unshackled themselves from rent and mortgages as a way to get by. They are surviving America.

But for them—as for anyone—survival isn't enough. So what began as a last-ditch effort has become a battle cry for something greater. Being human means yearning for more than subsistence. As much as food or shelter, we require hope.

And there is hope on the road. It's a by-product of forward momentum. A sense of opportunity, as wide as the country itself. A bone-deep conviction that something better will come. It's just ahead, in the next town, the next gig, the next chance encounter with a stranger.

As it happens, some of those strangers are nomads, too. When they meet—online, or at a job, or camping way off the grid—tribes begin to form. There's a common understanding, a kinship. When someone's van breaks down, they pass the hat. There's a contagious feeling: Something big is happening. The country is changing rapidly, the old structures crumbling away, and they're at the epicenter of something new. Around a shared campfire, in the middle of the night, it can feel like a glimpse of utopia.

As I write, it is autumn. Soon winter will come. Routine layoffs will start at the seasonal jobs. The nomads will pack up camp and return to their real home—the road—moving like blood cells through the veins of the country. They'll set out in search of friends and family, or just a place that's warm. Some will journey clear across the continent. All will count the miles, which unspool like a filmstrip of America. Fast-food joints and shopping malls. Fields dormant under frost. Auto dealerships, megachurches, and all-night diners. Featureless plains. Feedlots, dead factories, subdivisions, and big-box stores. Snowcapped peaks. The roadside reels past, through the day and into darkness, until fatigue sets in. Bleary-eyed, they find places to pull off the road and rest. In Walmart parking lots. On quiet suburban streets. At truck stops, amid the lullaby of idling engines. Then in the early morning hours—before anyone notices—they're back on the highway. Driving on, they're secure in this knowledge:

The last free place in America is a parking spot.

Part One

CHAPTER ONE

The Squeeze Inn

ON THE FOOTHILL FREEWAY, about an hour inland from Los Angeles, a mountain range looms ahead of northbound traffic, bringing suburbia to a sudden stop. This wilderness is the southern edge of the San Bernardino Mountains, a "tall, precipitous escarpment" in the words of the United States Geological Survey. It's part of a formation that began growing eleven million years ago along the San Andreas Fault and is still rising today, gaining a few millimeters each year as the Pacific and North American plates grind past each other. The peaks appear to grow much faster, however, when you're driving straight at them. They're the kind of sight that makes you sit up straighter and starts a swelling sensation in your chest, a feeling like helium crowding your ribcage, enough perhaps to carry you away.

Linda May grips her steering wheel and watches the approaching mountains through bifocals with rose-colored frames. Her silver hair, which falls past her shoulders, is pulled back from her face in a plastic barrette. She turns off the Foothill Freeway onto Highway 330, also known as City Creek Road. For a couple miles the pavement runs flat and wide. Then it tapers to a steep serpentine, with just one lane in either direction, starting the ascent into the San Bernardino National Forest.

The sixty-four-year-old grandmother is driving a Jeep Grand Cherokee Laredo, which was totaled and salvaged before she bought it off a tow lot. The "check engine" light is finicky—it has a habit of flashing on when nothing is actually wrong—and a close look reveals that the white paint on the hood, which was crumpled and replaced, is a half-shade off from the rest of the body. But after months of repairs the vehicle is finally roadworthy. A mechanic installed a new camshaft and lifters. Linda spruced up what she could, scrubbing the foggy headlights with an old T-shirt and insect repellant, a do-it-yourself trick. For the first time the Jeep is towing Linda's home: a tiny, pale yellow trailer she calls "the Squeeze Inn." (If visitors don't get the name on first mention, she puts it in a sentence—"Yeah, there's room, squeeze in!"—and smiles, revealing deep laugh lines.) The trailer is a molded fiberglass relic, a Hunter Compact II, built in 1974 and originally advertised as a "crowning achievement in travel for fun" that would "follow like a kitten on the open road, track like a tiger when the going gets rough." Four decades along, the Squeeze Inn feels like a charmingly retro life-support capsule: a box with rounded edges and sloped sides, geo-metrically reminiscent of the Styrofoam clamshell containers once used at hamburger joints. Inside it measures ten feet from end to end, roughly the same interior length as the covered wagon that car-ried Linda's own great-great-great-grandmother across the country more than a century ago. It has some distinctive 1970s' touches: quilted, cream-colored pleather covering the walls and ceiling, linoleum with a mustard and avocado pattern on the floor. The roof is just high enough for Linda to stand. After buying the trailer at auction for $1,400, she described it on Facebook. "It's 5'3" inside and I am 5'2"," she wrote. "Perfect fit."

Linda is hauling the Squeeze Inn up to Hanna Flat, a camp-ground in the pine forest northwest of Big Bear Lake. It's May and she plans to stay there through September. But unlike the thousands

Linda May with her dog, Coco.

of warm-weather visitors who travel for pleasure each year to the San Bernardino National Forest—a swath of wilderness larger than the state of Rhode Island—Linda is making this journey for work. It's her third summer employed as a campground host: a seasonal gig that's equal parts janitor, cashier, groundskeeper, security guard, and welcoming committee. She's enthusiastic about starting the job and getting the annual raise for returning workers that will bump her hourly wage to $9.35, up 20 cents over the year before. (At the time, California's minimum wage was $9.00 an hour.) And though she and other campground hosts are hired "at will," according to the company's written employment policy—meaning they can be fired "at any time, with or without cause or notice"—she's been told to expect a full forty hours of work each week.

Some first-time campground hosts expect a paid vacation in paradise. It's hard to blame them. Ads for the job are splashed with photos of glittering creeks and wildflower-choked meadows. A brochure for California Land Management, the private concessionaire that is Linda's employer, shows gray-haired women smiling delightedly on a sun-dappled lakeshore, arm in arm, like best friends at summer camp. "Get paid to go camping!" cajoles a recruiting banner for American Land & Leisure, another company that hires camp hosts. Below the headline are testimonials: "Our staff says: 'Retirement has never been this fun!' 'We've developed lifelong friendships,' 'We're healthier than we've been in years.'"

Newbies are known for balking—and sometimes quitting—when faced with the less picturesque parts of the job: babysitting drunk, noisy campers, shoveling heaps of ash and broken glass from the campfire pits (rowdy visitors like dropping bottles into the flames to make them explode), and the thrice-daily ritual of cleaning outhouses. Though tending toilets is most campground hosts' least-favorite chore, Linda is unfazed by it, even takes a little pride in performing the task well. "I want them clean because my campers are using them," she says. "I'm not a germaphobe—you snap on some rubber gloves, and you do it."

As Linda reaches the San Bernardino Mountains, the valley views are sublime but distracting. The roadside is narrow, with barely enough of an edge to call a shoulder. Along some stretches there's nothing but empty air past the ribbon of pavement that clings to the slope. Signposts warn drivers: "Rock Slide Area" and "Avoid Over-heating: Turn Off A/C Next 14 Miles." None of this seems to rattle Linda, though. Her stint as a long-haul trucker nearly two decades ago left her undaunted by difficult roads.

I'm driving a camper van just ahead of Linda. As a journalist, I've been spending time with her, on and off, for a year and a half. Between in-person visits, we've spoken on the phone so many times that, on every call, I anticipate her familiar greeting before she even picks up. It's a melodic "Hell-ooo-ooo," spoken in the same three-note singsong you'd use to say "I see you!" when playing peekaboo with an infant.

I'd originally met Linda while researching a magazine story on a growing subculture of American nomads, folks who live full-time on the road.* Like Linda, many of these wandering souls were trying to escape an economic paradox: the collision of rising rents and flat wages, an unstoppable force meeting an unmovable object. They felt like they were caught in a vise, putting all their time into exhausting, soul-sucking jobs that paid barely enough to cover the rent or a mortgage, with no way to better their lot for the long term and no promise of ever being able to retire.

Those feelings were grounded in hard fact: Wages and housing costs have diverged so dramatically that, for a growing number of Americans, the dream of a middle-class life has gone from difficult to impossible. As I write this, there are only a dozen counties and one metro area in America where a full-time minimum wage worker can afford a one-bedroom apartment at fair market rent. You'd have to make at least $16.35 an hour—more than twice the federal minimum wage—to rent such an apartment without spending more than the recommended 30 percent of income on housing. The consequences are dire, especially for the one in six American households that have been putting more than half of what they make into shelter. For many low-income families, that means little or nothing left over to buy food, medication, and other essentials.

Many of the people I met felt that they'd spent too long losing a rigged game. And so they found a way to hack the system. They gave up traditional "stick-and-brick" homes, breaking the shackles of rent and mortgages. They moved into vans, RVs, and trailers, traveled from place to place following good weather, and kept their gas tanks full by working seasonal jobs. Linda is a member of that tribe. As she migrates around the West, I've been following her.

When the steep climb into the San Bernardino Mountains begins, my giddiness at seeing the peaks from a distance fades. Suddenly I'm anxious. The idea of driving switchbacks in my clunky van

---

* When I first embarked on that story, little did I know it would grow into a larger project, with three years of reporting and hundreds of interviews.

scares me a little. Watching Linda pull the Squeeze Inn in her rattle-trap Jeep scares me a lot. Earlier she instructed me to drive ahead of her. She wanted to be in the rear, following. But why? Did she think her trailer could come unhitched and backslide? I never did find out.

Past the first sign for the San Bernardino National Forest, a shiny oil tanker truck looms up behind the Squeeze Inn. The driver seems impatient, a bit too close as they enter a series of S-curves that obscures Linda from my sight in the rearview mirror. I keep watching for her Jeep. When the road straightens out again, it doesn't emerge. Instead, the tanker reappears on the uphill straightaway. There's no sign of Linda.

Pulling into a turnout, I dial her cell phone and hope for that familiar "Hell-ooo-ooo." The call rings and rings, then goes to voicemail. I park the van, hop out, and pace nervously along the driver's side. I try again. No answer. By now, more cars—maybe half a dozen—have come out of the curves, onto the straightaway, and past the turnout. I try to push down a queasy feeling, adrenaline blooming into panic as the minutes slide past. The Squeeze Inn has disappeared.

FOR MONTHS, LINDA HAD BEEN YEARNING to get back on the road and start her job as a campground host. She'd been marooned in Mission Viejo, fifty miles southeast of Los Angeles, staying at the house rented by her daughter and son-in-law, Audra and Collin, with three of her grandchildren, all teenagers. There weren't enough bedrooms, so her grandson Julian bunked in a door-less dining space off the kitchen. (This setup was more comfortable than the family's last apartment, however, where a walk-in closet had doubled as a bedroom for one of her two granddaughters.)

Linda got what was left: the couch by the front door. It was an island. As much as she adored her family, she still felt stranded there, especially with her Jeep stuck in the repair shop. Whenever members of the household planned an outing that didn't include her, everyone had to walk past Linda's couch on the way to the door. That started getting awkward. Linda worried: Did they feel guilty spending time without her? She also missed her autonomy. "I'd rather be the queen of my own house than live under the queen of somebody else's house, even if it is my daughter," she told me.

At the same time, health problems had left the family stretched thin—emotionally and financially—making it even harder for Linda to lean on them. Her granddaughter Gabbi had been weak and intermittently bedridden for more than three years with a mysteriously malfunctioning nervous system; she later tested positive for Sjogren's syndrome, an autoimmune disease. Julian, her grandson, was managing type 1 diabetes. Her daughter, Audra, had bad arthritis. And if that weren't enough, Collin, the breadwinner, had recently developed severe migraines and vertigo that forced him out of his office job.

At one point, Linda had considered applying for a seasonal position at an Amazon warehouse through CamperForce, a program created by the online retailer to hire itinerant workers. But she had done the same job a year earlier and ended up with a repetitive motion injury from using the handheld barcode scanner. It left behind a visible mark, a grape-sized lump on her right wrist. Even worse was what she could not see: a searing pain that radiated the length of her right arm, from thumb to wrist, through elbow and shoulder, ending in her neck. Lifting an eight-ounce coffee cup or a cooking pan was enough to trigger an agonizing jolt. She believed it to be a bad case of tendonitis, but knowing that hadn't helped abolish the affliction. And without it healed, she couldn't go back.

Broke and confined to her couch-island, Linda tried to focus on her future as the proprietress—and sole occupant—of the Squeeze Inn. Before staying with her family, she'd been traveling from job to job in a twenty-eight-foot 1994 El Dorado motorhome that guzzled gas and was starting to fall apart. So downsizing to a tiny trailer felt good, even if the Squeeze Inn needed some work. The former owners had left it sitting in the salt air of the Oregon coast, where some of the metal parts had started to corrode; an orange rust streak marred the fiberglass hull. Linda began spending her downtime on mobile-home-improvement projects. Her first task was concocting an abrasive cleaner—the secret ingredient was eggshells run through a blender—that she used to remove the rust stain. Another task was creating a cozy bed. The trailer had a small dinette along its rear wall, so Linda removed the table and cut out a cardboard template to fit on top of the benches. When a queen-sized pillow-top mattress that looked brand-new appeared in the neighbors' trash, she scavenged it. Slitting it open, she removed and discarded the springs like a fishmonger deboning a very large catch. Next she pulled out the layers of padding, marked them to fit her template with a Sharpie, and cut away the excess material using a carpet knife. Once she'd pared down the outer fabric to match, she sewed the case back together—trim and all—and re-stuffed it, creating what appeared to be a perfect seventy-two-by-thirty-six-inch mini-mattress. "I didn't think any narrower would be fun to sleep on with my bed buddy here," she told me, gesturing to Coco, her Cavalier King Charles spaniel. "So I made it thirty-six for the both of us."

The day before Linda left for Hanna Flat, I asked whether she was excited. She looked at me as if this was the most obvious thing in the world. "Oh, yeah!" she said. "I've had no car. I've had no money. I've been stuck on that couch." Her $524 monthly Social Security checks would carry her to the first payday of her new job.* Linda was ready to feel her world opening up again after it had shrunk to the size of a sofa. For too long, she'd been without her accustomed freedom, that accelerated rush of newness and possibility that comes with the open road. It was time to go.

The morning of May 6 was mild and overcast. Linda and her family members exchanged hugs good-bye. "Call you when I get there," she promised. She loaded Coco into the Jeep and was off,

---

* In a few weeks Linda would turn sixty-five, bringing her already meager benefit down to $424 after the deduction of Medicare premiums.

heading to an automotive shop where she filled her mismatched tires, which were cracked and balding. The Jeep didn't have a spare. Next up was a Shell station. She topped off the tank and then went inside for a receipt and a couple packs of Marlboro Red 100s. The young clerk nodded when she reminisced about buying gas as a teenager for a quarter a gallon, a far cry from the going rate of $3.79. "You could put a dollar in the tank and drive around all day," she told him, shaking her head and smiling.

It seemed nothing could darken Linda's mood, not even returning to the Jeep to find the doors locked and the keys inside. Coco stood on her hind legs, paws up on the driver's side door, tail wagging. The dog had stepped on the latch, Linda guessed. The window was rolled down a few inches, though. I retrieved a long-handled BBQ lighter from the van, squeezed my hand in the crack and used it to pop the lock. And so the journey continued.

The Squeeze Inn was waiting in storage on the outskirts of Perris, a town on the far side of the Santa Ana Mountains, one of the peninsular ranges that separate California's coastal region from its harsher desert interior. Getting there meant traveling the Ortega Highway. This is one of the most dangerous roads in the state, "a place where urban sprawl, bad driving and obsolete road-building techniques collide head-on," in the words of one *Los Angeles Times* reporter. The winding thoroughfare is often clogged with commuters shuttling between Orange County and the Inland Empire, but at midday, traffic was mercifully light. Before long, Linda was on the other side, driving past some of the half-dozen trailer parks that cling like barnacle colonies to the western edge of Lake Elsinore. Three years ago she'd lived there at the Shore Acres Mobile Home Park, renting a $600-a-month trailer on a cracked asphalt lane that ran from the highway to the waterfront.

At a Target store, Linda bought food to last until her next Social Security check came in a week: a big cardboard canister of Quaker Oats, a dozen and a half eggs, ground beef, bologna, hamburger buns, Goldfish crackers, Nutter Butters, tomatoes, mustard, and a half-gallon of milk. Although her start date for work was still a few days off, she called her soon-to-be boss from the parking lot. Linda wanted him to know she was reliable and took the job seriously. She was on her way, she told him, and planned to arrive at Hanna Flat before dark.

Past a cyclone fence topped with barbed wire and sun-bleached American flags, the Squeeze Inn sat in a storage lot on the north side of Highway 74. Linda drove through the gate. The onsite handyman, a skinny guy named Rudy with a gray Van Dyke–style beard, came out to greet her. They joked around as Linda prepared the trailer, trying to remember everything on her to-do list. "I've got a mind like a steel trap: Nothing gets in, nothing gets out," Rudy quipped. They were still chatting away when she stepped down too fast from the trailer's door, tipping it off balance. The Squeeze Inn seesawed on its single axle. Its rear edge clattered to the ground. "Shouldn't have had that cinnamon roll this morning, huh?" Rudy teased. Linda steadied herself. "That was a rush!" she said. Fortunately nothing had broken, on her or the Squeeze Inn.

Linda tightened a rack on the front of the trailer, which held the pair of twenty-pound propane tanks that fueled her fridge, the stovetop burners, and a small furnace. Finally Rudy helped her hitch the Squeeze Inn to the Jeep. She started the ignition and pulled ahead, tentatively at first. Waving good-bye, she rolled out through the gate. Just like the old advertising brochure promised, the trailer "followed like a kitten."

———

WHEN LINDA DIDN'T REAPPEAR after the first set of turns in the San Bernardino Mountains, my brain shuffled through a deck of possible disasters. Maybe her engine stalled. Maybe she got a flat tire—bad news without a spare—or worse, a blowout. The apprehensions grew darker. What if the Squeeze Inn had disconnected and gone barreling back down the hill? What if a wide turn had sent the Jeep over the roadside, into the canyon, like a remake of that climactic scene from *Thelma & Louise*?

I was starting the van to go back and look for her when the phone rang. "I'll be right there," Linda said. I felt a surge of relief when she appeared at the turnout, but it was short-lived. Linda pulled up and pointed out something odd on her trailer: The propane rack was empty. Both tanks had flown off in the tight turns. One of them, still tethered to its hose, had bounced along after the Squeeze Inn, taking a four-inch bite out of its fiberglass shell. The other had detached completely and rolled across the highway like a combustible tumbleweed. The oil truck, still following close behind, swerved to avoid it and sped past Linda, who was lucky and had found a stretch of road with room to pull over. The runaway tank came to rest on the far side of the highway. Linda sized up her situation—perched on the outer edge of a blind curve, she was invisible to oncoming traffic—and resisted the urge to dart across and retrieve it. "That's a $20 propane tank, and I am a priceless person!" she remembers thinking. She unscrewed the remaining tank from its hose and stashed it in the trailer.

With that near-mishap averted, Linda continued uphill. She drove through the communities of Arrowbear Lake and Running Springs, whose alpine slopes brought skiers and snowboarders during the winter but were now drawing mountain bikers and hikers. She passed the century-old dam at Big Bear Lake, a snow-fed reservoir, and traced its northern shore through bald eagle habitat. Next came Grout Bay and the tiny town of Fawnskin, given its current name by early twentieth century developers who didn't think a place called "Grout" would attract vacationers. There the general store was stocked with everything a wilderness adventurer might need: fishing tackle, beer cozies, toboggans, tire chains, sleeping bags, sun umbrellas, and souvenir shotgun-shaped liquor bottles. ("Tequila shots," the cashier explained.) The nearby town park was full of fiberglass monuments to men in uniform, including a baseball player, an Indian chief, a cowboy, a fireman, a fighter pilot, a pirate, and a highway patrolman. They looked like they might start singing "Y.M.C.A." "All these statues!" Linda exclaimed during a later visit to Fawnskin. "Why aren't there any women?" Then she noticed other sculptures: a pair of oxen hitched to a covered wagon. Those two were probably female, Linda suggested, since they had no discernible genitalia and were the only ones doing any work. From then on, whenever she passed the park, she'd call out to them: "Heeeeeyyy, girls!"

On Rim of the World Drive, Linda cruised past a private estate whose incongruously tidy lawn was visible behind heavy locked gates and "No Trespassing" signs. She slowed the Jeep to a crawl as she turned onto Coxey Truck Trail. Here the asphalt gave way to a washboard dirt track flanked with yellow sprigs of western wallflower poking out between the boulders and manzanita shrubs covered in pink, urn-shaped blossoms. There were also remnants of the 2007 Butler II wildfire: charred tree trunks bristling up from the landscape like giant porcupine quills. That blaze had engulfed more than fourteen thousand acres of forest, including Hanna Flat, which was closed for repairs until 2009. As she neared the campground, Linda kept her speed down and focused on the rough road, dodging deep ruts in the hard-packed dirt. The Squeeze Inn bounced and clattered behind her.

It was around 6 p.m., still light out, when she arrived at the campground entrance. At seven thousand feet above sea level, Hanna Flat was more than a mile higher than Mission Viejo, where her journey had started that morning. The air was colder and thinner. She spied a bulletin board and got out of the Jeep to read it. Notices warned visitors to beware of snakes, to extinguish their campfires ("EVERY SPARK DEAD-OUT"), and to avoid bringing in firewood with invasive stowaways: insects like the gold-spotted oak borer and nefarious pathogens with names like "pitch canker" and "sudden oak death." A large map showed a road looping through eighty-eight numbered campsites that could each be rented for $26 a night. There was also a numberless tract, so close to the entrance that Linda could see it from where she stood. It had a few amenities: a paved parking pad, hookups for water and power, and a picnic area with a table and a campfire ring. Out front, near a rotting stump colonized by fire ants, a sign read "CAMP HOST."

Linda was home for the next four months.

———

APART FROM THE START OF HER JOB, something else had Linda counting the days: A friend was coming to work with her. Silvianne Delmars, sixty, had never been a campground host before, but she was excited to give it a try. "With Linda May at my side, I could face an army!" she'd declared a few months earlier. Silvianne was living in a 1990 Ford E350 Econoline Super Club Wagon, which had been a transit van for the elderly and a work vehicle for convict labor crews before she bought it off Craigslist, complete with leaky head gaskets, bad brakes, cracking power steering hoses, worn-out tires, and a starter that made ominous grinding sounds. Sometimes sunlight raked the passenger side at an angle that revealed the edges of long painted-over letters that spelled "Holbrook Senior Citizens Assoc."

Two of Silvianne's pals had suggested names for the vehicle: "the Queen Mary" and "Esmeralda." Not wanting to pick one over the other, she named it the Queen María Esmeralda. She transformed the interior with jewel-tone scarves, embroidered pillows, Christmas lights, and an altar bearing a Virgin of Guadalupe votive candle and a statuette of Sekhmet, the lion-headed Egyptian goddess. Silvianne had set out in her van following a string of challenges: her car stolen, her wrist broken (no insurance), and a house in New Mexico that she couldn't sell. "The first time you sleep in your car downtown, you feel like a horrible failure or a homeless person," she explained. "But that's the great thing about people: We make everything habit."

Silvianne had first encountered Linda a year and a half earlier, when they were both working as night-shift temps at the Amazon warehouse where Linda hurt her wrist. Silvianne was a tarot card

Silvianne in her van, the Queen María Esmeralda.

reader—she'd also held jobs in corporate healthcare, waitressing, retail, acupuncture, and catering—and she came to see the chain of events that put her in her van as divine influence, the goddess setting her on a gypsy path. (On her blog, Silvianne Wanders, she also characterized the transition like this: "A not-quite-retirement-age baby boomer gives up her sticks 'n bricks former miner's cabin, her three part-time jobs, and her attachment to any illusion of security this tattered remnant of the American Dream might still bring to her tortured soul. The goal: to hit the road for a life of nomadic adventure as the Tarot reader—Shamanic Astrologer—Cosmic Change Agent she was always meant to be.")

Silvianne wrote a song she called her "vandweller anthem." The first time she sang it for me, the Queen María Esmeralda was parked in a Burger King parking lot in Arizona and we'd been doing an interview inside while peeling the breading off chicken nuggets and feeding them to her green-eyed cat, Layla, who wouldn't eat them any other way. Set to the tune of "King of the Road"—and refined several times since Silvianne began writing lyrics on a lonesome stretch of Highway 95 in Arizona—the latest version goes like this:

Old beat-up high-top van,
Like livin' in a large tin can.
No rent, no rules, no man,
I ain't tied to no plot of land.

I've got cool forests for summer fun,
Winterin' in the desert sun.
I'm an old gypsy soul with new goals,
Queen of the Road!

My friends think I'm insane,
But for me their life is way too tame.
If sometimes I sing the blues,
Small price for the life I choose.

I've found all space is hallowed ground,
If we will but look around
In our sacred search for the New Earth.
Queens of the Road!

I know every back road in five western states.
If it's a blue highway I don't hesitate.
I learn every strange history of each little town.
I may get there slowly but I get around, in my . . .

Gas-guzzling high-top Ford
I'm sometimes scared, but never bored,
Because I've finally cut the cord
Unlike society's consumer hordes.

I've got a large feline to keep me sane,
Lovely Layla is her name,
Not really wild, but not too tame
Queens of the Road!

When Linda arrived at Hanna Flat, Silvianne was still two hours south in the Queen María Esmeralda, parked outside a friend's condo in Escondido, enjoying the access to laundry and hot baths. (She was "driveway surfing" in vandweller slang.) Down to $40, she was waiting on the mail for a credit card, the first one she'd had in ten years.

Linda's first few days at the campground were quiet. There were coyote sightings and rumors of a mountain lion. A couple inches of snow fell and she ran a space heater to warm the Squeeze Inn. She bought a replacement propane tank. She decorated her fridge with a magnet that said "Live each day as if Aunt Bee were watching," featuring a photo of the housekeeper from *The Andy Griffith Show*, along with an ode to nomadic living called "A Full Set of Stuff" by a writer named Randy Vining, who also referred to himself as the Mobile Kodger. It began, "I travel full time with a full set of stuff/ Not less than I need or more than enough." She read books. A vandweller friend had recommended *Woodswoman: Living Alone in the Adirondack Wilderness* and Linda devoured it, marveling at the independence and frugality of the author, ecologist Anne LaBastille, who was inspired by *Walden* and built her own cabin using just $600 worth of logs. Next she started *Making Ideas Happen: Overcoming the Obstacles Between Vision and Reality*, an entrepreneurial self-help tome that she scoured for advice on building a fulfilling future. And she snuggled with Coco, who nestled into her side on their shared mattress and sometimes scooted up to hyperactively lick her face. "Oh kisses, kisses!" she told the dog. "You're going to wear out that tongue! You're going to need a tongue retread, and guess who's gonna pay for that?"

On the Sunday Silvianne was due to arrive, Linda went to freshen up at the nearest showers, which were five miles away at Serrano

Snow blankets the Squeeze Inn at Hanna Flat Campground.

Campground on the shore of Big Bear Lake in chilly cinderblock stalls. To conserve water, the fixtures only turned on for quick intervals and taking a shower meant pushing the same chrome button over and over again. Back in the parking lot, Linda brushed her long locks in the sun, did a shampoo-commercial flip. "Is my hair shiny yet?" she asked.

Silvianne showed up that afternoon wearing a mustard yellow Frida Kahlo T-shirt, a flowing patchwork skirt, pink leggings, and suede moccasins. She hugged Linda and went to peek inside the Squeeze Inn. "It looked bigger in the pictures!" she said. Silvianne is tall and slender and wore her wavy, graying brown hair in bangs, with a few tendrils escaping a banana clip in the back. She had to duck to enter the trailer. Linda told her how much she liked living there. The only comforts she missed from her old RV were the shower and the toilet. She'd replaced the latter with a bucket, and so far, that seemed to be working out okay.

Camp host orientation began Monday at 8:30 a.m. and lasted two days at Big Bear Discovery Center, an education facility run by the U.S. Forest Service. To reward trainees who participated in the class, California Land Management supervisors tossed packaged Moon Pies at them. Mostly the workers looked forward to the free lunches: hot dogs on one day, chicken from El Pollo Loco on the other. Apart from food, each of the camp hosts received a maroon three-ring binder with the 350-page California Land Management operations manual, along with a detailed verbal rundown of the work to come. They were encouraged to scour their campgrounds for "microlitter"—bits of cellophane wrappers, foil scraps, cigarette butts, and other flotsam—and to keep individual campsites free of "trip hazards," such as the grapefruit-sized cones that fell from the forest's towering Jeffery pines. They heard cautionary tales, too, stories about mistakes they should avoid. One time a hapless worker forgot to check for live embers while shoveling ashes out of campfire rings and ended up setting his golf cart on fire. *Don't be that guy.* Another time a campground host broke a rib when she boosted herself up onto a dumpster to reconnect a bear-proofing chain. "That was me!" Linda exclaimed, to the chagrin of her bosses, who told the story without realizing its victim was present. (That accident had taken place the previous summer when Linda was working in Mammoth Lakes, California. For a while the injury made everything hurt: breathing, sweeping, driving bumpy roads in the golf cart, bending over, even laughing along with her campers. Friends and family insisted she see a doctor. He confirmed the rib was broken and urged her to avoid lifting anything heavier than ten pounds while it healed.)

At 8 a.m. on Wednesday, Linda and Silvianne set out for their first day of work in matching uniforms: brown pants and khaki windbreakers with a mountaintop logo stitched to the left breast. In those colors, they bore a passing resemblance to federal forest rangers; they'd been told this was a useful bit of camouflage when dealing with unruly campers. Silvianne had already been up for hours to follow her morning regimen—taking detoxifying herbs before meditating and eating a breakfast that, like the rest of her diet, contained no sugar, meat, dairy, or refined grains—a healing routine she hoped would help cure a basal cell carcinoma below her right eye. Their golf cart was loaded with tools: two rakes, two brooms, a spade, a metal can for ashes, and plastic buckets full of cleaning supplies. It was also stocked with leaflets advertising pricey wilderness tours via parasail, helicopter, Segway, zip line, off-road four-by-four, and a paddlewheel boat named *Miss Liberty*. Silvianne, who had just learned to drive the golf cart, was excited to take the wheel. Linda rode shotgun. The morning was cold but bright, with sun filtering through the pines. Ravens croaked in the branches and mountain chickadees sang a three-note melody that matched "Three Blind Mice." At the base of the trees, bright red snow plants—asparagus-shaped stalks that bloom in late spring and use a fungus to pull nutrients from the conifers' roots—were starting to poke through the pine needle carpet. Western fence lizards skittered across patches of gravel. Ground squirrels dove into their burrows as the golf cart approached.

You could tell Linda had done this kind of work before by her collection of tricks. When she disinfected the outhouses, she draped a paper towel over the rolls of toilet tissue to avoid misting them with chemicals. She talked about getting some Pam cooking spray—or WD-40, but Pam was cheaper—because coating the walls of the toilet chutes with it makes waste less likely to stick. After emptying a litter basket, she demonstrated a quick way to knot a new plastic liner so it wouldn't slide down past the lip. When raking dirt around the picnic tables, she added a wrist flick at the end of each stroke. "That way they can't tell where you stopped," she explained. "It looks more natural."

At one messy campsite—an unbundled sleeping bag and a roll of toilet paper were strewn in the dirt, along with empty Cup o' Noodles packages—a cooking fire had been left burning. Linda and Silvianne took turns dousing it with jugs of water, coughing as the smoke and steam billowed up and the embers hissed. They stirred the soupy, boiling ashes with a shovel to make sure no hidden sparks would reignite. Later that day, the campers—a crew of guys in their twenties—returned from a hike to their waterlogged fire pit. They were cold. Despite a snowy forecast, one wore short sleeves and hadn't packed a jacket, while another hiked in the only shoes he brought: bedroom slippers. Linda found them there, trying haplessly to restart the fire. "When you leave, you're supposed to be able to put your hand in your campfire," she said patiently. "It's lucky we found it and not the forest rangers." The rangers would have fined them. The guys apologized profusely. "Sorry ma'am!" they said. "Sorry about that."

Twice a week, Linda and Silvianne were responsible for all of Hanna Flat. On the other three days, they split the territory with another camp host who was familiar with the area. (That employee liked to tell a story from the year before, when she was working in the same forest and a flasher wrapped in the American flag—and nothing else—ran around exposing himself until police arrived to take him away.) Most of their time on the job went to cleaning Hanna Flat's eighteen toilets and eighty-eight campsites. Apart from janitorial tasks, they checked in new campers, collected fees, set out site reservation tags, gave hiking advice, settled petty disputes, shoveled out fire pits, and did paperwork. Campers came to them to purchase the company's $8-a-bundle firewood, which was locked in a cage on the camp host's site. Often they walked away without purchasing a thing, taking Linda and Silvianne's advice to scavenge wood from the forest that followed "the three Ds": already dead, down, and detached. Sometimes at the end of rounds, Linda was winded and had to take a nap.

Living next to a sign that says "CAMP HOST" isn't easy. It means you're captive to campers' needs at all times. So when were the off hours? If a camp host was around and there was work to be done, the host was expected to do it. When two trucks of campers showed up at Hanna Flat one night at 11:30, they went straight to the Queen María Esmeralda and woke up Silvianne to have her check them in.

Camp hosts were also expected to enforce nighttime "quiet hours" and handle noise complaints. Linda tried to pre-empt problems in a friendly way. When a group of folks who looked like they might be partiers first arrived, she'd tell them, "We want you to have fun, but after ten we want you to have fun *really quietly*." When she saw a campsite strewn with beer bottles, instead of demanding that the campers clean it up, she'd make a helpful offer: "I could bring you down some big trash bags."

Linda and Silvianne had been hired to work full forty-hour weeks, but there were no guarantees. Half a month into the job, their supervisor abruptly told them that campsite reservations were down and the company needed to cut costs. As result, Linda and Silvianne would work a three-quarter schedule for the next two weeks. That sent Linda's weekly pay under $290. (It was even lower for Silvianne, who hadn't received the returning-worker raises that Linda had.)

Linda and Silvianne didn't complain about the erratic and sometimes boundary-less nature of this low-wage labor, but other workampers have. A common frustration voiced by camp hosts is that they're expected to do more work than what fits within the fixed number of hours for which they can bill. One worker in his sixties, who was employed with California Land Management for the first time in 2016, emailed me from his post to talk about it. "Camp hosting is a trip," he wrote. "Lots of mixed messages from 'management.' I'm at a thirty-hour site, but some weeks clocked forty-five plus. I pushed back about that and they have reduced what they were asking." His managers did not, however, pay for the extra hours he'd already worked.

That echoed something a pair of campground hosts in their mid-sixties, Greg and Cathy Villalobos, told a legal news site in 2014. They said that, while working as campground hosts for California Land Management and another concessionaire, Thousand Trails, they were expected to work more hours than they were allowed to put on their time cards. "I mostly want to get this story told to help other seniors and stop this practice. It is pretty outrageous, especially because it comes down to the federal government who contracts these companies," Greg Villalobos told the reporter.

Another workamper, employed with California Land Management in 2015, gave the company a one-star review on Yelp, claiming she and her husband were often on the job for twelve hours or longer in a given day but weren't allowed to file for more than eight. "Them doing this to elderly couples that needed the income was wrong and needs to be investigated!" she wrote.

The U.S. Forest Service, which hires private concessionaires to manage public campgrounds, has also gotten complaints. I filed a Freedom of Information Act request with the agency's Pacific Southwest Regional Office so I could read some of them. When the documents finally arrived, censors had blacked out employees' names, ages, and contact information. In one letter, a fourteen-year California Land Management employee said coworkers weren't being provided with water while working in the heat. "Even field workers are provided with shade and cold water to drink. Why is this not being done for your own employees?" the letter read. It recounted the travails of one camp host who was assigned to work alone at two campgrounds—Upper and Lower Coffee Camp in the Sierra Nevada foothills—on 109-degree days and "was transported by ambulance twice already for heat exhaustion." The same employee, it added, "has worked many overtime hours [but] he has been told by the site manager not to write overtime on his time card. I'm sure other employees are being treated the same way as well."

In another complaint, a former camp host for California Land Management in the Sequoia National Forest wrote:

I received very harsh migrant labor-type treatment . . . I was employed at $8.50 an hour for "forty hours" but routinely had to work fifty to sixty hours plus for the same forty-hour pay with no overtime or even straight time. Therefore CLM is not paying a minimum wage. By "work" I do not mean standby time but rather a full eight hours intensive raking, debris removal, clean up in Hume, Princess and Stony Creek Campgrounds, as well as Ten-Mile and Landslide, cleaning numerous pit toilets several times a day, fire pits, blowing roads etc. And then doing registrations until almost 9 p.m. My first week they worked me six days straight, eleven to twelve hours a day . . . After some discussion where I finally voiced some of these concerns [my supervisor] called me a "punk" to "shut your punk trap" and "take your punk ass back to Oregon."

I wrote to California Land Management about these grievances and heard back from Eric Mart, the company's president. "I can assure you that our policies (copies of which are available to all employees), our training, and our standard operating procedures are all contrary to what these employees are claiming," he replied. California Land Management investigated at least three of these complaints, he continued, and found them without merit. (One worker, though, did get reimbursed on a claim of unpaid hours.) The last of the cases—which referred to a manager shortchanging an employee and calling him a "punk"—triggered a separate investigation by the U.S. Forest Service, he added.

Federal officials said otherwise. When I approached the U.S. Forest Service about these employees' specific letters, I was told the agency does not look into such grievances directly. Instead it forwards the letters to any concessionaire that the workers are complaining about—which in this case would be California Land Management. That is the agency's official policy, even though the U.S. Forest Service is responsible for issuing and renewing the concessionaires' operating permits and, ultimately, for how public lands are managed.

"The Forest Service does not have the authority to act on complaints of labor law violations, discrimination or any other type of complaints against private employers, including conducting any investigation," explained press officer John C. Heil III in an email.

During a follow-up phone call, I asked him if he really wanted that to be the agency's full response. "It seems odd that these are your contractors, ostensibly under your control, but you appear to have no control over them," I added.

Heil explained that he had researched the Forest Service's protocol, which was to forward all letters, and had nothing further to say.

AS LINDA GOT ACCUSTOMED to Hanna Flat, I observed her first two-and-a-half weeks there. We sat together for hours in her trailer at night. She doled out her life story in installments. The oldest of three siblings, Linda had adored her parents despite their shortcomings. Her father drank heavily, working on and off as a machinist in the San Diego shipyards, while her mother fought chronic depression. They bounced between apartments, moving seven times in a single year, and at one point left California for a stint staying with family in the Black Hills of South Dakota. On the drive east, Linda squeezed into a truck with her parents and two brothers, plus all their belongings and a dachshund named Peter Jones Perry. Linda's mother had to get some teeth pulled around the same time. "My father couldn't afford to put dentures in her mouth," she recalled. "So here we are in this big flatbed with all the furniture in the back, my mother with no teeth, three kids, some damn dog."

Over time Linda's father developed an increasingly violent temper. Sometimes at the dinner table he whacked her youngest brother over the head with a serving spoon. He beat Linda's mother, threw her down the stairs, and "tossed her around like a ragdoll." During one of the fights, Linda, who was about seven, hid in the back corner of the top bunk in her bedroom. There she made herself a promise: *This is never going to happen to me.*

Meanwhile Linda struggled with dyslexia, though no one knew it. When her report cards arrived, they said things like "Linda is college potential but does not apply herself." Linda felt like a duck. To observers on shore, she appeared to be drifting along without any effort, but underwater her feet were churning furiously.

She dropped out of high school but eventually got her GED, along with a certificate in construction technology and an associate's degree. She held jobs that included trucker, cocktail waitress, general contractor, flooring-store owner, insurance executive, building inspector, IRS phone representative, caregiver at a traumatic brain injury facility, dog-feeder and kennel-cleaner in a government program for seniors—she still bears the scar from a Shih Tzu bite—and de-featherer of ducks and quail at a hunting lodge. And Linda raised two daughters, mostly on her own.

I listened intently, absorbing as much as I could. I hoped it would help me understand some nagging questions: How does a hardworking sixty-four-year-old woman end up without a house or a permanent place to stay, relying on unpredictable low-wage work to survive? Living in mile-high alpine wilderness, with intermittent snow and maybe mountain lions, in a tiny trailer, scrubbing toilets at the mercy of employers who, on a whim, could cut her hours or even fire her? What did the future look like for someone like that?

Even though I'd had no epiphanies, the time came for me to go home. I left behind my extra groceries: some cold cuts, tomatoes, eggs, bacon, cheese, kale, soup, carrots, and tortillas. Most of it went to Linda because of Silvianne's restricted diet.

"This will help a lot," Linda said matter-of-factly. "I'm down to $10 until payday."

As I packed to leave, Linda and Silvianne built a campfire. For kindling, they used a stack of old paperwork—copies of the "DAR," or daily arrival report, showing which campsites had been reserved. The reports were supposed to get burned or shredded. If the smoke from the DARs could carry a message heavenward, I asked, what would it be? "We went camping! We had a great time! The bathrooms were immaculate!" Linda replied.

The sun was getting low and the cold crept in. Already bundled up in hoodies and their fleece-lined work jackets, Linda and Silvi-anne shivered and talked about getting dinner started. There would be no more campers to check in tonight. They'd already set out a sign that read "CAMPGROUND FULL" at the entrance.

So I said my good-byes and started up the camper van. The camp hosts stood and waved. "Don't let the campers burn the forest down!" I shouted. Linda shook her head and hollered back.

"Then I'd be out of a job!"

CHAPTER TWO

The End

ON THANKSGIVING DAY OF 2010—before her life as a nomad began—Linda May sat alone in the trailer where she was living in New River, Arizona. At sixty, the silver-haired grandmother lacked electricity and running water because she couldn't afford the utility bill. She couldn't find work. Her unemployment benefits had run out. Her older daughter's family, with whom she had lived for many years while holding a series of low-wage jobs, had recently downsized to a smaller apartment. With three bedrooms for six people, there wasn't enough space to move back in with them. She was trapped in a dark trailer with nowhere to go.

"I'm going to drink all the booze. I'm going to turn on the propane. I'm going to pass out and that'll be it," she told herself. "And if I wake up, I'm going to light a cigarette and blow us all to hell."

Her two small dogs, Coco and Doodle, were staring at her. (Doodle, a toy poodle, would later die before Linda moved into the Squeeze Inn.) She hesitated—could she really envision blowing them up as well? That wasn't an option. So instead she accepted an invitation to a friend's house for Thanksgiving dinner.

But that moment—the instant when she saw her resolve flicker—

wasn't something she could easily forget. Linda considers herself "a happy, joyous person." She had never seriously entertained the idea of giving up on it all. "I was just so down that I couldn't see a way out," she later recalled. Something had to change.

A couple of years later, Linda found herself close to the edge again. She was working as a Home Depot cashier for $10.50 an hour in Lake Elsinore, California. Some weeks she only got scheduled for twenty to twenty-five hours, barely enough to cover the $600-a-month trailer she was renting across town at the Shore Acres Mobile Home Park. Landing that job had taken months, never mind that her resume included two degrees in construction, plus a year and a half at a Home Depot in Las Vegas, where she'd made around $15 an hour as an expeditor, a position she'd enjoyed because it meant solving problems one-on-one for customers. Running the register felt like a comedown after all that. Still, she tried to make the most of it. "They made me a cashier, when I have all that experience," she recalled. "So I said, 'Okay, I'm going to be the best cashier here!'" Linda chatted up her customers, asking about their projects and helping where she could. When one homeowner arrived at the counter with the wrong lumber for a roof, she prescribed a different material called "oriented strand board," advising him that it would do the job better (and for $500 less). Why would Home Depot waste that kind of knowledge behind a register? "They are, in my opinion, a little age-prejudiced," she suggested.

Linda wondered, not for the first time, how anybody could afford to grow old. Of the many jobs she'd held in her life, none had brought even a modicum of lasting financial stability. "Never managed to get myself a pension," she said.

Linda knew she would soon be eligible for Social Security. She'd never paid much attention to her annual statements, though, so she was surprised when she read one and learned that her monthly benefit would be around $500, not even enough to cover the rent.

Linda had raised two girls as a single parent. She knew what it meant to scrape by. Her own mother had taught her as much, making one pound of hamburger last across a week's worth of meals to feed Linda and her brothers. When dinner was spaghetti bolognese— but no pieces of meat were visible in their bowls—the kids would tease their mother, saying she'd put the ground beef in a sock and waved it over the saucepan to impart some essence of flavor. From time to time, when the family took in an extra kid whose parents had run into trouble, Linda joked that her mother would just "wave the hamburger in a sock over the pan one more time" to accommodate the newcomer.

Perhaps because of this history, Linda was empathetic to folks who were down on their luck. In the early 1990s, she ran a carpet and tile shop called Cherokee Interiors in Bullhead City, Arizona, where, after business hours, homeless men congregated at an open spigot behind the building to wash up and fill their water jugs. "That's perfectly fine," she told them. "Just make sure you turn it off when you're done. Don't forget!" The log-cabin-style structure had a porch with hitching posts tucked below an overhang. When the men began overnighting there, she deputized them. "Okay, if you're going to sleep here, your job is night watchman," she said, suggesting they tell that to any police officer who might try to roust them.

One of the men, a former tree trimmer, told Linda he wanted to get off the street. He thought he could make some money working for the city, which dispatched contractors to clear weed-choked properties. She helped him collect donations to get started: rakes, a mower, a little gas money. Together they drove around looking at overgrown parcels the city had put up for bid. Using her business license, Linda was able to win him some contracts.

Then two bad things happened. The flooring store went under because her business partner had kept two sets of books, hanging on to some of the profits for his own use. And the former tree trimmer blew off the jobs Linda had lined up for him. When he got offered another gig painting a house in Las Vegas, he skipped town without clearing any of the lots.

Still Linda felt lucky. "Thank god, you know, I was provided for," she recalled. "I had no way to make money but I had all these con-tracts." Before long, she was pushing a mower on arid summer days, when temperatures sometimes climbed to 120 degrees. She familiar-ized herself with the symptoms of heatstroke: "If you're ever out in the sun and you start getting the chills, get the hell out of there!" The contracts earned her about $150 apiece. Often she started work at dawn and knocked off by noon, returning later in the day to finish raking and bagging the debris.

"The first time, before I got paid, I didn't have money to take it to the dump, so we took it out to the lake and we had a bonfire and it was very windy," she said, recalling a trip to Lake Mead. "The wind grabbed the dried weeds and started blowing them across the shore. The ranger came down and said, 'You cannot do that.' I'm like, 'I already got that. I'm already throwing dirt on it. I'm putting it out.'

"From there I thought, 'I cannot stay out in 120 degrees raking weeds. This is not why I went to college!'" recalled Linda, who had studied construction technology. Meanwhile, her older daughter and her son-in-law had both found employment in the bustling casino industry: She worked in a restaurant and he was a valet park-ing runner. Linda soon landed a job as a cigarette girl at the River-side Casino in the gambling boomtown of Laughlin, Nevada. (The town's namesake—Riverside owner Don Laughlin—originally wanted to call it "Casino" but was rebuffed by the U.S. Postal Service.) Linda was so grateful for the opportunity that she sent Don Laugh-lin two dozen roses. She got called to his office. "What is this?" he asked, perplexed.

"It's a heartfelt thank you, Don," she said. "It's no other reason. Just to thank you for the job. I'm not looking for anything else." At the casino, Linda sold candy, flowers, and tobacco from a tray on a shoulder strap. The tray was so heavy that, in the beginning, she had to wear a back brace to help support it. Even with the brace, she got a serious workout. "I went from a size fourteen to a size ten running cigarettes," she recalled.

Linda bought roses wholesale for 96 cents apiece and then sold them for $4, which usually came with a dollar tip. She purchased cigarettes by the carton, selling them at a profit of 50 cents a pack. Gradually she came to know the gamblers, like the guy who always got a headache and could be counted on to drop $5 on a 25-cent packet of aspirin. On a good night, she could clear $200 to $300. She'd also picked up a second source of income, hiring and supervising people to clean the casino's artificial silk plants.

But the heyday of cigarette girls at the Riverside ended abruptly with the arrival of tobacco vending machines. Don called Linda back to his office to break the news that her job was obsolete. But he didn't want to fire her. He suggested she speak with Dale, the general manager, to find another position. Linda went to track him down and got right to the point.

"Who makes the most money in this place?" she asked.

"Well, it's between being a dealer and being a cocktail waitress," Dale replied.

"I think I'd much prefer to be a cocktail waitress," Linda said.

The new job came with a uniform: a petite tailcoat over a silky red cummerbund with high-leg dance briefs, nylons, and heels. It didn't leave much to the imagination, and this made Linda nervous. "I don't know if I could ever wear that!" she thought, but she decided to give it a shot. When she put it on for the first time, her supervisor told her she looked beautiful. To Linda's surprise, she agreed. Out on the casino floor, she felt protected by the bouncers, who didn't tolerate gamblers disrespecting the cocktail waitresses. "I've seen security grab people by the back of the neck and just open the front doors with their face," she said.

Linda looks back on her Riverside years fondly. She still has a snapshot of herself in full uniform, smiling, her dark hair cropped short and the Colorado River at her back. But she was in her forties then. Her options for work would dwindle with age, rather than broadening to reflect her years of experience. There seemed to be no way off the treadmill of low-wage jobs.

By her sixties the question loomed: How would she ever afford to

Linda in uniform at the Riverside Casino.

stop working? She had spent most of her life living paycheck to pay-check, with no savings to speak of. Her only safety net, Social Secu-rity, was perilously thin. What would retirement look like on around $500 a month?

At the same time, Linda had a long-term dream for her future. It didn't include any of the old clichés—a gated community in Florida or even a few rounds of golf. Her hopes were, quite literally, down to earth, made out of dirt and other people's trash.

She wanted to construct an Earthship: a passive-solar home built using discarded materials such as cans and bottles, with dirt-filled tires for its load-bearing walls. Invented by radical New Mexico architect Michael Reynolds, who has been tinkering with them since the 1970s, Earthships are designed to sustain their inhabitants entirely off the grid. The tire walls act like batteries, absorbing the sun's heat through a bank of south-facing windows during the day-time and then releasing it at night to regulate indoor temperature. Rain and snowmelt drain from the roof into a cistern, providing water that gets filtered and reused for drinking and washing, feeding indoor fruit and vegetable gardens and flushing toilets. Electricity is supplied by solar panels and, in some cases, windmills.

For all their pragmatism, many Earthships have fanciful touches—spires and turrets, columns and arches, adobe-clad walls in vivid hues, or rows of bottles inlaid to resemble stained glass. Their construction does not require any sophisticated techniques, which makes them accessible to amateur builders and leaves room for creativity. Dozens of them dot the desert outside Taos, New Mexico, in a subdivision known as the Greater World Earthship Community. Together they look like a moon colony co-produced by Dr. Seuss, Antoni Gaudí, and the set designers from *Star Wars*.

The idea of creating a unique, self-sufficient, and ecologically sound dwelling appealed deeply to Linda. "It's not mass-produced," she said. "It's like living in a piece of art, and it's something I could build with my own two hands." Her fascination with Earthships began after *Gunsmoke* actor Dennis Weaver moved to Colorado in 1989 to build one. He made a documentary about the process that aired for years on public television, introducing the concept to mainstream America. When the film opens, the gray-haired actor stands atop a low wall, pounding dirt into a tire with a sledgehammer. He looks up and strides purposefully toward the camera. "How would you like to live in a house with no electric bills, no air conditioning, no heating ducts, and still be perfectly comfortable in the coldest winter or the hottest summer?" he asks. "Sounds crazy?" Joyfully he joins the construction crew. He shaves bark from a log to make a roof beam and then slathers a mix of mud, sand, and straw over the tires and cans that will become his bedroom wall.

Not everyone understood the actor's passion for living in a glorified tire pile. Locals nicknamed it "the Michelin Mansion." On *The Tonight Show*, Jay Leno asked him if his neighbors thought he was building an addition whenever he took out the trash. "When the garbage man comes, how does he know where the garbage begins and the house ends?" the comedian cracked.

Humble materials aside, Dennis Weaver's 10,000-square-foot

dwelling cost $1 million to build and is an extreme case of what one might call "Earthships of the rich and famous." Most Earthship dwellings end up costing about as much as a conventional house, though one New Zealand family managed on a budget of less than $20,000. "I believe in child labor," Brian Gubb, proud father of five, wrote online, adding that his wife initially thought he was a "nutter" for wanting to construct an Earthship. In Seattle, a group of Earthship enthusiasts decided to make a small, simplified version for free using scavenged materials, volunteer labor, and the generous donation of a friend's driveway. Their diminutive structure—the local-alt weekly called it an "earthdinghy"—is a work-in-progress.

Earthships exist on every continent except Antarctica. Globetrotting disaster-relief volunteers have built them in the aftermath of such catastrophes as the 2004 Indian Ocean tsunami, the 2010 Haiti earthquake, and Typhoon Haiyan in the Philippines in 2013. Probably the most infamous Earthship builders so far were Heaven's Gate cult members, who erected a tire house on their New Mexico compound. In the media frenzy following their 1997 mass suicide, architect Michael Reynolds assured America that Earthships had nothing to do with it. "Crazy occult people need housing" just like everyone else, he told the Associated Press. "We're teaching people here to connect with the planet, not leave it."

Linda is one of Reynolds's most ardent admirers. She respects how hard he's fought to realize his vision by pitting himself against bureaucrats who upheld arcane housing regulations, a struggle that was chronicled in the film *Garbage Warrior.*

"Michael Reynolds, wouldn't you like to take a walk through his mind? He's been fighting the fight since the 70s," she enthused. "They took his architecture license away once because his first houses were failures."

In recent years, Reynolds has argued that his Earthships could play a role in providing for basic human necessities in a way that's not at the mercy of the market. "We have to find secure sustenance for people that is not subject to the monster called the economy," reads a statement on his website. "The economy is a game. This game should be about nonessential things (motorcycles, computers, televisions). A person feeding their family, staying alive, having shelter . . . that should not be subject to an economy."

Around a decade ago, Linda began scouring the internet for Earthship floor plans, system diagrams, and interior photographs. The ones she likes best are printed out and neatly compiled in a three-ring binder with a wood-grain pattern on its vinyl cover. Her Facebook profile picture shows an Earthship rising from desert chaparral under a pink New Mexico sunset. "This is my dream house," she wrote beside the image. By way of explanation, she added: "Earthships are made of recycled tires, bottles and cans. They are self-contained, require no utility hookups, sun and/or wind for power, water from the sky. Water is used four times. Indoor gardens grow food. It means you can live free, no bills. How many times do I say I have to do this so I can pay the mortgage?"

Linda's hope was to find a cheap piece of land somewhere with lax building codes. Reynolds calls such places "pockets of freedom." She had rough ideas for sourcing free materials and recruiting volunteers to help with the work. But how would she embark on such an ambitious vision while she was stuck in low-wage work and funneling her paychecks into rent, knowing how little relief Social Security would bring? She needed a new way to live, a strategy that would enable her to keep earning income while whittling down her already slim living costs. In other words, she needed a bridge to the Earthship.

Linda knew she couldn't wait. She wasn't getting any younger, and creating her new home would require a reasonable level of physical fitness. Accumulating the resources would take time, too. But if she could pull it off, the project would be more than just a funky place to retire. The Earthship was her shot at posterity, a monument that might stand for a century or more. "It would take all my education and know-how and heart, and I'd leave something behind that would last," she said. "I would like to leave that to my children and my grandchildren."

Linda craved self-sufficiency. She reasoned that an Earthship, with its stand-alone systems for providing food, electricity, climate control, and water, would act almost like a symbiotic organism. If she could create and maintain such a dwelling, it would take care of her, too. That kind of stability felt reassuring. Linda, after all, was aging into a precarious demographic. According to 2015 census figures, among older women living alone, more than one in six are below the poverty line. Nearly twice as many elderly women in America are poor (2.71 million) than their male counterparts (1.49 million). And when it comes to Social Security benefits, female recipients get on average $341 a month less than men because of lower total payroll tax contributions, an under-recognized consequence of the gender wage gap. In 2015, women were still making just about 80 cents on the male dollar and more likely to work as unpaid caregivers to young children and aging parents. (Apart from raising her two children, Linda later became a live-in helper for her mother, who developed an aggressive brain cancer in the mid-1990s.) Women have lower lifetime earnings and accrue less in savings. And since they have greater longevity—outliving men by five years on average—those dollars must stretch further into the future.

On June 1, 2012, Linda May turned sixty-two. The next month, her first Social Security check arrived in the mail. "I shouldn't have started collecting until I was sixty-five," she later reflected, "but my benefit was so little, I thought, 'I don't care what percentage they put on it, it wouldn't increase it that much.'"

Either way, she had a problem. "How am I going to live and not have to work for the rest of my life and not be a burden to my children?" she wondered. Linda knew she wanted her long-term solution to be an Earthship. But how would she ever get there?

CHAPTER THREE

Surviving America

EXACTLY A WEEK AFTER LINDA DECIDED against blowing up her trailer on Thanksgiving Day of 2010, bad news came to Empire, a factory village of three hundred people that clung like a burr to the back of the Black Rock Desert in northwestern Nevada. One of the last traditional company towns in America, Empire was wholly owned by United States Gypsum, the company that makes Sheetrock. The place was a throwback to the much romanticized heyday of American manufacturing, when factory jobs offered workers a sure footing in the middle class and the chance to raise a family without fear of displacement.

Empire was six miles north of "the gyp," an open-pit gypsum mine nestled at the foot of the Selenite mountain range. There miners detonated blasts of anfo—an explosive blend of ammonium nitrate and fuel oil—to dislodge white, chalky chunks of ore from five terraced pits, the largest a half-mile across. Haul trucks shuttled sixty-ton batches of gypsum up the highway to a drywall plant on the edge of town. There workers pulverized it, heated it to 500 degrees in massive kettles, and shaped it into the wallboard found in homes across the American West.

Past Empire's factory, single-story cottages lined four main residential streets planted with cottonwoods, elms, and silver poplars. U.S. Gypsum subsidized the rents, which were as low as $110 for an apartment or $250 for a house. (Mechanics in the drywall plant made up to $22 an hour and equipment operators got a little bit less, which meant employees could typically cover a month's rent with a day or two of work.) The company also paid for TV, sewer, trash, and internet service. Since employees' expenses were low and their income reliable, the notion of living paycheck to paycheck—that nerve-wracking, precarious form of existence so common in the outside world—was relatively foreign here. Empire felt like a town suspended in the 1950s, as if the postwar economy had never ended. "It's a really good place to save money," Anna Marie Marks, a fifteen-year employee who worked in the factory lab testing Sheetrock, told me.

At the town's peak, more than 750 people lived there, as noted in the July 1961 issue of U.S. Gypsum's in-house magazine, *Gypsum News*. "The folks who make their homes in Empire are one big happy family," the magazine reported. Though the population dwindled amid modernization and was less than half of that by 2010, the sentiment hadn't changed. Since all the citizens of Empire knew each other, the front doors of houses stayed unlocked, and cars were often parked with keys left inside. "No gangs, no sirens, no violence," rhapsodized Tonja Lynch, who lived in town with her husband, a factory supervisor. And because Empire was so isolated—for years it was marked on state Highway 447 with a two-story sign that said "Welcome to Nowhere"—folks had no choice but to entertain themselves and each other, too. That meant a lot of block parties, potluck dinners, and gatherings to play a dice game called Bunco, along with excursions into the high desert wilderness to hunt deer, antelope, and chukar, a gray and cinnamon-colored partridge with striped wings and a bright red beak. Many of the townspeople cultivated improbably lush lawns, pushing back against the arid landscape and asserting something that looked like civic pride. Where the grass that marked their territory ended, the Black Rock Desert stretched unbroken all the way to the horizon. In satellite photos, Empire was obvious: a splotch of green in an otherwise brown and barren wasteland.

Isolation had its downside. "We've got the neighborhood watch program," quipped Aaron Constable, the factory's maintenance foreman. "Your neighbors watch you, whether you want them to or not." This had been the local way of life for decades, with coworkers dwelling in close quarters. In 1923 laborers established a tent colony on the site of what later became the town. By some accounts, Empire boasted the longest continuously operating mine in the country, excavating a claim first established by Pacific Portland Cement Company in 1910.

On December 2, 2010, that history came to a sudden stop. Workers in steel-toed shoes and hard hats gathered in the community hall at 7:30 a.m. for a mandatory meeting. Mike Spihlman, the gypsum plant's soft-spoken manager, delivered a grim edict to a room full of stunned faces: Empire was shutting down. Everyone had until June 20 to leave. First came silence, then tears. "I had to stand in front of ninety-two people and say, 'Not only do you not have a job anymore, you don't have a house anymore,'" Mike recalled later, sighing heavily. Employees got the rest of the day off. They wandered back out into the cold and overcast winter morning, returning to homes that wouldn't be theirs much longer, to mull over the news and break it to their families.

U.S. Gypsum, valued at $4 billion, had taken heavy losses in 2010, hemorrhaging $284 million by the end of the third quarter. William C. Foote, then CEO, attributed the company's declining fortunes to "continued weak market conditions and extraordinarily low shipping volumes." Beneath that jargon was a simpler story: Demand wasn't high enough for what Empire made anymore. The fortunes of wallboard manufacturers are tied to the domestic construction industry, and the slump brought on by the housing market collapse had lasted too long. So while many towns had been merely scarred by the recession, Empire would completely disappear.

In January 2011, I visited Empire to report a magazine story. Calvin Ryle, who had been the quality control supervisor and, before that, the general foreman, told me he started working at the factory on July 1, 1971. "I've been here for thirty-nine years and seven months," he said matter-of-factly. "I've never missed a single day, never been injured." Since he held the record for longest continuous service, the honor of halting the production line went to him. Standing beside a conveyor belt in the factory, where his son also worked as a maintenance mechanic, the sixty-two-year-old raised his right hand as his coworkers looked on. He pressed the stop button and wept. "The worst thing you can hear in a board plant is silence," Calvin explained. "You're a part of building America; it's not just making Sheetrock here." And Empire, he added, had been a great place to raise kids out in nature while earning a solid living. He planned to dig up the rosebushes he'd planted in his yard to bring with him, since he figured the town would be quickly overtaken by weeds. "It's probably going to look like that movie *The Hills Have Eyes*," he said soberly. (An abandoned nuclear test village full of decrepit houses and lurking cannibals figures prominently in the 2006 remake of that cult horror film.) "It's going to be the 2011 Nevada ghost town."

Within sight of the factory, the Catholic mission of St. Joseph the Worker was celebrating one of its last masses. The church had a new wooden sign carved by one of the parishioners, Tom Anderson, sixty-one, who'd been a full-time electrician at the factory with thirty-one years of service. Like Calvin with his plants, Tom said he'd reclaim his handiwork before leaving. He attended the service along with some two dozen neighbors. Toward the end, the pastor asked if anyone had special prayers to offer. A six-year-old girl in a lavender princess dress spoke up. "I want to pray about some of the people who need help to find homes," she said haltingly. "And the people who need the stuff to live." The room was silent.

At the quarry south of town, roads had already been choked off with giant gravel berms to keep out vehicles. Before long other signs of Empire's demise started to appear. An eight-foot chain-link fence topped with barbed wire rose along the perimeter of the town. Locals said it made the place look "like a concentration camp." The newly unemployed created a makeshift memorial, tossing their construction helmets into the branches of a tree across from the post office. (U.S. Gypsum hard hats had once brought pride to their wearers, the corporate equivalent of team jerseys. Many had been personalized with stickers, some with paint or permanent markers. And there were distinctive gold-colored helmets for workers like Calvin who'd surpassed twenty-five years of service.)

Slowly the diaspora began. The same economy that had been flattened by the housing crash saw gold prices skyrocket, and Nevada's mines were hiring. More than a dozen former Empire employees left for jobs with the Barrick Gold Corporation, which owned several nearby sites. But others among the dispossessed workers were having a harder time.

"I threw out a few resumes, haven't gotten any bites," former supply chain manager Dan Moran told me. "I might just end up cutting firewood for a living." Monica Baker, twenty-two, who grew up in Empire, had recently moved back to town from Oahu with two young children on the promise of factory work, only to be broadsided by the shutdown. "I was really pissed off about it because they kept telling me I'd have a job here," she said. Though she'd heard the gold mines were hiring, Monica worried about working near a toxic leach pond, noting that mercury from the industry had already made it so no one could eat the fish caught in northern Nevada. She figured she'd try her luck seventy miles south in the small city of Fernley, which had chain stores. She'd be riding the tide of the national economy: away from manufacturing, toward the retail and service industries. "I'll just get a job at Walmart or Lowe's," she said.

The exodus of workers' families continued through June. When the last of them departed, the town was sealed away behind chained gates, with security cameras and no trespassing signs. The cottages along with a public pool, two churches, a post office, and a nine-hole golf course were left to rot. Even the local zip code, 89405, was expunged. To keep the weeds down, the company imported two dozen goats, which roamed the new ghost town like a pack of organic lawn mowers. Years later, visitors would compare the place to Chernobyl, a catalog of interrupted lives. At the factory's office, unfinished cups of coffee remained on desks and calendars still showed the date of the shutdown.

Eerily, there's one place where Empire lives on. As of 2017, you could still go to Google Maps Street View, drop a tiny avatar on Circle Drive, and wander around looking at parked cars and lawn furniture and folks watering their yards uninterrupted, all frozen in a photographic landscape that hasn't been updated since 2009.

———

AT THE SAME TIME Empire was dying, a new and very different kind of company town was thriving seventy miles to the south. In many ways, it felt like the opposite of Empire. Rather than offering middle-class stability, this village was populated by members of the "precariat": temporary laborers doing short-term jobs in exchange for low wages. More specifically, its citizens were hundreds of itinerant workers living in RVs, trailers, vans, and even a few tents. Early each fall, they began filling the mobile home parks surrounding Fernley. Linda didn't know it yet, but she would soon be joining them. Many were in their sixties and seventies, approaching or well into traditional retirement age. Most had traveled hundreds of miles—and undergone the routine indignities of criminal background checks and pee-in-a-cup drug tests—for the chance to earn $11.50 per hour plus overtime at temporary warehouse jobs. They planned to stay through early winter, despite the fact that most of their homes on wheels weren't designed to support life in subzero temperatures. Their employer was Amazon.com.

Amazon had recruited these workers as part of a program it calls CamperForce: a labor unit made up of nomads who work as seasonal employees at several of its warehouses, which the company calls "fulfillment centers," or FCs. Along with thousands of traditional temps, they're hired to meet the heavy shipping demands of "peak season," the consumer bonanza that spans the three to four months before Christmas.

Amazon doesn't disclose precise staffing numbers to the press, but when I casually asked a CamperForce manager at an Amazon recruiting booth in Arizona about the size of the program, her estimate was some two thousand workers. (That was back in 2014. For the 2016 season, Amazon stopped hiring CamperForce workers earlier than usual because "it was a record year for applications," according to a Facebook post by a former program administrator.)

The workers' shifts last ten hours or longer, during which some walk more than fifteen miles on concrete floors, stooping, squatting, reaching, and climbing stairs as they scan, sort, and box merchandise. When the holiday rush ends, Amazon no longer needs CamperForce and terminates the program's workers. They drive away in what managers cheerfully call a "taillight parade."

The first member of CamperForce I corresponded with at great length, over a period of months, was a man I'll call Don Wheeler. (That is not his real name, for reasons I'll explain later.) Don had spent the last two years of his main career as a software executive traveling to Hong Kong, Paris, Sydney, and Tel Aviv. Retiring in 2002 meant he could finally stay in one place: the 1930s' Spanish Colonial Revival house he shared with his wife in Berkeley, California. It also gave him time to indulge a lifelong obsession with fast cars. He bought a red-and-white Mini Cooper S and souped it up to 210 horsepower, practicing until he was named third overall in the U.S. Touring Car Championship pro series.

The fast times didn't last. When I started exchanging emails with Don, he was sixty-nine, divorced, and staying at the Desert Rose RV Park near the warehouse in Fernley. His wife had gotten to keep the house. The 2008 market crash had vaporized his savings. He had been forced to sell the Mini Cooper.

Don was living with Rizzo, a fifteen-pound Jack Russell terrier, in a 1990 Airstream he called "Ellie"—a reference to its model number, 300LE—with a plastic hula girl on the dashboard and race car posters propped against the drawn blinds. In his old life, he'd spent about $100,000 a year. In the new one, he'd learned to get by on as little as $75 a week.

By the end of the 2013 holiday season, Don anticipated he'd be working at the Amazon warehouse five nights a week until just before dawn, on overtime shifts lasting twelve hours, with thirty minutes off for lunch and two fifteen-minute breaks. He'd spend most of the time on his feet, receiving and scanning inbound freight.

"It's hard work, but the money's good," he explained. Don was bald with wire-rimmed glasses and a snow-white goatee. He had an artificial right hip, a replacement from when he fell off a pickup truck during another temporary job at an Oregon campground. Don didn't abide complainers. Still, like most of his coworkers, he was counting down the days until December 23, the end of the CamperForce work season.

Don told me that he was part of a growing phenomenon. He and most of the CamperForce—along with a broader spectrum of itinerant laborers—called themselves "workampers." Though I'd already stumbled across that word, I've never heard anyone define it with as much flair as Don. He wrote in a Facebook direct message to me:

> Workampers are modern mobile travelers who take temporary jobs around the U.S. in exchange for a free campsite—usually including power, water and sewer connections—and perhaps a stipend. You may think that workamping is a modern

phenomenon, but we come from a long, long tradition. We followed the Roman legions, sharpening swords and repairing armor. We roamed the new cities of America, fixing clocks and machines, repairing cookware, building stone walls for a penny a foot and all the hard cider we could drink. We followed the emigration west in our wagons with our tools and skills, sharpening knives, fixing anything that was broken, helping clear the land, roof the cabin, plow the fields and bring in the harvest for a meal and pocket money, then moving on to the next job. Our forebears are the tinkers.

We have upgraded the tinker's wagon to a comfortable motor coach or fifth-wheel trailer. Mostly retired now, we have added to our repertoire the skills of a lifetime in business. We can help run your shop, handle the front or back of the house, drive your trucks and forklifts, pick and pack your goods for shipment, fix your machines, coddle your computers and networks, work your beet harvest, landscape your grounds or clean your bathrooms. We are the techno-tinkers.

Other workampers I spoke with had their own ways of describing themselves. Many said they were "retired," even if they anticipated working well into their seventies or eighties. Others called themselves "travelers," "nomads," "rubber tramps," or wryly, "gypsies." Outside observers gave them other nicknames, from "the Okies of the Great Recession" to "American refugees," "the affluent homeless," even "modern-day fruit tramps."

Whatever you want to call them, workampers ride a national circuit of jobs extending coast to coast and up into Canada, a shadow economy created by hundreds of employers posting classified ads on websites with names like *Workers on Wheels* and *Workamper News*. Depending on the time of year, nomads are sought to pick raspberries in Vermont, apples in Washington, and blueberries in Kentucky. They give tours at fish hatcheries, take tickets at NASCAR races, and guard the gates of Texas oil fields.* ("It was awful," said one workamper of a gate guarding job in Gonzalez, Texas, where she and her husband made about $125 for a twenty-four-hour day—working out to about $5 an hour—and were quickly exhausted because they could only sleep in short intervals. "You have to log everybody—license plate, name badge—at all hours of the night. When we left there my husband and I were total zombies.") They flip burgers during baseball games at the Cactus League, a spring training series in Phoenix, Arizona. They're in demand to run concession stands at rodeos and the 2017 Super Bowl at NRG Stadium in Houston. ("Must be comfortable with up-selling," insists the job listing.)

They maintain hundreds of campgrounds and trailer parks from the Grand Canyon to Niagara Falls, recruited by private concessionaires along with the U.S. Forest Service and the Army Corps of Engineers. They staff some of the nation's premiere tourist traps, including Wall Drug, with its eighty-foot-long concrete brontosaurus and animatronic singing cowboys, and The Thing?, a curiosities museum on a desolate stretch of Arizona freeway where dozens of yellow billboards tease "Seeing Is Believing" and "Mystery of the Desert."

The migrants work at roadside stalls during the holidays, selling pumpkins for Halloween and fireworks for the Fourth of July. (Camping for "a week next to a tent of explosives . . . Am I nuts?" wrote one workamping widow who was preparing to take a fireworks job.) Some vend Christmas trees. ("Give a Camp Christmas Tree a try!" beckons an ad aimed at RVers. "No grumps," grouses another.) Some run kiosks in shopping centers, selling seasonal gifts for See's Candies and Hickory Farms. Others get hired as leak detectors on natural gas pipelines, trudging along miles of buried conduit with "flame packs" that monitor hydrocarbon levels to prevent explosions.

---

* Some of these workampers made national headlines in 2010, when the U.S. Department of Labor claimed their employer, Gate Guard Services LP in Corpus Christi, had misclassified them as independent contractors rather than employees and therefore owed them $6.2 million in back pay. A federal judge later dismissed that order.

The Florida Department of Fish and Game hires them to run a check station for hunters, where they weigh the carcasses of wild hogs and deer and remove biological samples—specifically, deer jawbones—for testing to monitor the age and health of local herds. A pheasant hunting lodge in South Dakota has openings in its "bird processing" department.

Workampers run the rides at amusement parks from Dollywood in Tennessee to Adventureland in Iowa, Darien Lake in New York, and Story Land in New Hampshire. ("Workampers not only get to meet and work with new people from around the world, but also get to experience the pure joy of children's dreams coming true every day!" promises a Story Land recruitment ad.)

As compensation, some employers pay an hourly wage. One Georgia farm seeks workampers for "daily hands-on training of llamas," providing an RV spot with hookups in exchange for twenty to twenty-four hours of free labor a week, paying $7.50 an hour after that. Others offer only a version of bed and board—a parking spot that is not necessarily paved but hopefully level and flat, along with hookups for water, electricity, and sewage. (A classified ad for one such wage-less position asked "Can You Drive a Boat? Do You Enjoy It?" and sought a "volunteer" water taxi captain for the Port San Luis Harbor District in California. The job entailed working up to forty hours a week and getting an RV site—but no pay—in return.) And then there is the annual sugar beet harvest. The last week of September, the American Crystal Sugar Company brings hundreds of RV dwellers to Montana, North Dakota, and Minnesota. Weather permitting, they work day and night in twelve-hour shifts. In return they get a starting wage of $12 an hour plus overtime, along with the standard parking space.

There's no clear count of how many people live nomadically in America. Full-time travelers are a demographer's nightmare. Statistically they blend in with the rest of the population, since the law requires them to maintain fixed—in other words, fake—addresses. No matter how widely they wander, nomads must be officially "domiciled" somewhere. Your state of residence is where you get vehicles registered and inspected, renew drivers' licenses, pay taxes, vote, serve on juries, sign up for health insurance (except for those on Medicare), and fulfill a litany of other responsibilities. And living nowhere, it turns out, means you can live anywhere you want, at least on paper. So many folks opt for residency in the places with the fewest hassles—Florida, South Dakota, and Texas, which lack state income taxes, are longtime favorites—and use mail-forwarding services to stay in touch. The rules for becoming a South Dakotan are especially laid-back. Spend one night at a local motel and register with a South Dakota mail forwarding service. Then show both receipts to the state department of public safety and you're in.

Despite a lack of hard numbers, anecdotal evidence suggests the ranks of American itinerants started to boom after the housing collapse and have kept growing. "We find since 2008 a lot more people are looking for us. In fact I have a list of people interested in hearing about jobs. I had to cap the list at 25,000 names," Warren Meyer, the president of Recreation Resource Management, which manages 110 campgrounds and hires some 300 workampers, told an *Al Jazeera* reporter. "Most folks are couples so that's really probably like 50,000 people who are applying for the 50 jobs I have," he added. "In 2008 I used to have to go to these conventions of retirees and try and beg people to work for me."

Kampgrounds of America (KOA), a major employer of workampers, hires some 1,500 couples each year for its resorts and franchises across the country, a representative told AARP. *Workamper News*, a bi-monthly magazine whose website features a popular job-listing service, claims to reach 14,000 members, with more joining all the time.

Meanwhile, "living in a van, or 'vandwelling,' is now fashionable," proclaimed *The New York Times Magazine* in late 2011, adding that 1.2 million homes were predicted to be repossessed that year and noting that van sales were up 24 percent.

Of all the programs seeking workampers, the most aggressive

recruiter has been Amazon's CamperForce. "Jeff Bezos has pre-dicted that, by the year 2020, one out of every four work campers in the United States will have worked for Amazon," read one slide in a presentation for new hires. To find warm bodies, the com-pany has set up recruiting kiosks at nomad-friendly events—mostly RV shows and rallies—in more than a dozen states across the country. Recruiters wear CamperForce T-shirts and pass out "NOW HIRING" fliers, along with promotional stickers, note-pads, paper fans, tubes of lip balm, landscape calendars, and "koozies," the neoprene sleeves that keep beer cans cold. All the objects bear the CamperForce logo: a black silhouette of an RV in motion, bearing Amazon's "smile" insignia.

More recently, that logo and a link to the recruiting website for CamperForce have appeared on large magnetic sunshades, made to cover the windshields of parked RVs. In 2015 these were presented as gifts to a handful of CamperForce workers, who were urged to put

CamperForce recruiters hand out promotional items at RV shows around the country.

them up wherever they roam. Workers are also offered a referral bonus of $125—up from $50 in 2012—for each new hire they sign up.

CamperForce has also published digital newsletters for prospective employees with tips from veterans of the program, such as the following:

Donna Bonnett says, "Do not try working in brand new shoes! Be sure to break them in beforehand."

Joyce Cooley says, "The most important tip is a positive attitude. We do not need to expect everything to be given to us. We must work for it."

Carol Petty says, "The right outlook from the beginning will certainly help. This is a job, not a career."

George Nelson says, "Go with the flow and don't complain because this isn't our profession. It's just a seasonal job."

Brian Nelson says, "I took the perspective that I was getting PAID TO EXERCISE as a picker. When you have long distances between picks, power walk. You'll burn more calories and be more productive at the same time."

Sharon Scofield says, "Your hands may receive minor cuts, or chafe from box handling. Amazon provides gloves to protect your hands. Buy GOOD hand lotion and massage thoroughly."

The newsletters also recommended attractions near Amazon warehouses that workers might enjoy off-hours. "In October, Fernley celebrates the 'Hard Times Dance,'" one suggestion read. "Attendees come clad in Depression-era and 'hard times' apparel." Another, aimed at workers in Coffeyville, Kansas, said, "There are also nut trees in the parks [and] you can pick up black walnuts, pecans, and hickory nuts for free. One camper couple picked up and sold over one hundred pounds of pecans last year!"

An Amazon recruiting handout warns CamperForce candidates that they should be ready to lift up to fifty pounds at a time, in an environment where the temperature may sometimes exceed 90 degrees. Newsletters for the program repeat the company's motivational slogan, "Work hard. Have fun. Make history." And they emphasize the program's intangible rewards: "You'll be surrounded by fellow CamperForce associates who get together to make new friends and reacquaint with old ones, share good food, good stories, and good times around the campfire, or around the table. In some ways, that's worth more than money!"* In a closed, worker-run Facebook group called Amazon CamperForce Community, one woman talked about losing twenty-five pounds during her three months on the job. Another replied, "It's easy to lose weight by walking a half marathon every day. Bonus: you're too tired to eat!" A third worker boasted of walking 547 miles in ten weeks of work. He was later topped by another, who posted a Fitbit log showing 820 miles in twelve-and-a-half weeks.

———

I WANTED TO SEE this new kind of company town for myself. When I mentioned that to a former CamperForce recruiter, he suggested the best time to visit would be late October, because "folks wouldn't be quite so exhausted yet."

I took that advice, arriving in Fernley the week before Halloween in 2013. By then, workers had already crammed into lots as far as thirty-five miles away from the Amazon warehouse, including the RV parking area at the Grand Sierra Resort & Casino in Reno. (Linda was among this crowd, staying in the nearby town of Fallon, but I didn't know it at the time and wouldn't encounter her until three

———

* Not everyone seems to prioritize the touchy-feely incentives, however. "Bottom Line for Workampers at Amazon.com: Money" read the headline of a 2014 CamperForce cover story in *Workamper News*, which interviewed some of the laborers.

months later in Arizona.) Many of these mobile home parks had booked up months in advance and had long waiting lists. The most popular—it offered the shortest commute—was the Desert Rose RV Park, a gravel patch bounded by Highway 50 and bisected with high-voltage wires that crackled audibly overhead. There CamperForce workers had set out doormats and patio furniture. They'd hung wind chimes and bird feeders from the cottonwoods and raised flags emblazoned with "AMERICA THE BEAUTIFUL" and "IT'S FIVE O'CLOCK SOMEWHERE." A few displayed homemade yard art, which included a cantaloupe-sized flying eyeball mounted on an inverted steering column, with several forks welded to each side for wings. Others had put up Halloween decorations: hay bales, dried cornstalks, a pumpkin covered in pink glitter. And when they weren't beautifying their own parking spots, they engaged in the small social transactions that were making this place start to feel like a community: forming car pools to save gas money, swapping advice on inexpensive restaurants for a day-off treat. (Their favorite? The Gold Pan Special at the Pioneer Crossing Casino in Fernley: two eggs and two buttermilk pancakes with bacon, sausage, or ham, plus a side of hash browns or home fries, all for only $2.70, factoring in the 10 percent senior discount.)

I'd long assumed that most RVers were retirees tootling idly around America, sightseeing and enjoying the relaxation they'd earned after decades of employment. RV, after all, stands for "recreational vehicle." Those happy-go-lucky pensioners still exist, but they've been joined by the new nomads. Most of the denizens of the Desert Rose, for example, weren't thinking about recreation. New-comers were preoccupied with "work hardening," an acclimation period of half-day shifts. Earlier arrivals were already straining to keep up with the pace in the warehouse.

"This is the first time I've ever done factory work. I've got a whole new respect for it," Linda Chesser, a former Washington State University academic adviser, told me. She was hanging shirts in the

CamperForce workers Angela and Kenny Harper at Big Chief RV Park in Coffeyville, Kansas.

laundry room at the Desert Rose, where bookshelves held a modest lending library and a wildflower meadow was emerging from an unfinished 1,000-piece jigsaw puzzle. She was sixty-eight and told me she was thankful for ibuprofen. "I take four when I leave for work in the morning and four when I get back at night." For some campers, ibuprofen wasn't enough. Karren Chamberlen, a sixty-eight-year-old former bus driver with two hip replacements, told me she'd left CamperForce after five weeks because her knees couldn't handle the long hours walking on concrete. During a visit to another Amazon encampment—Big Chief RV Park in Coffeyville—I met Kenny Harper, who quit soon after. Later, in an email, he explained that "my left rotator won't take the job." Other workers talked about "trigger finger," a tendon condition that can be brought on by repetitive tasks such as UPC-scanner use. And many of the RVs I entered were stocked like mobile apothecaries, with Icy Hot Pain Relieving Gel, tubs for soaking tired feet, Epsom salts, and bottles of Aleve and Advil. If the workers ran out of pills, that wasn't a problem—Amazon had wall-mounted dispensers offering free over-the-counter painkillers in the warehouse.

"THIS IS A WHOLE BAND of housing refugees!" Bob remembered speculating to his wife, Anita, when they arrived in Fernley to join CamperForce. The Apperleys used to think they would retire to live aboard a sailboat, funding that dream with equity from their three-bedroom house in Beaverton, Oregon. They'd bought the home for $340,000 at the top of the market and put another $20,000 into it. Then the housing bubble burst and its value tumbled to $260,000. Before the crash, they'd been doing alright. Bob worked as an accountant for a timber products firm—he hated that job, but it paid the bills—while Anita was an interior decorator and part-time caregiver. Neither could imagine spending the rest of their lives servicing a loan worth more than the value of their house. So they bought a 2003 Cardinal fifth-wheel trailer and hit the road. "We just walked away," Anita said. "We told ourselves, 'We're not playing this game anymore.'"

Bob blamed the bad guys on Wall Street. He spoke almost defensively about his decision to abandon the house. He rushed to add that he'd always paid the bills on time and kept good credit. His downfall was putting his faith in the gospel of ever-increasing home prices. "I never had any experience that a house would drop in value," Bob said, shaking his head. He compared the "slow-dawning reality" of his new life to waking up in *The Matrix*: learning that the pleasant, predictable world you used to inhabit was a mirage, a lie built to hide a brutal dystopia. "The security most people take comfort in, I'm not convinced that isn't an illusion," he added. "When you find out what you believed to be true *isn't* true, it's disorienting. What you believe to be true is so embedded. It takes a radical pounding to let go." When I met the Apperleys, both were still a few years away from taking Social Security. Bob planned to keep doing seasonal work with

CamperForce until he was sixty-five. Anita wasn't eligible for a warehouse position because she lacked a high school diploma. So she picked up odd jobs from her neighbors. Their encampment, along with others inhabited by CamperForce workers, had developed small-scale economies, run by the stay-at-home partners of warehouse workers. They hawked their services—dog walking, cooking meals, sewing, upholstery repair, painting lessons for beginners—on bulletin boards in the communal laundry rooms.

The Apperleys weren't the only foreclosure victims I found in the ranks of Amazon's CamperForce. I spoke with dozens of workers in Nevada, Kansas, and Kentucky. Tales of money trouble were rampant. Sometimes I felt like I was wandering around post-recession refugee camps, places of last resort where Americans got shipped if the so-called "jobless recovery" had exiled them from the traditional workforce. At other moments, I felt like I was talking to prison inmates. It was tempting to cut through the pleasantries and ask, "What are *you* in for?"

Among the people I met, some had their personal savings wiped out by bad investments or saw their 401(k)s evaporate in the 2008 market crash. Some hadn't been able to create enough of a safety net to withstand otherwise survivable traumas: divorce, illness, injury. Others had been laid off or owned small businesses that folded in the recession. And though workers under fifty were a minority, I met them, too. They described jobs that they'd lost—or had never found to begin with—and problems compounded by student debt and degrees that turned out to have little practical value. Many hoped life on the road would be an escape from an otherwise empty future.

CamperForce began as an experiment, one that happened to coincide with the housing crash. Amazon's far-flung warehouses had been struggling for years to staff up enough to meet the demand for Christmas, so they'd tried out various hiring programs and even bused in workers from three to five hours away. Then, in 2008, a temp agency, Express Employment Professionals, brought in a bunch of RVers for the pre-Christmas rush at the company's warehouse in Coffeyville, Kansas. Pleased with the results, Amazon branded the program with the CamperForce name and logo, expanded it to warehouses in Fernley and Campbellsville, Kentucky, and began hiring for it directly, cutting out the temp agencies. Later managers created small squads of trusted CamperForce veterans—it called them "away teams"—to train workers at facilities that had just opened in Tracy, California; Murfreesboro, Tennessee; and Robbinsville, New Jersey. In early 2017, Amazon advertised the latest round of CamperForce openings at its warehouses in Campbellsville, Murfreesboro, and Haslet and San Marcos, Texas. (The Fernley, Nevada, facility had shut down, replaced by a new location in Reno that did not hire CamperForce employees.)

Workampers are plug-and-play labor, the epitome of convenience for employers in search of seasonal staffing. They appear where and when they are needed. They bring their own homes, transforming trailer parks into ephemeral company towns that empty out once the jobs are gone. They aren't around long enough to unionize. On jobs that are physically difficult, many are too tired even to socialize after their shifts.

They also demand little in the way of benefits or protections. On the contrary, among the more than fifty such laborers I interviewed in my first year of reporting on workampers, most expressed appreciation for whatever semblance of stability their short-term jobs offered. Take fifty-seven-year-old Joanne Johnson, who was dashing upstairs at Amazon's Campbellsville facility when she tripped and fell, striking her head on a conveyor-belt support bar. She was bandaged up at AmCare—an in-house medical facility—and then rushed to an emergency room. The episode left her with two black eyes and nine stitches along her hairline. "They let me continue working. They didn't fire me," Johnson recalled warmly. And the day after she was injured, a human resources representative visited the RV she shared with her sixty-seven-year-old husband, a former workamper.

Johnson, who had promised her employers that she would never run up the stairs again, was thunderstruck: "We thought that was one of the most amazing things in the world that he literally took time away to come to our door to see how we were doing."

I wondered why a company like Amazon would welcome older candidates for jobs that seem better suited to younger bodies. "It's because we're so dependable," suggested Johnson. "We know that if you commit to something, you do your best to get that job done. We don't take days off unless we have to." (While recuperating from her head wound, Johnson missed only one scheduled workday. It was unpaid.)

The folks who run CamperForce reiterate the belief that older workers bring a good work ethic. "We've had folks in their eighties who do a phenomenal job for us," said Kelly Calmes, an administrator for the program in Campbellsville, during an online job seminar hosted by *Workamper News*. "The benefit to our workamping population being, for the most part, a little bit older is that you guys have put in a lifetime of work. You understand what work *is*. You put your mind to the work, and we know that it's a marathon, it's not a sprint. It's kind of like *The Tortoise and The Hare*. We have some of our younger folks who will race through. You guys are pretty methodical—you just kind of work as you go, and work as you go—and at the end of the day, believe it or not, you both cross the finish line at about the same time."

Beyond that, Amazon reaps federal tax credits—ranging from 25 to 40 percent of wages—for hiring disadvantaged workers in several categories, including aging recipients of Supplemental Security Income (SSI) and anyone on food stamps. Savvy CamperForce members know all about that incentive. "The Work Opportunity Tax Credit is the reason Amazon can take on such a slow, inefficient workforce," noted one itinerant worker on her blog, Tales from the Rampage. "Since they are getting us off government assistance for almost three months of the year, we are a tax deduction for them."

———

THE PRO-ELDERLY LABOR ATTITUDE isn't unique to Amazon. During an online recruitment seminar for the annual sugar beet harvest, Scott Lindgren, a managing partner with temporary staffing firm Express Employment Professionals, praised the steadfastness of older RVers.

"We've also found that our workampers have great work ethics and for that we applaud you," he said. "We know that you've worked hard your whole life and we know that we can count on you to get the job done and you're some of our best workers."

David Roderick, a seventy-seven-year-old workamper, agreed. "They love retirees because we're dependable. We'll show up, work hard, and are basically slave labor," he told me, recalling the winter of 2012 when he and his wife, also in her seventies, sold Christmas trees at the San Mateo Event Center in California while living in their fifteen-year-old Lazy Daze RV. His job involved carrying conifers that were up to nine feet tall and boosting them atop customers' cars and trucks, for eight to ten hours at a time, six days a week. "I love the selling part, but the work behind the scenes of cutting and hauling the trees is a very, very young person's job. But a number of us were retired," he said of the team.

If not for the turquoise CamperForce T-shirt David was wearing when we first met at the Desert Rose RV Park, the white-haired and goateed grandfather wouldn't have seemed a likely candidate for itinerant labor. After starting his career teaching chemistry and oceanography at California community colleges, he'd launched a pioneering ecotourism company and later worked as a State Department English Language Fellow in Jordan. (David also received offers for subsequent teaching jobs in Saudi Arabia and Kuwait. Both were rescinded when administrators realized he'd turned seventy, passing regional age cutoffs.)

But the financial cushion David might have retired on had disappeared. During a divorce much earlier in his life, he had been forced to prematurely cash out his pension from sixteen years of teaching at California community colleges. If left alone, it would have grown to at least $500,000 with the state's match; at the time, it amounted to $22,000 that had to be split between him and his first wife. When David got married again later, it was to a woman who had also taken a financial hit, losing a $650,000 annuity from her first marriage in the 1991 collapse of Executive Life, which was, at the time, the largest failure in insurance industry history.

David demonstrated for me the squat-and-reach motions he made hundreds of times a day in the Amazon warehouse. He said he's lucky because, unlike his wife, he doesn't get aches and pains. He estimated that, at Amazon, he was making one-fifth of his peak earnings.

"I mean, I've never had any problem finding jobs ever, but the work is at these slave wages," David said. "This is the new age of retirees."

As workers like David told their stories, the Amazon encampments began to seem more and more like microcosms of a national catastrophe. The RV parks were jammed with workers who had fallen a long, long way from the middle-class comforts they had always taken for granted. These were standard-bearers for every economic misadventure to afflict Americans in recent decades. Everyone had a story.

One of them was Chuck Stout, seventy, who estimated he hiked thirteen miles a day as a warehouse "picker," pulling products from the shelves to fill orders. "People call it 'prison' because you walk single file, you clock in, you go do your thing," he told me. In a previous life, Chuck had spent forty-five years with the McDonald's Corporation, where he'd been a white-collar employee, serving as director of product development in the late 1970s for the company's world headquarters. But Chuck ended up declaring bankruptcy in 2011 after he and his wife, Barbara, a fifty-seven-year-old music teacher, saw $410,000 vaporize in the stock market. They lost their house on the golf course at Heron Pointe, a gated community in

Myrtle Beach, South Carolina, moving into a 1996 National Seabreeze motor coach they call TC. (On a good day, they explained, "TC" stood for "totally comfortable." On a bad day, it stood for "tin can.") Inside was a cross-stitch that says, "Home is where the hug is." After Amazon, their next job was selling beer and burgers at spring-training games for the Oakland A's.

Another one was Phil DePeal, a forty-eight-year-old Desert Storm veteran. "I keep telling myself it's just two months," he said. "If I can do the Army, I can do Amazon." Phil and his wife, Robin, forty-six, had started workamping after the market crashed in 2008 and the bank subsequently foreclosed on their home. Intense competition brought on by rising commodity prices had crushed Phil's Michigan scrap-metal hauling outfit, We-R-Junk. "Scrap went through the roof," he said. "Anyone who could put something on top of their car would haul it." Now they were living in a fifth-wheel trailer. They pulled it with a 1993 gold and maroon Dodge P350 pickup. On the side of the truck was a decal with the words "Easy Money."

"That was on there when we bought it," Phil said.

———

MANY OF THE WORKERS I met in the Amazon camps were part of a demographic that in recent years has grown with alarming speed: downwardly mobile older Americans. In the heyday of a place like Empire—the era of a strong middle class, complete with job stability and pensions—their circumstances had been virtually unimaginable.

Monique Morrissey, an economist at the Economic Policy Institute, spoke with me about the unprecedented nature of this change. "We're facing the first-ever reversal in retirement security in modern U.S. history," she explained. "Starting with the younger baby boomers, each successive generation is now doing worse than previous generations in terms of their ability to retire without seeing a drop in living standards."

That means no rest for the aging. Nearly nine million Americans sixty-five and older were still employed in 2016, up 60 percent from a decade earlier. Economists expect those numbers—along with the percentage of seniors in the labor force—to keep rising. A recent poll suggests that Americans now fear outliving their assets more than they fear dying. Another survey finds that, although most older Americans still view retirement as "a time of leisure," only 17 percent anticipate not working at all in their later years.

THE VERY IDEA OF RETIREMENT is a relatively new invention. For most of human history, people worked until they died or were too infirm to lift a finger, at which point they died pretty fast anyway. In 1795, forward-thinking founding father Thomas Paine penned a pamphlet called "Agrarian Justice" that proposed an annual pension of ten pounds sterling starting at age fifty, which he regarded as a typical life expectancy. Americans ignored him and more than a century passed before the German statesman Otto von Bismarck created the world's first old-age insurance. Adopted in 1889, Bismarck's plan rewarded workers who reached their seventieth birthdays with pensions. This move was designed to fend off Marxist agitation—and to do so on the cheap, since few Germans survived past that ripe old age. It also landed Bismarck, a right-wing empire builder nicknamed the Iron Chancellor, in the crosshairs of conservative critics, who accused him of going soft. But he'd been brushing aside their complaints for years. "Call it socialism or whatever you like; it is the same to me," he said to the Reichstag in 1881, at an early debate over state-run insurance.

The notion of retirement was evangelized in early twentieth-century America by William Osler, a celebrated and outspoken physician who helped found the Johns Hopkins School of Medicine. Workers peaked at forty, he argued in a 1905 speech, then went downhill until they hit their sixties—at which point, he prankishly suggested, they might as well be chloroformed. These remarks came to be known as the "chloroform speech" and they provoked a national scandal. *The New York Times'* editorial board likened his position to that of "savage tribes whose custom it is to knock their elders over the head whenever the juniors find their elders in their own way." Meanwhile, "Oslerize" enjoyed a brief heyday as a popular verb. (That coinage wasn't entirely fair, however, since the plan for compulsory euthanasia had been borrowed from Anthony Trollope's *The Fixed Period*, a dystopian tale that was quite possibly that author's least popular work, selling just 877 copies.)

The pension advocate Lee Welling Squier expressed a similar sentiment in 1912, in considerably less comic terms:

> After the age of sixty has been reached, the transition from non-dependence to dependence is an easy stage—property gone, friends passed away or removed, relatives become few, ambition collapsed, only a few short years left to live, with death a final and welcome end to it all—such conclusions inevitably sweep the wage-earner from hopeful independent citizen into that of the helpless poor.

Many industrialized nations followed Germany in adopting some form of old-age insurance. But the United States, land of the rugged individualist, lagged. By the early twentieth century, Americans who grew too old to work had two choices. They could move in with their kids, if they had any. Or they could go to the poorhouse, a dismal institution imported from Great Britain, where life was so wretched that residents—called "inmates"—might actually prefer to be Oslerized. One observer of such a facility in Sandusky, Ohio, described it thus: "Building very old and dilapidated; walls in terrible condition; no screens; swarms of flies everywhere; no comfortable chairs; rooms very dirty; inmates do the work; food very poor. The so-called hospital is a miserable place, more like a prison." An equally wretched institution appeared in a 1920 report to Colorado's state board of charities: "Building an old church condemned five years ago as unfit for habitation; walls unsafe and falling in; little protection from the cold; old floors cracked and dirty; miserable beds and bunks; a bedridden inmate with tubercular hips who has been in this bed since September and has not had a bath . . . in another dilapidated room sits a woman in rags, past ninety, over an old stove trying to keep warm."

So iconic—and dreaded—was the poorhouse that it was awarded a square in the earliest version of Monopoly. Situated on a corner of the board, this civic institution was the space of last resort for any player who "has not enough money to pay his expenses, and cannot borrow any or cannot sell or mortgage any of his property," according to the 1904 rules. In later versions, game designers paved over the poorhouse and put up a "free parking" space.

It took the Great Depression to make retirement into a reality in the United States. There were too many workers, too few jobs, and a consequent sense that the elderly needed to be nudged out of the labor pool. At the same time, older Americans weren't faring so well. By 1934, more than half lacked the means to support themselves. Some individual states had devised a patchwork of old-age pension systems, but these managed to serve just a fraction of the indigent elderly. Francis Townsend, a California physician who had also farmed hay and managed a failing dry-ice factory, began lobbying for what came to be known as the Townsend Plan: If a worker retired at sixty, the federal government would reward him with a monthly pension of up to $200. In short order, thousands of grassroots "Townsend Clubs" sprung up around the country. It was partly in response to this populist initiative that President Franklin D. Roosevelt and a Democratic Congress passed the Social Security Act of 1935—which, unlike the Townsend Plan, required future retirees to chip in to a common fund throughout their working lives. Five years later, the first Social Security check was issued to one Ida Mae Fuller, a sixty-five-year-old retired legal secretary in Vermont. It was in the amount of $22.54.

After the New Deal, economists began referring to America's retirement-finance model as a "three-legged stool." This sturdy tripod was composed of Social Security, private pensions, and combined investments and savings. In recent years, of course, two of those legs have been kicked out. Many Americans saw their assets destroyed by the Great Recession; even before the economic collapse, many had been saving less and less. And since the 1980s, employers have been replacing defined-benefit pensions that are funded by employers and guarantee a monthly sum in perpetuity with 401(k) plans, which often rely on employee contributions and can run dry before death. Marketed as instruments of financial liberation that would allow workers to make their own investment choices, 401(k)s were part of a larger cultural drift in America away from shared responsibilities toward a more precarious individualism. Translation: 401(k)s are vastly cheaper for companies than pension plans.

"Over the last generation, we have witnessed a massive transfer of economic risk from broad structures of insurance, including those sponsored by the corporate sector as well as by government, onto the fragile balance sheets of American families," Yale political scientist Jacob S. Hacker writes in his book *The Great Risk Shift*. The overarching message: "You are on your own."

All of which is to say that Social Security is now the largest single source of income for most Americans sixty-five and older. But it's woefully inadequate. "Instead of a three-legged stool, we have a pogo stick," quipped economist Peter Brady of the Investment Company Institute.

That means barely enough for necessities. Nearly half of middle-class workers may be forced to live on a food budget of as little as $5 a day when they retire, according to Teresa Ghilarducci, an economist and professor at the New School in New York City. "I call it 'the end of retirement,'" she said in an interview. Many retirees simply can't survive without some sort of paycheck. Meanwhile, she noted, jobs for older Americans are paying less and becoming ever more physically taxing. She worries we're returning to the world that Lee Welling Squier described more than a century ago. And any serious discussion of that problem, she added, is complicated by a cultural stigma. "I never talk about this issue in terms of 'retirement,'" she said. Americans traditionally abhor "the idea that you are mooching or you're not productive."

After all, the very mention of "retirement" risks summoning the stereotype of the "greedy geezer": a boogeyman conjured by critics of Social Security at the turn of the twenty-first century, foremost among them ex–U.S. Senator Alan Simpson of Wyoming. The "greedy geezer" spends his golden years in affluent leisure while draining the lifeblood from younger generations. He's a geriatric vampire, a septuagenarian version of Ronald Reagan's "welfare queen." Except that she drove a Cadillac, and the caricature Alan Simpson described drives a Lexus. Simpson also famously railed against the "Pink Panthers," a pro–Social Security lobbying group that does not actually exist; he invented it as a straw man—or straw woman?—to make an argument. When an actual advocacy group, the Older Women's League, accused him of spewing ageist and sexist vitriol, he dug in deeper, emailing them to say that Social Security has become "like a milk cow with 310 million tits!"

That email ended with a sarcastic sendoff. It seemed to suggest that the legislator had never set foot in a place like Amazon's new company towns or met any of the many older Americans who must labor long hours to supplement their meager benefits.

It read, "Call when you get honest work!"

CHAPTER FOUR

Escape Plan

FACING AN INSURMOUNTABLE PROBLEM—her low Social Security benefit—Linda did what anyone would: consulted the internet. She came across a website with the following words:

> Maybe you were a gypsy, vagabond or hobo in a past life,
> but you think you could never afford to live the life of freedom
> you long for?
>
> Perhaps you are just sick of the rat race and want to simplify
> your life.
>
> We have good news for you, you can, and we are here to show
> you how!

Linda had discovered CheapRVLiving.com, the creation of a former Safeway shelf stocker from Alaska named Bob Wells. Imagine an anti-consumerist doctrine preached with the zeal of the prosperity gospel—that was Bob's message. He evangelized living happily with less. One principle underscored all his writings—the best way to find freedom, he suggested, was by becoming what mainstream society would consider homeless.

"The key is eliminating the single highest expense most of us have, our housing," Bob wrote. He urged readers to eschew traditional homes and apartments in favor of what some nomads call "wheel estate": a van, car, or RV. He noted that there were vandwellers subsisting on $500 a month or less—a sum that made immediate sense to Linda—and drafted a sample budget stretching that pittance across life's necessities, including allowances for food, car insurance, gas, cell service, and a small emergency fund.

Bob's own vandwelling odyssey had started nearly two decades earlier, with considerably less enthusiasm. In 1995 he was struggling through a bitter divorce with his wife of thirteen years, the mother of his two young sons. And he was what he calls a "debt addict," with $30,000 on maxed-out credit cards. He was getting ready to declare bankruptcy.

When the time came for Bob to move out of his family's crowded trailer in Anchorage, he decamped to Wasilla, where years earlier he'd bought a couple of acres with plans to build a house there. So far he only had a foundation and a floor. Undeterred, he stayed in a tent, using the place as a base camp from which he could travel the fifty miles into Anchorage for work.

Before long, he yearned to be closer to his kids and to the Safeway where he held a steady job. (His father had been a Safeway manager and Bob had scored his first job there, as a bagger, on his sixteenth birthday.) But apartments in Anchorage were expensive and sustaining two separate households seemed next to impossible. Of the $2,400 he took home each month, half went to his ex. "She got $1,200 of it, and that left me $1,200, and you can't rent an apartment in Anchorage on that," he said. "Most places you can, but I certainly couldn't there." Meanwhile, he was burning time and gas money every day as he commuted between Anchorage and Wasilla. He started feeling desperate.

So Bob tried an experiment. To save on fuel, he began spending the workweek in the city, sleeping in an old Ford Courier pickup with a camper shell, and then returning to Wasilla on the weekends. That relieved some of the pressure. When he was in Anchorage, he parked right outside the Safeway. The managers didn't mind. If someone didn't show up for a shift, they'd offer it to Bob—he was right there, after all—and he'd score overtime that way. All of which made him wonder: Could I do this permanently?

Bob couldn't imagine living full-time in his tiny camper, but he started to mull over other options. On his commute, he'd been driving past a battered Chevy box truck with a "For Sale" sign parked in front of an electrician's shop. One day he went inside to ask about it. The vehicle had no mechanical problems, he learned. It was just so ugly and beat up that the boss was embarrassed to send it on service calls. The asking price was $1,500, the same amount Bob had left in savings. He went all in.

The walls of the box truck were seven feet tall with a roll-up back door. The floor was eight-by-twelve feet. It was really the size of a small bedroom, Bob reasoned, rolling out his sleeping pad and blankets. But as he lay there that first night, he found himself weeping. No matter what he told himself, immersion in this new life felt soul-shattering. It didn't help that, in his forty years, Bob had never been a particularly cheerful or optimistic person. From childhood on he'd learned hard lessons about impermanence as the ground shifted, sometimes literally, under his feet. When he was a toddler, his unhappily married parents had moved between Flagstaff and Prescott, Arizona, and Ponca City, Oklahoma. In 1961, the year he turned six, his family settled in Anchorage. Three years later, the world came to an end. Or at least it felt that way. The second-largest recorded earthquake in history struck south-central Alaska at 5:36 p.m. on March 27, 1964, when a fault ruptured between the Pacific and North American tectonic plates. The Great Alaska Earthquake, also known as the Good Friday Earthquake, registered 9.2 on the Richter scale and lasted four and a half terrifying minutes, with numerous aftershocks. Tsunamis swept Alaska's coastal towns, while

Anchorage was devastated by landslides that demolished entire city blocks. The sixty-foot control tower at Anchorage International Airport collapsed. Concrete slabs tumbled from the façade of the five-story J. C. Penney building, crushing people and cars below. At Bob's school, Denali Elementary, the foundation was riven with cracks and a brick chimney crashed through the roof, shuttering the building for the next year.

Bob remembers cowering at home with no light, no heat. Outside the weather was below freezing and there was snow on the ground. "I mean the earth opens up around you and all night we had after-shocks," he said. "You'd hear houses exploding. You'd be laying there in bed and a house would explode. There'd be a natural gas leak and it'd ignite somehow."

His home didn't blow up that night. But it did, in a sense, seven years later, when he was sixteen and his parents finally split up. His sister chose to live with their mother. Bob felt sorry for his dad and decided to stay with him. Before long he was also sharing a roof with a stepmother he hated. As Bob grew into adulthood, he fended off feelings of emptiness. In the coming years, he'd try to fill that void with whatever was at hand: debt, food, sex, religion.

Bob had never been especially proud of the life he was building. But when he moved into a box truck at age forty, any remaining scraps of self-worth disappeared. He feared he'd hit rock bottom. He saw himself critically: a working father of two who couldn't keep his marriage afloat, reduced to living in a vehicle. He told himself he was homeless, a loser. "Crying myself to sleep was a routine event," he said.

That box truck, which he often referred to as a van, would be his home for the next six years. Living there wasn't the descent into misery he expected, though. Things started to change as he made the place habitable. He built bunk beds out of plywood and two-by-sixes. He slept on the bottom one and used the top as a storage loft. He lugged in a cozy recliner. He screwed plastic shelving into the walls. For a makeshift kitchen, he had an ice chest and a Coleman two-burner stove. For water, he visited convenience store restrooms and filled up a gallon jug. On his days off from work, his sons came to visit. One slept on the bunk bed and the other on the recliner.

Before long, when Bob remembered how he used to live, he found he didn't miss much. On the contrary, thinking about some of the things he now lacked—in particular rent and utility bills—made him giddy. With the money he was saving, he kept making the van more comfortable. He insulated the walls and roof. He bought a catalytic heater with a forty-gallon propane tank to stay warm when winter temperatures plunged to thirty below and installed a through-ceiling fan to keep cool in the summer. After he added a generator, battery, and inverter, it was easy to run lights at night. Soon he even had a microwave and a twenty-seven-inch tube TV.

He grew so attached to this new lifestyle that, when the engine blew on the box truck, he didn't falter. Bob sold his land in Wasilla, along with the shell of the house he'd continued to build there on credit cards. Part of the proceeds went to fixing his engine.

"I honestly don't know if I would have been brave enough to do it if I hadn't been forced into it," Bob admits on his website. But in retrospect, he's glad the change happened. "When I moved into the van, I realized that everything that society had told me was a lie—that I had to get married and live in a house with a white picket fence and go to work, and then be happy at the very end of my life, but be miserable until then," he told me in an interview. "I was happy for the first time ever living in my van."

In 2005, Bob started CheapRVLiving.com. The website began as a modest collection of how-to articles for readers hoping to live in a vehicle on a shoestring budget. The key was "boondocking": going off the grid rather than relying on the kind of hookups for water, sewage, and electricity that come with a paid spot in an RV park. (Though its informal usage has broadened, the word "boondocking"—as purists will quickly point out—also implies that one is parked way out in the wilderness. Vehicle dwellers who are doing this sort of thing in cities are technically not boondocking—they're "stealth parking" or "stealth camping." In any case, Bob's website shared strategies for both kinds of living.)

After the financial meltdown of 2008, traffic to CheapRVLiving.com exploded. "I started getting emails almost daily from people who had lost their jobs, their savings were running out, and they were facing foreclosure on their home," he later wrote. Cast out of the middle class, these readers were trying to learn how to survive. Googling phrases such as "budget living" and "living in a car or van" brought them to Bob's website. And in a culture where economic misfortune was blamed largely on its victims, Bob offered them encouragement instead of opprobrium. "At one time there was a social contract that if you played by the rules (went to school, got a job, and worked hard) everything would be fine," he told readers. "That's no longer true today. You can do everything right, just the way society wants you to do it, and still end up broke, alone, and homeless." By moving into vans and other vehicles, he suggested, people could become conscientious objectors to the system that had failed them. They could be reborn into lives of freedom and adventure.

ALL OF THIS HAD A PRECEDENT. In the mid-1930s, with America in the grip of the Great Depression, house trailers went into mass production for the first time. Hobbyists and small-batch builders had been constructing the curious contraptions for years, but now their popularity skyrocketed. "At first . . . the trailer was just something different in camping . . . then people discovered you could live in them," *Fortune Magazine* recounted two years later.

At the time, millions of dispossessed Americans shared the sentiments Bob later echoed. They'd upheld their end of the social contract, yet the system had let them down. Some of those people had a revelation—that they could escape the stranglehold of rent by moving into house trailers. Becoming nomads. Getting free. Heck, it beat Hooverville. "Go anywhere, stop anywhere, escape taxes and rent—this is irresistible. Nothing but death has ever before offered so much in a single package," read an article in *Automotive Industries* in 1936.

"We are rapidly becoming a nation on wheels," wrote one prominent sociologist in *The New York Times* in 1936. "Today hundreds of thousands of families have packed their possessions into traveling houses, said goodbye to their friends, and taken to the open roads . . . [soon] more families will take to the road, making an important proportion of our people into wandering gypsies." Roger Ward Babson, a financial oracle who'd foreseen the 1929 market crash, turned heads when he announced that half of all Americans would be living in house trailers by the 1950s. *Harper's Magazine* proclaimed that "homes on wheels" represented "a new way of life which will eventually change our architecture, our morals, our laws, our industrial system, and our system of taxation."

Over the next quarter century, Americans bought—or built in their garages or backyards—an estimated million and a half to two million house trailers. The fad ended around 1960 with the rise of the so-called "mobile home": inexpensive manufactured housing units that were roomier than their wandering cousins but offered less freedom since, after getting towed to a trailer park, they typically stayed there.

Social critics were split on the trailerites, depicting them as either liberty-loving pioneers or harbingers of social disintegration. The writer David A. Thornburg, whose parents lived for fifteen years in a house trailer, saw in their push for self-determination a quiet revolution. In a poetic history called *Galloping Bungalows*, he wrote:

> And so, right out of the heart of the Great Depression a new dream was born: the dream of escape. Escape from snow and ice, from high taxes and rent, from an economic system that nobody trusted anymore. Escape! For the winter, for the weekend, for the rest of your life. All it took was a little courage and a $600 house trailer.

He went on to elaborate:

> The Great Depression reduced millions of Americans of every age and class to the powerless condition of adolescents . . . But a few people saw opportunity amid all this chaos— opportunity to rebuild their world, their values along more personal and perhaps less vulnerable lines. Among these rebuilders were the pioneer trailerites of the 30s, over a million strong, idealists and iconoclasts, thoughtful and deliberate drop-outs. People who chose not to wait for government or big business to save them, who chose to take their economic destiny into their own hands. People who elected to slip the middle-class noose and form for themselves a wholly new subculture—a life just a little freer, a little more autonomous and less anxiety-ridden, a little closer to their hearts' desires.

EVEN AS THE STOCK MARKET IMPROVED, Bob kept hearing from new economic refugees for whom the "jobless recovery" had brought little relief. It seemed that, unlike the trailerites of the thirties—most of whom eventually went back to "stick and brick" housing—the new wave of nomads were girding themselves for a more permanent transition.

"Money is a major issue for all of us, especially in today's very bad economy," Bob wrote in a 2012 post about budgeting. "Almost every week I get an email from a reader telling me they lost their job a while ago and now they are being evicted. Among their other questions, they ask me if they can afford to be a vandweller. I write back and answer their other questions and then ask them, 'How can you afford to *not* be a vandweller?' I am convinced that living in a car, van or RV is by far the cheapest possible way to live long-term."

By then Bob's website included reports on residing in vehicles of all sizes, from a subcompact Ford Festiva and a Toyota Prius to vans of every conceivable vintage and even a decommissioned U.S. Air Force bus. Some of their inhabitants were featured, too, including Charlene Swankie (aka "Swankie Wheels"), who moved into a van at age sixty-four when she was too broke to rent a decent apartment and was struggling with bad knees and asthma. The lifestyle suited her; she dropped sixty-five pounds and embarked on a quest to paddle all fifty states in a yellow kayak that she transported atop her van. (Swankie ended up completing her mission at age seventy and set a new goal: hiking the 800-mile Arizona Trail.) In another article, a nomad called Trooper Dan described losing his job in Ohio and living in a white Toyota pickup with a red camper top, which he'd driven to southern Florida and called his BOV, or bug-out vehicle. As an ardent survivalist, he'd long been ready for WTSHTF, or When The Shit Hits The Fan. "I'm just an average guy that has fallen victim to the current economic downturn. Basically I feel like I am camping and I do not consider myself homeless," he wrote on the website. "I think this is a sign of things to come and we will be seeing people

Swankie Wheels has a map in her van that commemorates kayaking all fifty states.

living in tents and vehicles everywhere (remember 'Hoover towns'?). The 'mobile homelessness' is so bad that the cops don't even stop people from doing it anymore."

CheapRVLiving.com covered topics from choosing and outfitting a vehicle to finding seasonal jobs and eating healthy on the road. Tutorials explained how to install rooftop solar panels, which had plunged in price over the previous decade, putting a technology that was once only available to relatively affluent folks within reach of low-budget vandwellers.

For purposes of stealth—to avoid getting harassed by passersby or, worse, rousted and maybe ticketed by police—readers were advised to hide their solar panels between the bars of a luggage carrier or ladder rack.

While many of the articles he published were purely pragmatic, Bob also dabbled in philosophy. He posted inspirational quotes from a grab bag of thinkers, from Braveheart and Dale Carnegie to Kahlil Gibran, Hellen Keller, Henry David Thoreau, and J.R.R. Tolkien. Pairing this borrowed rhetoric with personal existential musings, Bob suggested that a pared-down and peripatetic lifestyle could go far beyond meeting basic needs, becoming a portal to loftier aspirations: freedom, self-actualization, and adventure.

To mainstream Americans this kind of transience may suggest a modern-day version of *The Grapes of Wrath*. But it's worth noting a critical distinction. For the nomadic Dust Bowl–era refugees who were once snubbed as "Okies," self-worth meant keeping alive the embers of one precious hope: that someday the status quo would return, moving them back into traditional housing, restoring at least an iota of stability.

Along with many of the wayfarers he came to inspire, Bob saw things differently. He envisioned a future where economic and environmental upheavals had become the new American normal. For this reason, he didn't package nomadic living as a quick fix, something to tide folks over until society had stabilized, at which point they could reintegrate with the mainstream. Rather he aspired to create a wandering tribe whose members could operate outside of—or even transcend—the fraying social order: a parallel world on wheels.

By late 2013, a discussion forum on Bob's website had attracted more than 4,500 registered members. Less than three years later, the number had grown to over 6,500. Nomads swapped advice on everything from keeping up with snail mail to coping with loneliness and police harassment. In this supportive environment, even a basic question like "how do I shower?" generated an outpouring of clever solutions. Some commenters, for example, recommended joining a no-frills gym chain—Planet Fitness was a popular pick—and treating the membership like a nationwide washroom pass. Some swore by sponge baths and the liberal use of baby wipes. Some preferred solar showers, which resemble giant IV bags, with one side painted black to trap heat. Some bathed using pressurized garden sprayers. Some knew about Laundromats with pay-per-use shower stalls in the back. Others visited truck stops like Flying J, Love's, and Pilot, which reward drivers with shower credits when they fuel up. Long-haul truckers often accumulate more freebies than they need and gift their credits to fellow travelers in the checkout line.*

The conversations grew intense, and they weren't limited to CheapRVLiving.com. Bob's site was just one node in a rapidly expanding network of internet gathering places where far-flung, low-budget nomads could learn from and support each other. The online

---

* I got my first-ever truck stop shower for free during the winter of 2014–15 at the Pilot in Quartzsite, Arizona. I left my van carrying soap, shampoo, and flip-flops in a plastic bag, walked inside to pay, and probably made a face when I heard it would cost $12. A trucker at the register to my right slid his rewards card over the counter and told the cashier to comp my shower. "Sir, you realize that if you use your card now, you can't use it again for another twenty-four hours," the cashier told him. The driver raised his elbows and sniffed under each armpit—first left, then right—and shrugged. "Awwww, it's already been a week," he said.

community goes back to at least November 2000, when a mysterious figure calling himself "lance5g" created "Live in Your Van," a Yahoo message board, with this simple introduction:

Welcome. I wish to teach interested parties the technique of living in your van for the purpose of saving, what else? $.

Obviously, this subject is best suited to the single male, but the woman can also learn . . .

Categories: bathing, sleeping, parking, going to the bathroom, safety, avoiding detection, interior organization, winter nights.

After that, lance5g never posted again. Like a low-rent version of the "watchmaker god" devised by Enlightenment-era theologists, he built a world, set it in motion, and walked away. His creation grew without him, though, populated with what would become a tight-knit group of friends posting under such names as vangypsy and vwtank-girl. Then came a problem: Yahoo decided to move all of its message boards to a new platform. Groups with absentee owners seemed unlikely to survive that transition.

One of the most active members of "Live in Your Van" was a gregarious wanderer called Ghost Dancer. On January 1, 2002, Ghost Dancer was parked outside a McDonald's on Highway 41 in Vincennes, Indiana, in his home, a brown 1989 Ford F150 pickup. He'd heard that the changeover deadline for message boards was the end of the day. He worried: Were his new friends, already scattered across the country, about to lose their clubhouse on the internet? Not knowing what would happen was eating him up, like the buildup to Y2K writ small. Yet he had done nothing to prepare.

When the solution came, it seemed obvious: Why not create a new gathering place before the old one went dark? To do this, Ghost Dancer couldn't just stroll into McDonald's with a laptop. For starters, he didn't own a laptop, and WiFi hotspots wouldn't be ubiquitous for another a few years. So he jury-rigged an internet connection

Ghost Dancer sits in the van that is his current home.

between the pay phone and the limited equipment he carried in the truck. "Freejack style," he called it. The setup relied on a Konexx acoustic coupler: a device that attached to a pay phone handset to receive and transmit analog data by holding a microphone to the earpiece and a loudspeaker to the mouthpiece. The other end of this coupler was plugged into a WebTV box, which had a built-in modem and offered basic browsing services; such boxes had started appearing in the mid-1990s, when computers were more expensive and less intuitive. To save space, Ghost Dancer had hung the WebTV from his CB radio. From there, it was connected to a thirteen-inch Philips television sitting on the passenger-side floor. After hours of fiddling with the setup, he fed thirty-five cents into the pay phone to get online, then logged into Yahoo and started a message board called "Vandwellers: Live in Your Van 2." He was proud of that success, a bit of cyber-McGyvering that became a well-worn tale and led one popular blogger to call him "vandwelling's founding father."

Only later did Ghost Dancer realize he'd screwed up. Working across time zones, he'd blown the purported deadline by a few hours.

It didn't matter, though. Members followed him over to the new message board. And though Yahoo never shut down the original "Live in Your Van," it became a virtual ghost town, overrun by adult-industry spambots that hawk "casual encounters" and "kinky cybersingles" to an audience of none. Meanwhile, "Live in Your Van 2" attracted thousands of newcomers, including Bob Wells, and kept gaining momentum. In the four years following the 2008 economic crash, the ranks more than doubled, growing to 8,560 people. A description of the group read:

> VanDwellers is the meeting place of [a] far-flung tribe. It is
> the Circle of Elders, the Nurturing Cradle for those who
> find themselves entering this cultural world by choice or by
> circumstance, the place for the Rites of Passage of newbies,
> a place where the Hunters and Gatherers of Information
> share the bounty with the tribe.

Their conversation spread across platforms. In 2010, a member of the Yahoo tribe started a Facebook group called "VanDwellers: Live in Your Van," with a similar mission statement appearing in a FAQ file:

> It is all about caring, sharing, giving of knowledge, forming
> friendships and looking after one another.

The same document also raised the thornier issue of participating in a mutual-support network whose members were frequently strapped for cash:

> Most of us in the group are poor. When disaster strikes it often
> leaves us with nothing or no money and depending on the
> kindness of relatives, friends and sometimes strangers. While
> we don't want the group to turn into a cyber-begging den, from
> time to time when people are broke and are desperate they will

ask the group to help. We encourage you to use your own
judgment here as to what you can and want to do.

On Reddit, a thread called "vandwellers" began in 2010 and grew
to include more than 26,000 readers. On YouTube, dozens of do-it-
yourselfers competed to be the Bob Vila of vandwelling, showing off
tricks for transforming humdrum passenger vehicles into well-
appointed cabins on wheels. Some websites compiled tips and updates
from travelers across the country, feeding them into searchable maps
of nomad-friendly places. One of them, FreeCampsites.net, logged
idyllic places in nature where visitors could stay for free, from small
city parks to sprawling national forests. Another, AllStays.com, tracked
businesses that allow overnight parking, from truck stops to casinos,
Cabela's sporting good outlets and Cracker Barrel restaurants. It also
sold a smartphone app dedicated to "Wallydocking," or boondocking
at Walmart.

Walmart has long endeared itself to RVers by letting them stay
overnight in its parking lots. Some believe founder Sam Walton, an
avid bird hunter, started the tradition in solidarity with outdoorsy
types. Others think it's a canny strategy to capture more shoppers.
Either way, nomads appreciate the invitation, though it frustrates paid
campgrounds and RV parks that don't like losing business. The policy, however, isn't in effect everywhere. Some Walmarts are located
in cities that ban the practice. Others have revoked the privilege
because visitors started overstaying their welcome, setting up barbe-
cues and lawn furniture, building semipermanent encampments. In
March 2015, a melee between police and an eight-member family of
Christian musicians from Idaho, who'd been living out of their Chevy
Suburban in the parking lot of the Walmart Supercenter in Cottonwood, Arizona, ended in a struggle over an officer's gun that left one
of the travelers dead. The store started rousting overnighters after
that. ("It is so sad that a few morons have to ruin a good deal for
everyone," wrote the editor of the *RV Daily Report* website.) Some
Walmarts are in a gray zone, struggling to manage the swelling ranks

of nighttime visitors—many living out of automobiles—brought on by the precarious economy. Food trucks from an outreach group called Mobile Loaves and Fishes make regular visits to the retailer's parking lots around Austin, Texas. "Customers of Walmart probably get wigged out a little bit by people sleeping in their cars in the Walmart parking lot," Alan Graham, the organization's founder, told a local radio reporter. "But god bless [management] for continuing to allow that."

With thousands of Walmarts across the country, how is a bleary-eyed traveler supposed to keep track of which ones are welcoming? The AllStays "Walmart Overnight Parking Locator" app marks every store in the United States and Canada with a little "W" icon. Some are red. Park there and you may get rousted or, worse, towed. Most are yellow. Clicking on them brings up user experience reports, like the following from a Walmart in Pahrump, Nevada:

#5101 Supercenter

Jul 2015: Stayed fine in my van. There were two other traveling vans.

May 2015: One other RV. Permission was granted by night customer service manager. Parked near truck dock by first concrete island with trees. Many trucks delivering early in the AM, so give them plenty of room.

Sept 2010: Manager welcomes RVers. Park in the south end of the parking lot and be careful not to block their delivery trucks.

The little "W" icons and notes feel like an updated version of hobo signs, the glyphs used by drifters to share place-based knowledge in what passed for crowdsourcing during the late nineteenth and early twentieth centuries. Marked on walls and doors with chalk or coal, sometimes carved into trees, the signs warned of threats—zealous police, vicious dogs, bad water—or pointed out resources: safe campsite, kindhearted lady, work available.

The proliferation of blogs through the mid-2000s encouraged otherwise solitary travelers to chronicle their adventures before a wide audience, giving rise to microcelebrities. Among the earliest and most prolific was George Lehrer, aka "Tioga George," a cancer survivor who began posting in 2003 when, in his mid-sixties and lacking the income to afford both his apartment and food, he moved into a twenty-seven-foot Fleetwood Tioga Arrow motorhome with solar panels and satellite internet. On his blog, The Adventures of Tioga and George, he and his trusty rig were "The Greatest Vaga-bonds in the History of the World" and ventured forth with a stir-ring motto: "Never pay rent!" George posted whimsically about his travels with "Ms. Tioga" (his RV) and their crew of similarly anthro-pomorphized companions: Mr. Sony Mavica (a camera), Mr. Chips (a desktop computer), Mr. Sunny (a solar power system), Mr. Data-Storm (a satellite antenna), Mr. Dometic (a fridge), Mr. DeLorme (a GPS system), and so on. Often he'd write several updates over the course of a day, from tales of befriending fellow travelers to battling an infestation of tiny ants, to getting shaken down by crooked cops in Mexico, where he especially loved to travel. He posted detailed accounts of his income and expenses, including revenue from Google ads. (In August 2010, it topped $1,300). He wrote movingly about the suicide of his son, David, and reminisced about sleeping on the din-ing room floor at David's tiny home after the recession of the early 1990s wiped out the company that had employed George to sell AutoCAD software. Less than a decade after George started writ-ing, his blog had attracted some seven million visits.

Tioga George influenced a generation of boondocking bloggers. They included Tara Burns, a twentysomething sex worker in a '98 Chevy Astro. Her popular blog, Hobo Stripper, chronicled what it was like to "live in a van and drive all over the country getting naked for cash." When she wasn't traveling between strip clubs with Bro, her border collie, she was at the keyboard, instructing readers how to sell a lap dance or how to change an engine's cooling system water pump. Another crowd favorite was RV Sue & Her Canine Crew, the blog of Susan Rogers, a sixtysomething retired math teacher from Georgia who credited Tioga George with inspiring her to hit the road. Posting daily dispatches from a '05 Chevy Express van towing a seventeen-foot Casita trailer, she accrued a lively following and, in 2012, made national news after her blog helped reunite Rusty Reed, a military veteran living out of a camo-painted pickup camper, with his lost shepherd mix dog, Timber, in Arizona. Pursuing what she called "low-budget, high-experience living" and "living on less and enjoying life more," Sue became a role model to many readers. "I think of RVSue as my RV Fairy Godmother," wrote one blogger who lives in a truck camper and calls himself ZenOnWheels. "Through Sue's humor and humility I read story after story of her daily life on the road and, slowly, over many months, realized that yes, I could definitely do this too," he added, expressing gratitude for her "openness, kindness, and darned good storytelling."

Like Tioga George, Sue shared financial reports that, starting in 2013, included income from ads on her site. By the end of that first year, it wasn't unusual for her to earn more than $1,000 a month. Sometimes this agitated less popular bloggers who'd tried monetizing their own posts with little success. (While most readers don't seem to begrudge traveling bloggers compensation for the work they do, it's easy to see how ads running on minimalist, anti-consumerist sites might sometimes seem off-key. On Cheap RV Living, for example, a post called "Getting Rid of Stuff" with a quote from Bertrand Russell—"It is preoccupation with possessions, more than anything else, that prevents us from living freely and nobly"—strikes an odd chord positioned beside a column of Amazon links flogging such products as a twelve-volt portable stove and a "luggable loo" toilet seat.)

Inevitably the online conversations between kindred wanderers spilled into real-world gatherings. As the nomads met over campfires in forests and deserts around the country, they began to form the kind of improvised clans that the novelist Armistead Maupin called "logical"—rather than "biological"—family. A few even called it a "vanily." For some of them, spending holidays together became more appealing than reuniting with actual kin. A typical scene: Christmas dinner on a barren, moonscape-like stretch of desert near Interstate 10 in California draws more than a dozen vehicles, whose inhabitants range in age from their twenties to seventies. They share a fifteen-pound turkey that has been deboned, halved, and cooked on a pair of portable grills, with sides of mashed potatoes, gravy, and cranberry sauce and two kinds of pie, until even the dogs licking leftover crumbs from the plates are sated.

Much of the action was happening out West, but get-togethers—also known as GTGs—were also coalescing back East, from Ohio down to Alabama, Georgia, and Tennessee. When folks caravanned from place to place together like wagon trains of yore, setting and breaking camp along the way, they called it a "roving GTG." In 2011, Bob organized for the first time what became one of the most antici-pated gatherings of the year. The Rubber Tramp Rendezvous, or RTR,* was inspired in part by the rough-and-ready mountain men of

Bob Wells holds a map of national parks during a talk on boondocking at the Rubber Tramp Rendezvous.

---

* When I first attended this gathering in 2013, there were about sixty mobile dwell-ings there. Four years later, in 2017, there were an estimated five hundred rigs.

the nineteenth century, who spent much of the year in hardship and isolation, trapping critters in remote places but reuniting each year at an annual fur-trading rendezvous. Held on public desert land near the town of Quartzsite, Arizona, for two weeks in January, the winter RTR was a chance for nomads to share skills and stories, make friends, and mentor newcomers to the lifestyle. Vandwelling aspirants sometimes showed up with tents or borrowed vans to learn everything they could before hitting the road themselves. The event was free and awareness spread mostly by word of mouth.

For this community, making an effort to gather in person was no trifling thing. Members spend much of the year scattered across the country. Often they lack the gas money to drive long distances in a straight shot. And many consider themselves loners. Among the hermits, RV Sue has cultivated an especially solitary reputation, pleading with her blog readers not to drop in on her campsites unannounced, explaining that "blogging suits me well because I can interact with all kinds of interesting people without having to actually meet them." Some of her fans have written about coming across a familiar seventeen-foot Casita during their travels—then realizing who that trailer belonged to and immediately hightailing it in the other direction.

Some folks who attend the Rubber Tramp Rendezvous deliberately park on the outermost edge of the camping zone, while others can only handle human company in small doses and stay for a short while rather than the full two weeks. When Swankie arrived at an RTR session wearing a T-shirt that said "Introverts Unite: We're Here, We're Uncomfortable, and We Want to Go Home," she got smiles and nods of acknowledgment all day.

Increasingly Bob Wells found himself the de facto social coordinator for this growing band of isolates. And after the rendezvous dispersed each year, some of them started migrating with Bob to his next campsite. (Many free public camping areas, including where the RTR takes place, enforce a fourteen-day limit; when that expires, you've got to move to a new site at least twenty-five miles away.) Bob welcomed them, and they parked at a respectful distance to give him space. When a blog reader noted that folks had taken to following Bob around and referred to them, tongue-in-cheek, as his "disciples," he joked back, "Despite my best efforts at mind-control, brain-washing, and manipulation, I still don't have any disciples!"

Bob's tone wasn't always so upbeat, though. In a more serious conversation with a reader, he wrote, "I think you are right, many, many more people are going to be forced into a much simpler life. My goal is to help them make the transition as easily as they can and hopefully eventually find joy in it, just like so many of us have."

———

BROWSING CHEAPRVLIVING.COM, absorbing the tales of transformed lives, Linda had a revelation of her own. "Holy crap!" she thought. "If they could do it, I'm sure I could, too." Bob made extreme frugality sound like a path to freedom: liberation instead of deprivation. Or in Linda's words: "Living a life of plenty with what you have." Besides, even as a solo traveler, it was clear she would never be truly alone— there was a whole band of wanderers to meet, including many solo women around her age who were also on the road. Together they were a subculture, building their own set of customs, experimenting with survival strategies and circulating the best ones, writing a playbook for life on the underside of the economy. That kind of fellowship was important to Linda. "I'm a real social person," she explained. "I didn't feel like I would be out there by myself lonesome and depressed and just scraping by. My life could be exciting and fulfilling and creative."

Linda began dreaming of the right vehicle and browsing Craigslist. She looked at dozens of ads and found one strong candidate, but she didn't have enough money to buy anything yet. So her oldest grandchild, who is autistic, ended up purchasing it for himself, lured by the promise of cheap rent: $500 a month plus electricity for a space in an RV park that wasn't too far from his parents and three siblings. Linda was glad to see him get it since he had few other options for living independently. "Part-time at Burger King is not enough money to live on," she said drily.

Then came a windfall. Collin, Linda's son-in-law, worked in sales for a commercial storage firm that installed everything from gun and evidence lockers to museum archive cabinets, often on government contracts. He noticed a gap in the plans for an upcoming project at a Veterans Affairs hospital. New signs were going up throughout the facility, but no arrangements had been made to do the prep work: tearing the old signs down, patching and painting the walls beneath. So Linda's daughter Audra took on the job and delegated some of the work to her. "Fifty dollars an hour to paint and prep for the VA hospital was such a blessing to me," Linda recalls. Within a couple months, she'd amassed $10,000.

In April 2013, Linda was perusing Craigslist when she saw a 1994 El Dorado motorhome with teal and black stripes. With only 29,000 miles on its odometer, the twenty-eight-foot RV should have been worth about $17,000. The asking price, however, was just $4,000.

Excited, Linda set up a meeting and brought along a girlfriend for moral support. Together they checked out the RV. The outside was in reasonable condition, apart from rotting tires and a football-size crater in the loft above the cab on the passenger side. It had been patched with a smear of caulk that looked like dried toothpaste. ("That caulk didn't need to be there," Linda reflected. "I don't know what he was thinking. We call that 'building material abuse.'") The owner explained that he had been driving on a crowned road—high in the center and low on the sides, which made the vehicle tilt outward—when he collided with an inward-leaning telephone pole.

Opening the door to the RV, Linda was hit with a stale, musty odor. Pond-liner and plywood covered the floor. The walls were draped with more trash bag–type plastic. *Water damage*, she thought, and her hopes sagged. But as she inspected the inside more closely, she realized the bad smells were wafting out of the shower, which had a hole that wouldn't be too hard to repair. The rest of the interior was immaculate, from a cozy bedroom in the back to a dinette beside the kitchen. The upholstery, window coverings, and carpet all looked great; she pegged the owner as a type A personality, someone who'd never stepped inside the RV without removing his shoes. Compared to some of the vans she'd been reading about, this place was the Ritz Carlton. The generator was broken, but just about everything else worked, including the flush toilet, which made her glad. (While Linda had read about vandwellers lining five-gallon buckets with plastic to use as portable toilets, she'd already decided that was most definitely not for her.)

Linda could feel her optimism returning. Then a familiar voice cut in. "Oh, no. You can't. You *can't* fix that," her friend said. But it was too late. Linda had already made up her mind. "Oh, come on, Mrs. '*I can't!*'" she retorted. "I live by '*I can.*'"

Linda bought the RV. She fixed up the shower, abolishing the funky smell. She didn't mess with the caulk-filled crater over the cab—while unattractive, it seemed to be holding for now. The tires couldn't wait, so she spent $1,200 to replace them. That was a major expense, but Linda was investing in her future—her freedom—and already had some ideas about how to keep money flowing in once she was on the road.

Bob had blogged about the three seasons he'd spent working for California Land Management as a camp host in the Sierra National Forest. Following his lead, Linda applied to the same company and landed a gig near Yosemite. "I can't believe how easy it is to get a job in an RV," she later reflected. She'd once waited six months for an opening at the Home Depot in San Clemente, and that had been a transfer. Ageism, she knew, could make it painfully hard to find a new job in one's later years, but the people who hired itinerants for seasonal work didn't seem to be reading from the same script as other employers. "If you have an RV, go on the internet and you get a job in six seconds," she marveled.

Linda had also become a fan of Jimbo's Journeys, the blog of Jim Melvin, a former Lowe's appliance salesman in his late sixties with a white push-broom mustache. After he realized he'd never be able to afford retirement in his home state of California, Jim took off in a 1992 white and powder blue Lazy Daze RV, citing Tioga George as his inspiration. He traveled between seasonal jobs, first alone and then with Chica, a hungry stray Chihuahua that wandered up to his RV in a trailer park and was thereafter Jim's declared "soul mate." Jim did many kinds of work: groundskeeping at Piney Ridge RV Estates in Texas as July temperatures soared past 100 degrees; camp hosting at Ochoco Divide Campground in central Oregon; flipping burgers at Tempe Diablo Stadium in Arizona during spring training for the Los Angeles Angels; and joining CamperForce at the Amazon.com warehouse in Fernley. He described the last of these jobs as the hardest he'd ever had. Getting through it meant taking two Aleve each day. The aches and pains didn't subside for months. But it paid more than the other gigs and he liked bonding with fellow RVers who were working there. "I have met a lot of very friendly, fun people," he wrote. "Would I return next year? You bet your sweet bippy!!!"

Linda decided to apply to Amazon, too. The company was offering a $50 referral bonus so she put down Jim's name. "Thank god for the bloggers, man," she said. "Can you imagine? We didn't have that when I was young. If you needed something it was like, 'Does your neighbor know? Where do you get this information?' You wouldn't have known about this community unless you knew somebody from it."

If Linda survived back-to-back seasonal jobs as a camp host and a CamperForce warehouse worker, she figured she could probably take a break afterward and collect unemployment for a bit. She'd also be able to afford a trip to the Rubber Tramp Rendezvous to meet her new tribe, the family she had joined but had yet to meet.

As for Linda's actual kin, they were supportive when she announced her plans. "That sounds really exciting!" Audra said. She insisted that Linda would need a smartphone to stay connected and offered to cover her bills on the family plan. "We'll make sure there's plenty of data," Collin added.

Would all of this work out? There was no way to tell. One thing was certain, though: Linda's life was about to change and, for now, that was enough.

Part Two

CHAPTER FIVE

Amazon Town

IN JUNE 2013, Linda turned sixty-three and drove the El Dorado RV she'd bought on Craigslist to Junction Campground, two miles from the eastern entrance to Yosemite National Park. This is where her new life as a workamper began—surrounded by wildflower-filled meadows, sparkling creeks, and stands of lodgepole and white-bark pine, with bracing mountain air and postcard views of the snow-dappled Sierra peaks. As a first-time employee of California Land Management, she would be working thirty hours a week for $8.50 an hour. (At this wage, even if Linda convinced her employer to give her full-time, forty-hour weeks all year long—and didn't take any vacations—her annual salary would amount to $17,680, with no benefits.)

Linda was only a half day's drive from the Home Depot in Lake Elsinore where she'd been a cashier, but the wilderness felt utterly remote. This new camp hosting job was the antithesis of running a checkout line under the sallow lights of a big-box store. It felt nothing like her gigs at restaurants, construction sites, casinos, or corporate offices, all the other places where she'd traded time for money.

Best of all, she'd be getting paid while living rent-free. Though the campsite lacked utility hookups, her supervisor lent her a generator and dispatched a water truck each Tuesday to fill the fifty-five-gallon tank on her RV. Her living expenses were now pared down to groceries, diesel for the generator, and propane for the stove. Linda was elated.

Junction Campground wasn't very demanding. Its thirteen sites were filled on a first-come, first-served basis—eliminating the hassle of reservations and the resulting time-consuming paperwork—and there were only two outhouse toilets to clean. So for part of her stay, Linda agreed to handle another small campground on nearby Tioga Lake.

Linda loved the social aspect of her work, chatting up vacationers. One of her favorite visitors was a solitary sixty-nine-year-old rock climber who she knew as "Mr. Brown." He ascended popular routes all over Yosemite, scouring the rock face for decades-old fixed anchors that were starting to corrode. Since those anchors secure climbers' safety ropes, when they go bad, the consequences can be deadly. Whenever Mr. Brown found a piece of failing hardware, he pried it out and installed a fresh one. He told Linda he'd been doing this for fifteen years. "The pack he carried," she marveled. "Oh my god! What a monster that was." While she admired his generosity and stamina, she was concerned for him, too. "Don't you worry that you could fall to your death?" she demanded. "Awww, nawwww," Mr. Brown replied in a craggy, mountaineer's grumble. "I know what I'm doing." Another pair of campers Linda met on the job, Billy and Helene Outlaw—their real last name—were septuagenarian RVers. When they mentioned they were looking for camp hosting work, Linda introduced them to her bosses. Before long, they had taken over her duties at Tioga Lake. Around the same time, Linda learned that camp hosting wasn't a good fit for everyone. One of her coworkers, a former border patrolman, insisted on making his daily rounds with a firearm. "He decided he couldn't exist without a gun on his side," she explained. "But the camp host can't be packing. They're not gonna take it at a National Forest if the camp host is packing. They had to let him go."

Linda's summer near Yosemite went smoothly until mid-August. That's when investigators believe a solitary bow hunter used twigs and pine needles to build a small campfire—illegal at the time—to heat soup and burn garbage from his backpack. He had been seeking deer in the remote Clavey River Canyon of Stanislaus National Forest, just fifty miles west of Junction Campground. When embers blew into the dry brush, the third-largest blaze in California history began. Over the next two months, the Rim Fire incinerated an area more than seventeen times the size of Manhattan.

By September, with smoke thickening the air at her campground, it was time for Linda to move on. She said her good-byes, then drove north to Fernley to join Amazon's CamperForce—the second workamping job she'd applied for. The trailer parks near the warehouse were already bustling and fully booked with itinerant workers; space was so tight that Amazon trainers were telling CamperForce members at orientation that the company was considering buying land nearby to build its own trailer park. Linda hadn't made a reservation; she'd spent most of the summer cut off from cell and internet service. Twenty-three miles southeast of the warehouse, she found the Sage Valley RV Park: a fenced-off gravel patch just off Highway 50 in Fallon, Nevada, dotted with cottonwoods and perfumed with the funk of nearby cow pastures. It was also fully booked with CamperForce, but she talked a sympathetic manager into making room for her.

Before the 2013 peak shipping season began, Amazon had put out the latest round of digital newsletters for prospective workers. The front page of the June edition read "CamperForce: The Value of Friendship." Echoing the cheery tone of the camp hosting brochures, it made a tough physical job sound like summer camp. "One benefit that's worth its weight in gold is the benefit of building lasting friendships!" it enthused. "While the monetary reward is a big part of the reason [to work], friendship is very close to the top! Each year we hear stories about friendships and relationships that are made that will continue once the 'Tail Light Parade' has left Amazon."

That contrasted with the March edition. In a section called "Getting Ready to Make History in 2013!" it recommended a preparatory fitness regimen and addressed some challenges of aging:

Getting prepared both physically and mentally will be the key to you having a successful peak season at Amazon. We cannot stress enough the importance of arriving at Amazon physically prepared. If you've not exercised regularly, consult your physician about a conditioning program, then get active! Here's a low cost suggestion: Get out and walk! Walking is a great form of exercise. It doesn't cost anything and is easier on the joints than other forms of exercise. Before setting out, warm up those muscles by stretching. Experts say that as we get older, the collagen structure in our bodies changes, reducing our flexibility and range of motion.

The April edition went on to mention some psychological challenges of the work. Under the headline "What to Expect Your First Few Weeks in the Amazon CamperForce Program," it read:

Your first few weeks at Amazon can be a little intimidating. The size of the facility, the acronyms that seem to be a different language, the hand-held scanners that act as if they have a mind of their own, all contribute to that feeling of being overwhelmed . . .

Meanwhile, Amazon's treatment of warehouse workers had been making headlines since 2011. That's when an investigation by the *Allentown Morning Call* newspaper revealed what were—quite literally—sweatshop conditions. When summer temperatures exceeded 100 degrees inside the company's Breinigsville, Pennsylvania, warehouse, managers wouldn't open the loading bay doors for fear of theft. Instead, they hired paramedics to wait outside in ambulances, ready to extract heat-stricken employees on stretchers and in wheelchairs, the investigation found. Workers also said they were pressured to meet ever greater production targets, a strategy colloquially known as "management by stress." Amazon monitors productivity in real time, analyzing data from networked scanner guns that employees use as they move and sort merchandise. Laura Graham, a CamperForce member who worked as a picker in the Coffeyville, Kansas, warehouse, told me each time she scanned a product, a countdown began on her screen. It indicated how many seconds she had to reach the next item, as if she'd graduated to the next level in a video game. Her progress toward hourly goals was also tracked. When an accidental trip down the wrong aisle left her more than five minutes behind schedule, a supervisor arrived to scold her. (Apart from the mental pressure, Laura's body rebelled against the demands of the device, which directed how she walked from ten to twenty miles a day on concrete in the 915,000-square-foot complex for $11.25 an hour. "There's nothing to describe the misery, physically," she told me. "I started getting these really sharp pains through my arches . . . it ended up being plantar fasciitis." Putting new insoles in her shoes didn't help. To cope, she took two ibuprofen tablets halfway through the graveyard shift, which ran from 5:30 p.m. to 3:30 a.m., and another two at the end. On days off, she tried to keep from using her feet, lying in bed except for visits to the bathroom or shower.)

———

LINDA, HOWEVER, WAS NOT intimidated by anything she'd heard about the warehouses. Nor was she a stranger to tough, physical labor. "I was in construction and I cocktail-waitressed, which was harder work than construction," she recalled. "What would I be worried about?" Besides, she had just finished camp hosting at more than nine thousand feet above sea level. In terms of getting in shape, she figured that had to count for something.

When her first week began, Linda sat through orientation and safety workshops. She learned that she had been assigned to be a "stower," someone who shelves inbound freight. To learn the particulars of that job, she went to what the company calls "process school."

Stowers push carts loaded with yellow plastic tubs—aka "totes"—full of newly arrived items through the aisles of library-style shelving where Amazon stores merchandise. (In company jargon, these areas are called "pick modules.") Each shelf is split with plastic dividers into units called "bins," and stowers are constantly hunting for bins with free space, so they can unload their wares. When shelving an item, the stower must point a handheld scanner gun at a code on the front of the bin and also scan the product that will be placed there. The process is slow, because employees are told to distribute identical items that arrived in the same shipment across different bins, spreading them out, rather than keeping them grouped together. This makes work more efficient for the "pickers," workers who rush through the aisles collecting products to fill customer orders. "It's weird!" Linda said, recalling the motley assortment of items that might share the same bin. "Brake fluid, baby formula, eyeshadow, a book, a tape . . . it's all in there."

After her introduction to stowing, Linda finished her first week with what Amazon calls "work-hardening": a series of half-days to acclimate newcomers to walking on concrete, so they'll be able to do it for ten hours or more when the orientation period ends. Linda had requested the overnight shift, since its hourly wage was 75 cents higher, bringing it to $12.25 an hour plus overtime. "I wanted all the money I could make," Linda said. When her full schedule began, she worked from 6 p.m. until 4:30 a.m., with two fifteen-minute breaks and thirty minutes for a quick meal. "I was sleeping all day," she added. "That kind of changes your life." After rising in the early afternoon, she typically had a three-hour window to do chores, prepare a bag lunch, and walk her dogs around Sage Valley RV Park. Then she made the twenty-five-minute commute back to the warehouse.

When each shift started, Linda donned an orange reflective vest and a lanyard with her security badge, grabbed a freshly charged battery for her handheld scanner, and went to "stand up"—a gathering where workers do stretches as supervisors rattle off productivity goals. Next she hit the floor, scanning UPC barcodes while shelving thousands of products. "You have a cart with fourteen tubs of Chinese junk," she told me. "One of the depressing parts was I knew all this stuff was going to end up in a landfill." That part demoralized her. "You think about all the resources it took to get it there," she mused. "And then it's 'Use it up. Throw it away.'" The work was tiring. Apart from walking up and down endless aisles, she was bending, lifting, squatting, reaching, and climbing and descending stairs, all while traversing a warehouse roughly the size of thirteen football fields. The place was so immense that workers used the names of states to navigate its vast interior, calling the western half "Nevada" and the eastern half "Utah."

In early October, after Linda's first two weeks on the job, she posted to Facebook, "If I live through this I'll be in great shape. I keep thinking of *The Biggest Loser*"—referring to the televised weight-loss competition—"and if they can do it so can I." She also repeated to herself a mantra she knew from Alcoholics Anonymous: "Don't give up before the miracle happens."

At that point, Linda had been sober for more than two decades. Earlier in life she'd faced a struggle that had felt almost inevitable—a taste for liquor was etched into the family genes and, even if it hadn't been, Linda's alcoholic father seemed determined to pass the trait along. Toward the end of Linda's high school years, he'd introduced her to sloe gin fizzes, which he made in the blender each night with fresh lemon and powdered sugar. He and Linda would stay up late, drinking and talking. He'd started playing the stock market and would try to teach her about finance; she thought he was a genius. They developed a morning routine. He'd open the door to her bedroom. "Are you going to school?" he'd ask. "I'm hung over," she'd moan. "Oh, poor baby!" he'd reply, gently closing the door.

As an adult, Linda had become a very busy, impressively high-functioning and increasingly hard-core alcoholic. Briefly she dabbled with meth—not so much for the speedy high but because it enabled her to consume the ever greater quantities of alcohol she needed to get drunk.

Linda had tried to quit and backslid a couple times. But after one all-night bender, she couldn't take it anymore. She returned home around 6 a.m. Her children watched wordlessly as she came inside. "Their faces told the story though—the disappointment," Linda recalled. "It's horrible to wait for somebody to come home. You expect them to come home, and they don't come home. It's not a nice thing to do to people that you love."

After that, Linda rededicated herself to quitting with a new vigor. This time it stuck. When she worried about slipping between AA meetings, she called her sponsor. Oddly, that's how she learned some of the same techniques that helped her keep going through long shifts at Amazon. She became an expert at focusing on whatever challenge lay immediately ahead, parsing large problems into bite-sized chunks until she felt she could manage anything.

"Are your dishes done? Okay. Go do your dishes then and call me back," her sponsor used to tell her. Linda would scrub the plates and glasses until they gleamed, then call again. "Did you make your bed?" was the next question. Linda went and did that, too. And so on, and so on, until she had muddled through.

LINDA WASN'T THE ONLY ONE having a challenging time in the warehouse. On October 1, Nevada OSHA received a complaint about workers getting back injuries from lifting heavy boxes. A week later, two inspectors went to the Fernley facility. They reviewed the company's injury logs and walked around the plant, escorted by Amazon managers. The visit took no more than four hours. The case was closed later that day, with an official report concluding: "The facility had numerous strain injuries including back strain, but nothing out of the norm for this type of work setting."

Apart from exertion, Linda said her biggest challenge was tedium. She played mind games to carve up the hours. "I'm only staying here five more minutes, then I'm leaving. I'm quitting. This is it!" she told herself over and over. That's how she lasted until a couple of hours before sunrise, when her shift ended. Then she and her coworkers clocked out and exited the building through a station with metal detectors and security guards, part of the company's anti-theft strategy. (Mark Thierman, a Reno attorney, represented a group of temps from Amazon's Fernley and Las Vegas warehouses who claimed they were owed back wages for the time they spent waiting in line to pass through the company's security stations, up to thirty minutes a day. While the Ninth U.S. Circuit Court of Appeals ruled in their favor in 2013, the U.S. Supreme Court overturned that decision the following year.)

Despite the boredom, Linda was grateful for one part of her job. "The best thing was the camaraderie," she said. "I made friends there."

Amazon is where Linda first met Silvianne, the astrologer who would later work with her as a camp host in the San Bernardino Mountains. Before Silvianne arrived at Fernley for CamperForce, she had written on her blog:

> Scene 1: Leaving northern New Mexico, headed towards northern Nevada for a seasonal workamping job as a ware-house associate for the online lynchpin of the Evil Consumer Empire, facing a temporary adventure in the belly-of-beast. A drastic although necessary step to fund the first stages of the journey. . .

Silvianne was one of Linda's neighbors at the Sage Valley RV Park. There she often walked Layla, her cat, using a leash with a pink harness. The habit had made her something of a local celebrity. Even on the floor of the warehouse, people approached her and asked, "You're the one who walks the cat, aren't you?"

Like Linda, Silvianne was a stower on the night shift. As a self-described type A personality, she found the job maddening. Often all bins were full. There was nowhere to put things, no way to do the work well, and it made the warehouse feel like a version of Kafka's castle designed to torture perfectionists. Silvianne had been watching *Orange Is the New Black* and found herself comparing the inmates' lives with her own. In the beginning, she cried two or three times a week. ("I'm an emoter," she explained. "It was so embarrassing. It's because I care too much.") Her back hurt all the time, which was new—apart from a twinge or two in her catering days, it had never bothered her before. And she was one of many workers who had problems with static shocks. Rolling a cart full of plastic bins through the warehouse seemed to build up a charge, she later explained. One time she wheeled over to a bank of metal shelves and tried to stow a book on the top level. Her hand glanced over the metal and a jolt coursed up her arm, which recoiled reflexively, sending the book flying into her face. This left her with a fat lip and bleeding gum. The book had landed face down on the floor. When she looked down at it, a photograph of a Tibetan monk smiled up at her from the back cover. "This is my goddess's sense of humor," she later reflected. (This problem wasn't new. Fernley employees had been filing formal complaints about getting shocked by the shelves for two years by the time Silvianne joined CamperForce. During state workplace safety inspections, Amazon officials said they knew about the problem and had bonded the shelves to grounding rods, along with installing tinsel on the carts to help them discharge electricity. When the shocks continued, they applied a product called Staticide to the floor. A company official stated this "had reduced the instance of static shock to employees." The inspectors called for no changes.)

Linda also befriended Jen Derge and Ash Haag, a couple in their late twenties who arrived at Sage Valley in early October. They were

Jen Derge and Ash Haag pose with their van, the Manatee.

living in the Manatee, a navy blue and white 1995 GMC high-top camper van, bought on the way to Nevada for $4,500. The seller had shaved $1,000 off the asking price. After having it on his lot for six months, he wanted it gone.

Jen recalled how Linda first summoned them out of their van to say hello, and how she'd breeze past with calls of "pancakes, pancakes!" to announce she was making enough breakfast to share. "You know Linda," Jen said. "She is the social hub!" When Ash was waiting for a special letter from her niece—it was addressed "To Auntie, Miss Jen and Van"—it was Linda who first heard from the front desk of the RV park that it had arrived. "So Linda busts into the bathroom and is like, 'Are you in here?' and I'm like, 'Yes!' And she's like 'What are you doing?' And I'm like 'I'm having private time, Linda!'" Ash recalled. "She's like, 'You have mail!' I love her."

Before becoming nomads, Jen and Ash had rented a house together in Colorado Springs, where both grappled with spells of depression and were increasingly disenchanted by their job prospects.

Jen had grown up watching her parents work at King Soopers—a

Kroger-owned grocery store—a job her father hated. "We want better for you kids," they always said, urging her toward college. Independence was important to Jen. In high school she started working as a bagger and courtesy clerk at the grocery store for around $6 an hour. Later she earned an associate's degree on scholarship. But she couldn't see the point of going further. "It's the same story everywhere," she said. "You see all your friends who get their bachelor's degree and higher and they can't get a job. So I just don't see a reason to go back even though I love learning. Just the money part of it, going into debt . . . the idea of it just scares me so bad, I don't want to."

Jen took jobs at a craft shop and some used bookstores and then became a school library assistant. In that role, she ended up working under a library software administrator for the largest district in Colorado Springs. Jen loved the position. "It was so much fun, communicating with all these librarians, getting into their computers and showing them all this cool stuff," she said. But it quickly became evident that her boss, who held a master's degree, was getting pushed into retirement, while Jen was taking over the same level of work at a much lower wage.

"The older generation that has advanced degrees, they're cleaning them out and putting techs into those positions. It's very sad for the people who have those degrees who've worked so hard for them," Jen said. "I felt like I betrayed my boss by taking her job, because she was an amazing lady."

At the same time, Jen figured she'd never be able to get a job like the one her boss held—it was getting reclassified to a lower-tier position—regardless of whether she went back to college. "Why go to school when the workforce is only entry-level positions?" she mused.

Meanwhile, Ash had watched her own parents fall out of the middle class after her father, an electrical engineer with a six-figure salary, got laid off in 2001. He was too proud to take a lower-paying job, at least before the family's finances were depleted. Then he ended up driving school buses in the morning and working at Walmart at night.

"Anyway, I'm seeing my parents in their mid-sixties with no

retirement, you know, everything that they built over their entire life just disappeared. And then with the recession you see that happening to more people," Ash said. Though she'd always considered herself a "follower," she began to worry that, even if she adhered to all of society's rules for living an upright middle-class life, she'd have no guarantee of stability. She was skeptical that Social Security would be around to support her generation in old age. And though she had a couple 401(k)s and a Goldman Sachs IRA that her parents set up during her childhood, she worried that, by the time she needed them, they would be worthless.

Ash was also grappling with student loans. The $30,000 she'd borrowed had mushroomed with interest to $37,000, all for a degree she hadn't completed after six years of classes. She'd felt obligated to go straight from high school to college—even though she believes "you don't know what you want, you don't know what you need, and you don't know who you are" at that age—and ended up studying everything from art history to physics.

During and after college, Ash worked at a mom-and-pop pharmacy that to her had felt like a family. But a leadership shakeup had changed her supervisors' attitudes; she watched as loyal, longtime staff got pressured to quit. "Our society is turning to that a lot," she said. "They don't want long-term employees, because then you do have pensions, then you do have to keep giving them cost-of-living increases and, if they've been working for the company a long time, they're going to want a merit-based raise." The new management, she said, "literally wanted disposable people. And to make disposable people you have to have a disposable job. And so everything became automated."

Meanwhile, Jen had been scouring the internet for alternate ways to live. She'd researched minimalism and the tiny house movement. She'd also come across CheapRVLiving.com. Gradually, she began thinking she'd found a way out. To Ash, moving into a vehicle and becoming a nomad wasn't initially the most appealing choice. She thought of the classic *Saturday Night Live* sketch in which Chris Farley plays a vandweller and motivational speaker named Matt Foley. He warns kids to shape up unless they want to end up living in a van, too. "My first thought was that we were going to be like that guy, saying 'I live in a van down by the river!'" Ash said. Despite this, she came to embrace the idea.

The plan was to alternate between work and adventuring while living in a Subaru Impreza hatchback, a hand-me-down from Jen's mother. As it turned out, that wasn't an easy car to turn into a home. Though the rear seats were collapsible, there wasn't enough space to lie down unless you crammed stuff into the foot wells behind the front seats, creating a headrest. Still, Jen and Ash prepared the best they could. Jen cut black wool felt into panels that could be Velcroed over the windows for privacy. To pare down their possessions, they put a message on Craigslist—CURB ALERT: FREE—and hauled everything they no longer needed out to the lawn. The posting told people to come at 9 a.m. By 8:30 a.m., everything on the lawn had disappeared. "If you say, 'It's free,' people will find a use for everything," Ash said. "Somebody even picked up the trash!" (She figured that was a mistake.)

Their first adventure was hiking the Colorado Trail—more than 480 miles from Denver to Durango—nonstop for fifty-two days. Then they headed to the Amazon warehouse in Fernley. Initially, they planned to do CamperForce while living out of the Subaru. ("That wouldn't have worked," Jen said, matter-of-factly. "We would have quit.") Fortunately they found the van. Buying it, however, left them pretty much broke.

After they got settled at the Sage Valley RV Park, the couple decided to bike to the warehouse for their first full-length work shift. They figured it would be fun, since the route was mostly flat, and also help them save on gas money. But then one of Jen's tires got a slow leak. They had to stop every fifteen minutes to pump it up. The trip took three hours but they still made it in time to start the ten-hour shift. When they got out at 5 a.m., it was dark and cold enough to make their teeth chatter. They stopped at Walmart to get extra layers of clothing and then biked alongside rush-hour traffic into a blinding sunrise. "We were known forever as the girls that rode their bikes to work," Jen said, laughing. After that, they decided to stay near the warehouse during the week to save on gas. They parked the Manatee at Walmart or a gas station, returning to the Sage Valley RV Park only on their days off.

As stowers, they found that all their recent hiking experience helped. Still, Jen said, "it takes a while to get used to all the bending but you get the muscles after a couple of weeks. You see all these older people there and you're like 'Oh, gosh, if they can do it, what am I complaining about?'"

Ash found the work "monotonous and isolating." To help allevi- ate the tedium, she sometimes entertained herself by creatively matchmaking items as she shelved them, putting, for example, a case of condoms next to a case of pregnancy tests. She used the wish list feature on Amazon's website to catalog "all the amazing and awe-inspiring shit we put on shelves." These included live wax- worms, a five-pound gummi bear, a diver's speargun, a book titled *Venus with Biceps: A Pictorial History of Muscular Women*, a butt plug attached to a plush foxtail, a pound of obsolete U.S. coins, a set of cotton briefs with four leg holes called "undies for two," and a Batman-themed dildo.*

By late October, temperatures in Fernley had dipped below freezing. Flurries dusted the trailer parks around Halloween. Real

---

* America's appetite for sex toys—indicated by the sheer number and variety of dildos and butt plugs passing through Amazon warehouses—is a subject of fasci- nation to many workers. And though most "adult novelties" get wrapped in black plastic as soon as they come off the loading docks, a few squeak past unnoticed. One CamperForce stower recalled gleefully the time she received a case of sixty suction-cup mounted dildos. She arranged them on the shelves with each one suctioned at the front of a bin and standing upright. "When you turned the cor- ner, around that aisle all you see is these peckers," she said, laughing. "Of course, we all had to go around, telling everybody, 'Go look at C23!'" Usually she would have worried about pissing off management, but "it was the last two weeks of work there, so what are they going to say?"

snow arrived a week before Thanksgiving. The bitterest weather hit in December—there were single-digit temperatures and one miserable –2-degree night. To sleep in the cold, Jen and Ash began wearing every piece of clothing they owned, then burying themselves in a collection of quilts and sleeping bags, along with a comforter and a down army blanket. On work nights, when they were stealth camping near the warehouse, they ran a Little Buddy propane heater for ten minutes before bed; holding their feet over it, they'd watch the sweat from hours of walking turn to plumes of steam. Though the night shift left them feeling like "Amazombies," they were grateful they'd chosen it. "During the coldest part of the twenty-four-hour cycle, we were going to be inside a heated environment, and that's a major thing," Ash said.

When wintry weather hit the Sage Valley RV Park, Linda had a CamperForce neighbor, Carl, who lived in a tent. He was on the day shift. Since Linda was in the warehouse all night, she urged him to just sleep in her motorhome where it was warm—she'd been running a heater off the park's electricity to save on propane—but he always said, "No, no, no. It's comfortable, I'm good." Meanwhile, even the experienced RVers were having a hard time. Some of them had tricks to stay comfortable, such as wrapping water hoses in electric heating tape and covering windows with reflective bubble wrap insulation. (A few years later, Amazon created a webpage for CamperForce applicants called "Winterizing Your Rig" that advised covering windows in shrink-film and putting reflective insulators over vents. Links were provided so readers could purchase both materials at— where else?—Amazon.com.) But there were limits. Linda disconnected her water lines. When she tried to unplug her sewage hose, she found the waste inside had already frozen. "There was a huge poopsicle just sitting there. I was like, 'That's nasty!'"

Phil and Robin DePeal, the Michiganders who used to own a scrap business, were fighting a similar battle. They bought a flood-light and tried using it to thaw out their iced sewage hose, to no avail. Meanwhile one of Linda's heroes—Jim Melvin of the blog Jimbo's

Journeys, which had pointed her to Amazon's seasonal jobs—rushed into town to buy an electric pet-bed warmer and a space heater for Chica, his two-pound Chihuahua.

Linda began fantasizing about her next destination, which would be warmer and less exhausting. Like many of her neighbors, she planned to camp on the public lands surrounding the town of Quartzsite, Arizona. That region, a migrants' Shangri-la in the Sonoran Desert, drew tens of thousands of winter visitors and hosted various events through the season, from sprawling acres of swap meets, to shows for rock collectors and RV enthusiasts, along with hundreds of looser social gatherings. Linda couldn't wait to check out one of those get-togethers, the Rubber Tramp Rendezvous, which happened there in January. When she mentioned that to Jen and Ash, who had heard of the event but were still figuring out what to do after Amazon, they decided to join her. "I had not solidified that plan of RTR but then when Linda said it, I was like 'Okay we have to do it,'" Jen recalled. Silvianne planned to go, too.

But the winter didn't let go so easily. There were mandatory fifty-hour overtime weeks. With Christmas coming on, the bins on all of the shelves were overstuffed with merchandise, a stower's nightmare. "We were at 120 percent capacity for the last month and a half, so whenever you scanned a bin to try to put one thing away, the scanner would go 'EE-nu! EE-nu! EE-nu! EE-nu!' and you'd have to wait before you could try the next bin," Ash said. "People were going around just like insane. There was nowhere to put anything, you wanted to beat your face against a wall." Stowers had to keep hunting, frustrated, until they found the rare bins that had space. At the same time, supervisors were telling them to pick up the pace, to make "rate," that "we've gotta get our numbers." Amazon would later recount that this period was its strongest ever holiday season. On December 2 (aka Cyber Monday, the first Monday after Thanksgiving) alone, customers ordered some 36.8 million products—or about 426 orders a second—helping to bring the company's overall sales for 2013 to a record high of $74.45 billion.

Amid this Linda had a health scare. She had been holding up well, despite straining her right wrist with the UPC scanner. But on December 15, two weeks before her last day at the warehouse, she began having dizzy spells. She didn't know what caused them. Other workers had been feeling that way, too, and some believed it was due to poor air quality in the warehouse. Linda toughed it out for an hour, but attempts at deep breathing weren't helping, so a coworker escorted her to AmCare. There the medical staff took her blood pressure: sixty over forty-eight—low enough to call an ambulance.

At the hospital in Reno, half an hour's drive west, Linda underwent a CAT scan and an X-ray but received no conclusive diagnosis. "The nurse at the hospital said I could have compressed something on the vagus nerve," Linda recalled. "That'll make you pass out. You can get it from straining." She sounded skeptical, since she didn't think she had been pushing herself that hard. In any case, she was instructed to follow up with her primary-care physician. "Yeah, I'd do that if I had one," she said, laughing. Like most workampers I met right before the Affordable Care Act took effect, Linda was uninsured. And since she didn't have a ride back to the Sage Valley RV Park, she sprung $172 for a cab. For the next few days, she felt weak and took unpaid time off.

CamperForce was winding down. Most workers left right before Christmas so they could celebrate with far-flung families. Linda volunteered to stay through December 30. She wanted to earn as much as possible. Besides, she wasn't feeling festive. After more than four months on the overnight shift, she'd been bored into a fugue state interrupted only by pains radiating from her right wrist, the one wielding the scanner gun. The job was repetitive, mindless: shelve merchandise, point the gun at one item after the next, pull and hold the trigger, wait for the beep that meant the red laser had found its mark—the barcode—before moving on. What did it add up to, apart from a paycheck? Each item Linda scanned was a pixel in a picture that depressed her. Some CamperForce workers called themselves "Santa's elves." That gave them a way to take pride in their work because it meant they were sending out gifts, spreading joy. Linda didn't drink the Christmas Kool Aid, though—she felt less like an elf, more like a cog in the world's largest vending machine, and the experience left her numb. "I wanted to disconnect from Christmas after seeing all that junk," she said. Apart from sending gifts to her grandchildren, she ignored the holiday. When the warehouse shut down for Christmas, so did she. Linda spent the day alone, resting in her RV.

Beneath the fatigue, however, was a slow-dawning sense of pride. Linda had achieved a goal, getting through her first half-year as a workamper, completing two seasonal jobs—camp hosting and CamperForce—while acclimating to a frugal and nomadic life in her RV. She felt self-sufficient and free. But that was only the beginning. The next step was finding a tribe, a community, what some nomads called a "vanily." The best place for that was the two-week winter Rubber Tramp Rendezvous, which was soon to begin in Quartzsite.

"Let me get the hell out of here!" she thought. "Put the pedal to the metal. Let's go!" Ready for a break and warmer weather, she set out for Arizona.

As the rest of CamperForce rushed away from Fernley and into the New Year, one worker stuck around. That was Don Wheeler, the former jet-setting software executive who'd written me a proud paean about workamping and who appears here under a pseudonym. Don was the first member of CamperForce I met, a sharp and entertaining storyteller who spent long hours regaling me with tales of life on the road. He was originally scheduled to work his last CamperForce shift on December 21. His post-Amazon plans included passing through Quartzsite—he called it "Burning Man for geezers"—and visiting friends in the Colorado Rockies. But something very unusual took place instead. In what would become three years of reporting on CamperForce workers, I would never witness anything like it happen again—Amazon offered Don a full-time, year-round job. "Hey, I'm seventy, who else is going to hire me?" he joked by email. In company jargon, Don was about to become an "Amazon associate." On the warehouse floor, he'd be what CamperForce workers and other temps called—with envy or sometimes derision—a "blue badge," referring to the blue worker ID cards worn by permanent employees.

In another email, he asked me to keep his name out of my writing. He explained:

> As entry-level apparatchiks, we may not even speak to the media on pain of death, dismemberment or worse. So now I'm worried. It was different before—as a workamper I could afford an insouciant, devil-may-care attitude toward the ponderous machinations of Corporate America, but now I am them. I need this job . . .
>
> I can't afford to be famous. If I pop up on national media, even as a sidebar, HR will make short work of me and when I show up at the warehouse one day, my badge won't let me into the building. That's called the ACS (Amazon Cold Shoulder) and there is no recourse since I am an employee at will.
>
> I'm sorry for my seeming paranoia but HR is NOT my friend, however much they insist they are. Their role is validated when they get rid of the bad apples and troublemakers. I am not as brave as Nadezhda Tolokonnikova (nor as good looking).*

Within a few months, Don had paid off debts, gotten some long-deferred dental work, bought new glasses, contributed to his Roth IRA, and began saving for a Harley.

---

* When Don wrote this email, Tolokonnikova, a member of the Russian dissident punk band Pussy Riot, had just been freed from a Siberian prison.

CHAPTER SIX

The Gathering Place

This was a peaceful place, this camp—a Garden of Eden on wheels, capable of picking its own latitudes and following the gentle weather round the year, a haven in which every occupant had brought his life into focus by compressing it into the minimum space, a miracle of internal arrangement plus mobility.

—E. B. WHITE

AS YOU DRIVE WEST ON INTERSTATE 10 into a January sunset, a strange vision appears in the desert. Thousands of gold specks glitter at the base of the Dome Rock Mountains, as if the peaks are surrounded by a vast reflecting pool. Up close, the sparkling dots break apart into a sprawl of RVs, their windshields catching the last rays of daylight. This is the town of Quartzsite, Arizona. Most of the year, it lies dormant, a lonesome outpost between Los Angeles and Phoenix with two truck stops and temperatures high enough to make you hallucinate. In the inferno of summer it has fewer than four thousand inhabitants. Visitors are outnumbered by tumbleweeds. But every winter when days grow mild and pleasant, hundreds of thousands of nomads stream in from all over the country and Canada, turning the town into a pop-up metropolis nicknamed "The Gathering Place." Some of the arrivals are leisure-loving snowbirds—folks with generous pensions or lucky retirees whose savings made it through the financial meltdown of 2008—while others are survivors, clinging to the ragged edge of the social contract. Their circumstances are reflected in the range of dwellings parading along Main Street.

Cars and trucks arrive towing all kinds of shelters, from shiny aluminum Airstreams to cargo boxes retrofitted with doors and windows, to teardrop-style trailers the size of pup tents. You might see a tiny house with gabled dormer windows and gingerbread trim mounted on a tandem axle platform, or a truck hauling a live-aboard sailboat that will get dry docked here as a makeshift apartment. There are dozens of decommissioned school buses. A few are still as yellow as a number-two pencil, while others are airbrushed with wilderness scenes or psychedelic swirls. Some have been converted into elaborate homes with couches and woodstoves. A handful are live-in businesses, including the Bus Stop Ice Cream & Coffee Shop—a rainbow-colored throwback that looks like it could belong to a latter-day Ken Kesey whose drug of choice is espresso—and a blacksmith's studio with an anvil logo and the slogan "Recycling Society's Waste by Hammer & Hand." There are also rattletrap pickups with cabins built into their cargo beds, fancy fifth-wheel RVs with satellite dishes, and jalopies so overburdened with possessions that their chassis scrape the asphalt. Some of the vehicles are immaculate, with chrome trim sparkling in the sunshine. Others are pitted with rust, wheezing plumes of dark exhaust. A few convey pleas for donations. One station wagon with an empty gas can tied to the roof has been painted to read "HELP OUR FAMILY START A BUSINESS" and shows the web address for a Go Fund Me campaign. An old pickup camper has "HOMELESS SHELTER" and "GOD BLESS" written on

A pickup camper bearing religious inscriptions and pleas for help parks at the McDonald's in Quartzsite.

the back in neat block letters. Below is a wish list: "NEEDS: GAS, CASH, BIGGER RV."

It's worth noting—you can't always size up folks' economic circumstances just by looking at their RVs. Some of the dwellings parked around workamping sites, for example, resemble the kind of pleasure craft one might associate with well-to-do vacationers. When I started visiting the RV parks where Amazon's CamperForce workers stay, I wondered, *What are those shiny land yachts with satellite dishes doing here?* And I learned two things: First, a few of the RV parks were also temporary homes for high-paid oil field workers, who had cash to burn on fancy toys. Second, plenty of folks don't own their RVs free and clear. Just like in the housing market, it's possible to overspend and get trapped in a debt cycle, struggling to make payments. And unfortunately, just like traditional homes, RVs can also go underwater.

Traffic crawls. No one seems to be in a hurry, though. Along with the mobile homes are dusty all-terrain vehicles coming back from zipping around the desert—the riders wear scarves and goggles and look like they've been sprinkled with confectioner's sugar. Tractor trailers creep toward crowded truck stops, clogging the turning lanes. At intersections, elderly people on mobility scooters and baby boomers pushing small dogs in strollers wait for the crosswalks to clear. Dreadlocked teens and twentysomethings in weatherbeaten backpacks sit on the curb. Their tribe calls itself by many names—crust punks, dirty kids, travelers, and Rainbows, a reference to the Rainbow Family gatherings that many attend. Some of the kids are hitching rides out of town—to Yuma, to Phoenix, anywhere. Others hold cardboard placards that ask for cash. They don't call this panhandling, though. It's "flying a sign," or "jugging," or "spanging"—short for spare-changing—and it's what you do when the gas money runs out. Many of the older folks give them dirty looks, but others play along. A white-haired cashier at Dollar General rings up two six-packs of Miller Genuine Draft for a guy in a brown hoodie and blond dreadlocks; she laughs when he jokingly extends a palm full of colored stones in payment instead of dollars. A spirited debate rises on the post office line between a snowbird and a young drifter with a handlebar mustache. *Are humans spiritual beings who transcend this planet? Or just fuck-ups trashing the earth?* When evening comes, the kids retreat to desert encampments. They pass bottles of whiskey around the bonfire, strum guitars, roast hot dogs, roll joints, kill time.

Most of the restaurants in town are packed by dinnertime, which starts in the late afternoon. At Silly Al's, a popular pizzeria, seniors do the Electric Slide and listen to a house band, whose set includes a Barenaked Ladies song that begins "If I had a million dollars, I'd buy you a house." On other days they sing karaoke. A wizened woman in a red straw hat rides her mobility scooter onto the dance floor and warbles "Lookin' out My Back Door" by Creedence Clearwater Revival in a heavy vibrato. During the twangy guitar solo, she drives figure eights around the middle of the room and the audience breaks into cheers.

The Main Street Eatery and Laundromat bustles with customers who show up to get fed, clean their clothes, even wash themselves. In back, showers cost $7 and come with a litany of posted rules: "Twenty-Minute Limit," "No Smoking," "No Dying or Tinting Hair," and "No Shoes in Stall." Cops hassle Rainbows hanging around the side door. A laundry customer rants about a comet that will destroy the universe (and how Obama can't do anything about it). A grizzled old man sits in the parking lot, his back against a chain-link fence, throwing a rock for a Jack Russell terrier that dutifully retrieves it for him, over and over. "He's a rockhound!" the man guffaws when he sees me watching. (Hunting for semiprecious stones in the desert—better known as rockhounding—is a favorite local hobby.)

Restaurant owners aren't the only ones scrambling to make a buck. Every year, vendors descend on Quartzsite, setting up temporary booths or reopening storefronts that closed for the off-season, posting signs all over town. "Mr. Motorhome Has the CLEANEST RVS in QUARTZSITE" claims one pitchman, whose photo appears on a series of posters, his grin unsettlingly white. "It's not a mirage, the deals are real," blare ads for a competitor, RVs for Less. "FREE PANCAKE BREAKFAST" reads a banner outside La Mesa RV, another dealership. Six mornings a week, seniors line up there for a hot meal in a room called the Silver Buckle Customer Corral, amid televised ads for motorhomes most cannot afford. (They treat the ads like soup-kitchen sermons—obligatory background noise to ignore.) There are dozens of RV supply and service stations, from waste dumping sites to solar panel vendors and roving windshield repair shops. Some use silly names to stand out: Passmore Gas, A Toe Truck, the RV Proctologist. Others make a loftier appeal. At Schartel Pinstriping Services, there's a tent topped with a giant cross and a sign that says "Hope for America. America for Jesus."

Everyone's angling for a quick payday, promising rock-bottom prices. "We Stack It Deeper & Sell It Cheaper," promises one sign. "Everything Must Go!" says another. At salvaged grocery outlets—known as "scratch-and-dent" stores—shoppers find deeply discounted food past its sell-by date in crushed boxes and dinged cans. Behind the lurid pink façade of an outlet called Addicted to Deals, they buy DVDs—three for $10—and expired vitamins. "This place is freaking crazy," one shopper wrote online. "It's like a college dorm room and an abandoned Kmart had a forbidden lovechild, painted it Pepto-Bismol pink, and gave it a phrase for a name."

Quartzsite doesn't offer much in the way of what city folks consider culture, but almost everyone visits Reader's Oasis on the east end of Main Street. The bookstore is owned by septuagenarian nudist Paul Winer, who has skin like burnished leather and wanders the aisles in nothing but a knit codpiece. When it's cold, he dons a sweater. Paul can afford to keep his bookstore going because, technically, it isn't a permanent structure, and that keeps the taxes down. It has no real walls—just a ramada roof above a concrete slab. Tarps span the space between them. Shipping containers and a trailer are annexes. *Trailer Life* magazine called it "the ultimate in Quartzsite architecture." In an earlier career Paul toured as Sweet Pie, a nude boogie-woogie pianist known for his sing-along anthem "Fuck 'Em If They Can't Take a Joke," and he still performs spontaneously on a baby grand near the front of the shop, not far from a discreetly covered adult book section. There's a Christian section, too, but it's in the back and Paul usually has to help people find it. "They follow my bare ass to the Bible," he declares.

Those seeking more old-fashioned religion go to the other end of Main Street, west of Reader's Oasis, where a purple and white big top houses Last Call Tent Ministries. At 7 p.m. revival meetings, a traveling preacher strums a gold Stratocaster while spreading the light of Jesus. "That light's gonna be seen around the world!" he whoops. "It's not just contained in this tent. It's not just contained in Quartzsite. It's not just contained in Arizona. It's laaaarge! Bigger and better!" After each service, parishioners approach the pulpit to be anointed with oil. The preacher speaks in tongues and grips their shoulders, prompting the faithful—including one woman on crutches—to fall limp into attendants' waiting arms.

Tens of thousands of nomads partake each year in the winter spectacle that is Quartzsite. The town has only three small motels, but more than seventy RV parks with names promising relaxation: Arizona Sun, Desert Oasis, Holiday Palms, La Mirage, Paradise, Winter Haven, the Scenic Road. (The last has a motto—"Enjoying Life in the Slow Lane"—that sums up the general sales pitch.) They charge on average $30 a night for a parking spot on asphalt or gravel with hookups for water, electricity, and sewage, access to showers and laundry rooms, sometimes WiFi and cable TV. Many parks ban guests who are underage—which means "born after the Eisenhower administration"—and post warning signs that read "55+." When a reporter for *The Scotsman* newspaper wrote about this scene, he called it "Jurassic Trailer Park."

Most folks who stay in Quartzsite don't bother with the RV parks, though. Instead they gather on the local equivalent of a low-rent district—the public lands just outside of town—like pioneers swarming the site of a latter-day gold rush. ("The old rush," the same *Scotsman* reporter quipped.) There they camp on the hardpan mix of dust and gravel known as "desert concrete." Rather than pay for amenities, they boondock, using solar panels and gas-powered generators for electricity, hauling their own water in jugs and tanks. What creature comforts they sacrifice are made up for by the scenery. They park beside giant, open-armed saguaros that grow thick and tall as telephone poles; from a distance, the cacti look like giant hitching posts for the motorhomes. They cluster along the edges of desert washes, seeking out rare patches of shade among the creosote, mesquite, ironwood, and palo verde trees. For neighbors they have kangaroo rats, Gambel's quail, lizards, scorpions, and roving packs of coyotes, whose nighttime yipping competes with the hum of their generators. (There are rattlesnakes, too, but most are dormant and won't stir until spring, when shimmering waves of heat scour the desert, clearing out most human visitors.) As the campers settle in, they put out welcome mats, barbecue grills, and lawn chairs; unfurl awnings, Astroturf lawns, and weatherproof carpet; fly colorful flags and set up fenced-in dog runs. It looks like a sprawling tailgate party, a spectacle that *National Geographic* once called "America's Largest Parking Lot." It's earned other nicknames, too, including "Spring Break for Seniors" and "Poor Man's Palm Springs."

This open desert is federal territory. Run by the Bureau of Land Management, it includes free camping spots that welcome nomads for up to two weeks at a time. After that, they have to move along to another patch of federal desert at least twenty-five miles away, or to the La Posa Long Term Visitor Area, which is just south of Quartz-site on more than eleven thousand acres. Staying there costs $40 for two weeks or $180 for up to seven months. The camping permits are brightly colored stickers with images of a roadrunner and a giant snowflake. Once applied to windshields, they seem to stay there, identifying Quartzsite's far-flung nomads to one another during the off-season like badges from a secret society.

It's estimated that more than forty thousand RVers dwell in the desert near Quartzsite from December through February. Bill Alexander has watched them come and go for what seems like forever. The outdoor recreation planner and lead park ranger at the Bureau of Land Management's Yuma Field Office, he's been working in this region for seventeen years. And after all that time, he says, he's still impressed by the campers' neighborliness. "We can have that guy who rides up on a bike with his dog on a leash and throws down his tent next to a guy in a $500,000 custom-built motorhome, and they get along just fine," Bill told me. "That ability to coexist is based sim-ply on their desire to enjoy the public land, and the fact that it belongs equally to the guy riding the bicycle as to the guy in the motorhome."

His observation echoed the thoughts of Iris Goldenberg, an Amazon CamperForce worker I'd met in Fernley. At sixty-two, Iris was living in a ten-and-a-half-foot Carson Kalispell sport trailer that she shared with Madison, a Shih-Tzu; Pancho, a lovebird; and Kas-par, a loquacious African Grey parrot named for a sixteenth-century theologian. We were all crammed in there together, chatting, when she brought up Quartzsite. I'd never heard of it before. Like Bill, she

Iris Goldenberg holds her parrot, Kaspar.

was fascinated by the blurring of class lines. That's no small thing against the backdrop of modern America, where income-segregated neighborhoods are on the rise, isolating—and insulating—the wealthy from the poor. Quartzsite isn't like that. "It's anybody's yard," Iris explained. "Whatever you have, you're welcome."

When Iris first told me about Quartzsite, she rhapsodized about how healthy she felt in the dry climate and how affordably she could live there. Apart from the inexpensive camping, it's an easy place to land short-term employment—temporary towns need temporary labor, after all—at a time of year when workamping gigs are scarce in most of the country. One of her jobs was washing dishes for $8 an hour at Sweet Darlene's Restaurant & Bakery (motto: "Great Food, Reasonable Prices"), where early-bird diners start lining up at 4 p.m. each Friday for a fish fry and, in the kitchen, stacks of dirty plates teeter toward the ceiling. Iris has also worked at a Chinese food take-out trailer called Rockin' Wok; when I went to visit her there, she came running out with a handful of fortune cookies.

Though the desert draws out civic spirit, people are still people—

they mark their turf and splinter into tribes. Using rocks to draw fake property lines is a well-established tradition. Stones also get arranged into shapes and initials, a sort of landscape tattoo. Campers create neighborhoods with names like "Coyote Flat" and "Roger's 1/2 Acre Lazy Daze Homeless Camp" and post homemade signs, from tidy wooden plaques that look like they were made in a high school shop class to hastily lettered paper plates duct-taped to wooden stakes.

So far as tribes go, there are dozens of desert "rallies": gatherings of RV clubs whose members share common traits. Some of these organizations are age-based. One of them, called Boomers, is for members of the postwar generation, though so many RVers fit that profile, it almost seems beside the point to have a club. Other groups, including Xscapers and NuRVers, target a slightly younger demographic—the giveaway is the erratic spelling and capitalization, a dot-com-era dog whistle. There are additional sects for fishermen (the Roving Rods), disaster relief volunteers (the DOVES), and gays and lesbians (Rainbow RV, with no relation to the traveling kids called "Rainbows"). There are singles clubs including the Wandering Individuals Network, SOLOS, and Loners on Wheels, the last of which has very strict rules. "If there's any hanky-panky, you get kicked out," one member told *The Victoria Advocate*, a Texas newspaper. The Loners' credo instructs everyone to "conduct yourself as a mingling single" and states that "members of the opposite gender, not blood related, must not occupy the same camping unit." There's even a dedicated group in the desert for nudists. A seventy-five-acre zone at the southern edge of the long-term visitors' area, called The Magic Circle, is surrounded with posters reading "ATTENTION: BEYOND THIS POINT YOU MAY ENCOUNTER NUDE SUNBATHERS." (Quartzsite denizens have jokingly referred to it online as "wrinkle city" and "floppy and saggy town.")

Other camps are made up of matching rigs. Dozens of La-Z-Days RVs, Casita trailers, or Montana Fifth Wheels park together, forming same-species herds amid an otherwise anarchic sprawl of vehicles across the desert. Encountering such groups is like stumbling on sub-urban tract housing—with its cookie-cutter neighborhoods—in the middle of nowhere.

―――――

THE LONDON *FINANCIAL TIMES* called Quartzsite "one of America's more bizarre and seriously demented places." But Quartzsite is not a national aberration. You'd be hard-pressed to find a town that is so quintessentially American—hyper-American to the point of carica-ture. Here the native inhabitants are mostly gone and, in their place, visitors snap up souvenir dreamcatchers made in Pakistan and beaded moccasins from China. Winter doesn't exist. Soothsayers and spiri-tual seekers and discount shoppers come together around the shared belief that the best way to escape life's problems is by filling up the gas tank and hitting the road. Quartzsite has always been a refuge for travelers, outsiders, people trying to reinvent themselves. And it has perfected the art of the boom and bust cycle.

The town traces its roots to 1856, when white settlers built the private Fort Tyson to repel Mojave Indians. The fort later became a stagecoach stopover, Tyson's Wells, whose ruins are now the site of a tiny museum next to Silly Al's pizzeria. (The town has two other museums—one featuring a collection of chewing gum from all over the world and another with military memorabilia—but they seem less popular.) In 1875 the memoirist Martha Summerhayes stayed at Tyson's Wells overnight and described it as "most melancholy and uninviting. It reeks of everything unclean, morally and physically." When the stagecoach was discontinued, the settlement became a ghost town. In 1897, it was revived amid a mining boom, when the post office reopened and the municipality got a new name: Quartz-site. (It was supposed to be "Quartzite," after the mineral. The "s" was a typo that stuck.)

Quartzsite's most famous historical figure was a Syrian-born camel driver named Hadji Ali. Buried in town after his death in 1902, he is better known by the nickname "Hi Jolly," an American bastardization of his name. Ali was recruited in 1856 to the U.S. Army's camel corps, a brief experiment using the notoriously cantankerous beasts to ferry cargo across the Southwest. (At some point camels even carried mail from Tucson to Los Angeles. The program was abandoned in 1861 with the start of the Civil War.) Hadji Ali's grave marker is a pyramid made of quartz and petrified wood with a steel dromedary on top; all together it stands about ten feet tall. A plaque on the front reads: "THE LAST CAMP OF HI JOLLY, BORN SOMEWHERE IN SYRIA ABOUT 1828" and "OVER THIRTY YEARS A FAITHFUL AIDE TO THE U.S. GOVERNMENT." It's rumored that the ashes of Topsy, one of his camels, are buried with him.

Apart from maybe the naked bookseller, Hadji Ali is Quartzsite's most famous citizen. In tribute, the town uses his camel as an unofficial mascot. Visitors to Quartzsite pass monument-sized welcome signs that sport metal dromedaries like the one on Ali's tomb. One of the local trailer parks calls itself the Stuffed Camel. Near the western end of Main Street, automotive wheel rims and other debris have been welded together into a large sculpture of a camel. And Quartzsite celebrates an annual Hi Jolly Days parade; in more prosperous times, it was a full-blown festival that included, in different years, demolition derbies and camel races. At the Quartzsite Yacht Club—a bar and restaurant with off-track betting whose motto is "Long Time No Sea"—the owner's son used to don a head-to-toe camel costume and get loose on the dance floor as a band played "Hi Jolly," a folk hit by the New Christy Minstrels that depicts the camel driver as both a tireless worker and a skirt-chasing bon vivant.

But Quartzsite's quirky history wasn't enough to keep the town from sinking into obscurity. By the mid-1950s, the population had shrunk to just eleven families. Then, as the story goes, it was resurrected by heaps of junk and pretty rocks. Widespread flea markets started here in the 1960s after a station wagon broke down on Interstate 10. The driver, a mother traveling west with four young daughters, couldn't afford repairs and sold her kids' toys for cash. Others followed her lead, hawking wares off the tailgates of their pickups. This grew into a sprawling bazaar. In 1967, a town improvement group started a gem and mineral show called the Pow Wow, capitalizing on the influx of shoppers. The event became so popular that many credit it with bringing Quartzsite back from the brink of extinction. Over time, it was joined by numerous flea markets and swap meets. During the winter, they crowd acres of blacktop and hardpan desert that stand empty the rest of the year. There is the Greasewood Park n' Sell. The Prospector's Panorama. The Main Event. The Sell-A-Rama at Tyson Wells. It feels like a hoarder's estate sale, with tables offering cattle skulls, cast-iron cookware, and concealed carry women's handbags.

At one such vending area, the Hi Ali Swap Meet on Main Street, I encountered Sharen Peterson, seventy. Everyone called her Chere (pronounced "Sherry"). She was using old wooden doors as tables to display the odds and ends she had for sale. These included a katana, an elk hide, Hawaiian shirts, and housewares she no longer needed, since she was living in a Ford E350 van. Scattered among her wares were scraps of paper on which she'd written bits of bumper-sticker wisdom: "Due to rising cost of ammo do not expect a warning shot" and "We're not snowbirds, we're snowflakes." Browsers passed through. One bought four shirts for $17. "The world would be a better place if everyone wore Hawaiian shirts!" Chere exclaimed. Another paid $25 for a brown and turquoise flatware set that Chere had gotten for $20 in Santa Barbara. "It's the only addiction where you can get your money back!" she said of thrift-store shopping.

Chere wore a baseball cap studded with gold and silver pins of a seahorse and other marine life, with blond braided pigtails poking out underneath. Her eyes crinkled at the corners and she had a permanent tan, possibly a legacy of surfing Manhattan Beach just south of Los Angeles in the 1960s. (She still has wallet- and poster-sized pictures of herself in a Gidget haircut and bikini, sidled up to a yellow longboard.) Back then, she reminisced, it was easier to get by. She lived by the rule of twenty-fives: "Hamburger, cigarettes, and gas were twenty-five cents a gallon, twenty-five cents a pack, and twenty-five cents a pound."

Chere had been staying in the van ever since she was forced to sell her house in Minnesota. She'd bought the house in 1989 and, for twenty-three years, was a live-in landlord there, renting out extra bedrooms to cover expenses. Then she got caught without a necessary permit and had to stop, which meant losing the house. "The bureaucrats are getting ridiculous," she lamented. She'd originally planned to live on equity from selling the place. But her home, which had been appraised for $300,000 in 2002, went for just $140,000 in the wake of the housing crash. After the mortgage and broker's fees, there wasn't much left over, but she was making the best of it. Her van had originally been a fifteen-seater. She told me it was like living in a mobile mansion with picture windows all around, except the view was constantly changing. Her Social Security was $600 a month, after a $100 deduction for Medicare. "I seem to have enough for gas," she said, laughing. "If I don't, I just stay in one place." She crammed all her clothes in three plastic bins in the van and also rented a $600-a-year storage unit. She said she was paying $300 a month for her swap meet space, along with $50 for a town vending permit. When she wasn't at the swap meet in Quartzsite, she sold jewelry on the Santa Barbara seaside, where a season pass cost just $100 but didn't include the period between 2 a.m. and 6 a.m. each day, when the beaches were closed. Where did she go during those hours? "I hide," she said matter-of-factly, explaining there were many places to park unobtrusively and that, unlike an old hippie van she once owned that was covered in stickers, her current home was plain white, attracting no attention.

A couple days after we first met, Chere and I got together for dinner at the Quartzsite Yacht Club. Chere ordered a double hamburger, eating just one of the patties. The second she wrapped carefully in a napkin to bring back to Skittles, a dog she'd been watching for another vendor who'd left on a quick trip to Phoenix. She made a side salad from the burger fixings—lettuce, tomato, and onion—

topping them with a blend of ketchup and mayo that looked like Thousand Island dressing. She drank two O'Doul's non-alcoholic beers and sipped a glass of ice water with lemon. When the meal was over, she refused to let me pay her share and then carefully poured the remaining water into a Styrofoam takeout cup. It was cold and refreshing and ice was a small luxury, since she couldn't make any in the van.

We walked back toward the Hi Ali swap meet together. When I asked where she slept at night, she replied that it was easy to stay in her van, which was parked just across from her vending tables. Nobody bothered her there. She told me I was crazy to live in New York and that she was grateful she wasn't stuck in a "concrete jungle" somewhere.

"If the birds can live in the park—or they can live in the city— then why can't I?" she said. "We don't have to live wherever people are supposed to live—that's what it's all about!"

———

LIKE A LOT OF SMALL TOWN AMERICA, Quartzsite has come on hard times. Amid the bustle of commerce on Main Street, you can also see businesses that didn't make it. A restaurant has been boarded up. At one gas station, the paint is chipped and faded into pastel; the pumps appear to have been abandoned for decades.

Old-timers say the high season used to bring so many RVs to Quartzsite that you could cross the desert by stepping from roof to roof. But attendance has gone down sharply in recent years. No one seems to know quite why, but everyone has a pet theory, from local political strife, to property tax hikes and increased fees for flea market vendors, to the U.S.–Canadian exchange rate and fluctuating gas prices. Some think the thousands of rockhounds who visit Quartzsite's gem and mineral shows are defecting to similar events in Tucson. Yet others believe it's symptomatic of a larger economic malaise, meaning fewer people can afford long drives in a gas-guzzling motorhome, let alone the luxury of free time.

"As a Quartzsite native, I remember the early 1980s when we would have over one million visitors during the height of the season. Now it is more around 300,000 people," Philip Cushman, the president of the local chamber of commerce, told me in an email.

"It is ironic that before air conditioning, people were content to camp out in the desert for six months. Now as soon as it hits 100, folks are in a mad rush to go somewhere else," he said, adding that "the demographics of winter visitors are changing. The World War II generation was content to play bingo, go to dances, go rockhounding, and volunteer in our several community service organizations. As the Baby Boomers replace them, we observe that they want more things to do or they get bored." He's not willing to believe that Quartzsite's best days are over. In recent years the community has experimented with new events like the Grand Gathering, a four-day grandparents' celebration where 631 attendees stood (and sat) in the form of a giant "Q" to set a Guinness World Record for Largest Human Letter.

Despite these efforts, many of the people who visit Quartzsite are struggling, not the kind of free-spending tourists it would take to revive the town. At the Church of the Isaiah 58 Project on South Moon Mountain Avenue, a biker-turned-pastor named Mike Hobby and his wife, Linda, started a seasonal soup kitchen to help them. After experiencing homelessness firsthand—a medical crisis drowned the uninsured couple in unpayable bills—they founded the church in 2003 with a mission to help the dispossessed. The program grew and now serves thousands of meals to elderly and homeless people from November through March each year. Unlike many church missions where guests aren't served until they sit through a sermon—"ear banging" is what insiders call it—there's no such requirement here.

Mike told me that transient old folks flock to Quartzsite because it's "a low-income retirement town" and "a cheap place to hide." Hide from what? I asked. His answers: shame, poverty, cold weather. In the desert, he explained, "they don't have to worry about freezing out. They tell their kids they're doing fine."

One night when I visited, diners lined up with plastic trays to receive spaghetti with chicken cacciatore ladled on top, along with salad, garlic bread on hamburger buns, and apple crisp. They sat at long tables in a warehouse space behind the church that opened onto the parking lot. The mood was convivial. Retirees swapped stories with freight-train hoppers and bicycle tramps. Overhead on a hand-painted banner, a stick figure approached a doorway with red flames to the left and a golden cloud to the right. "Time Is Up!" it proclaimed. "Which Did You Choose? If You Don't Choose Jesus, You Do Choose Hell."

Over that dinner I met Leonard Scott, a former gas station owner who went by "Scottie" and wore his hair in a stringy gray ponytail under a "Jesus Is Lord" trucker hat. The sixty-three-year-old was living in a 1995 Winnebago: "I lost my empire"—two homes and a duplex he had bought as investment properties—"when the economy collapsed." Scottie had worked at a hot spring in Tonopah, Arizona, to supplement his monthly $590 Social Security check, and was planning to join friends in the Pacific Northwest picking morel mushrooms, which he heard fetch $10 an ounce. Eventually, he added, he hoped to move to a beach in Kauai and live off fruit from the trees.*

The church is near the town food pantry. I spent some time there with Carol Kelley, an eighty-year-old widow who ran the place tirelessly from a cluttered desk below a wall covered in nutritional posters. "I will die in this chair," she joked. An unexpected bonanza had arrived by way of an overturned semitrailer—crates of sugar snap peas, cucumbers, green beans, and mangoes—and she was foisting

---

* He's not the first down-on-his-luck person to consider that. Hawaii's largest homeless shelter operator, the Institute for Human Services, gets between 100 and 150 calls and emails a year "from people who are actually looking to be homeless here in Hawaii," a representative of the agency told a local television reporter. The homeless population has grown by more than a third in recent years and now is higher, per capita, than anywhere else in the nation, prompting the governor to announce a state of emergency and the mayor of Honolulu to call for a "war on homelessness." Meanwhile Hawaii's tourism industry has been funding an initiative to fly homeless people back to the mainland.

the spoils upon her visitors with the enthusiasm of a farm-stand operator holding a fire sale. A couple from Oregon came by. They were living out of a van. The woman told me her coffee shop business had gone under and they were starting over with nothing. She was good at painting pictures of dogs, so they were on the way to a nearby flea market, in hope of selling some of her work.

Carol sent them off with a box of vegetables. After they left, she looked stressed. It was tough enough to keep up with the needs of Quartzsite's full-time residents, she explained, let alone the visitors. "Our little town has to feed all these people who wander here for the winter," she said. "It's not fair." One of the regular volunteers chimed in, as if to steady her.

"We feed everyone," he said quietly. "We treat everyone alike."

———

FOR THREE WINTERS IN A ROW, I camped in the desert around Quartzsite—at first in a tent, and later in a van—to get acquainted with the nomads who live there for months on end. I managed to catch up with some of the same people during all three trips, including Barb and Chuck Stout, the music teacher and former McDonald's vice president I'd originally interviewed in Nevada.

When Barb and Chuck showed up in Quartzsite for the first time, they were still recovering from their three-month stint at CamperForce. Like their coworkers, they'd faced a triple trial there. First came physical exhaustion. ("Muscles I never knew I had are shouting at me after ten hours of lifting, twisting, squatting, reaching," Barb reflected.) Then came Kafka-style madness. (After forty-five minutes spent hunting for a bin with enough room to stow a product, Barb had to repeat "breathe, breathe" to stay sane in the warehouse, which she nicknamed "Amazoo.") Last came flat-out survival: the stress of subzero temperatures in an RV built for warmer climes. (The rig's water supply got cut off after a filter froze and burst. Then its pump broke. Chuck lost a day of work getting repairs done.)

After all that, they were ready for some Arizona sunshine. But as first-timers at "the Q," they didn't know where in the vast desert wilderness they should boondock. Another couple had invited them to an annual gathering called the Birds of a Feather Quartzsite Rally. They decided to check it out. What they found: More than eighty-five Bluebird Wanderlodge luxury motor coaches parked side by side in a giant circle, like the rays on a child's drawing of the sun, in an area the rigs' owners called "the nest." Their front bumpers were pointed inward, aligned with X's that had been scratched into the dirt at perfect twenty-five-foot intervals. When the gathering began, a dry erase board reading "Welcome to Q" was updated daily with a schedule of events from a "Ladies' Walk" (the caption read: "walk, bitch, walk, bitch . . . ") to a "Men's Tech Walk Around," a firearms session called "Tactical Shooting" and "Ray's Prime Rib Dinner." (A tongue-in-cheek note warned folks that, if they forgot to pay for their steaks, they'd arrive at the dinner to find "Ray donated your piece of heaven to the homeless in town!")

The Stouts quickly learned that their 1996 National Seabreeze motor coach was an "S.O.B."—slang for "Some Other Brand." It was not allowed to join the members' circle. They had to park off to the side. On some nights, they had their own bonfires.

Though the Stouts felt out of place at the rally, they quickly reconnected with a more welcoming tribe—one whose bonds had been forged by hard labor. An unofficial CamperForce reunion sprang up on a patch of desert called Scaddan Wash. Nine Amazonians and one retired police officer, who'd tagged along for kicks, sat in camp chairs and reminisced about warehouse work while munching on pork rinds, tortilla chips, baby carrots, and Barb's homemade vegan egg salad sandwiches. They sang "The Twelve Days of Amazon," a workers' parody of the holiday classic that replaced "lords a-leaping" with "horns a-beeping"—a reference to warehouse noise—and added other gifts like "an ID badge for security," "two pairs of gloves," "three orange vests" and, eventually, "ten sore muscles." Then they drew names from a hat to award door prizes: Amazon-branded swag including key chains, bottle openers, lanyards, and flash drives. (Offered a box cutter, I politely declined, explaining I'd have to fly home later.) Someone threw a blue plastic Frisbee and Sydney, the Stouts' Australian shepherd and heeler mix, trotted after it. Folks mused about how, at Amazon, they'd been counting down the days until the season ended whereas in Quartzsite, it was easy to lose track of time altogether.

Barb and Chuck came to enjoy Quartzsite and made it into an annual pilgrimage. Like Iris, they found short-term jobs there. These included gigs at an RV show: picking up litter, guarding a vendors-only entrance, and staffing a booth that sold angler's tools, sport beverage holders, and other novelties. Barb liked working that booth the best—she got to be a cross between a carnival barker and a Home Shopping Network host. She handed out samples of bloody Mary mix and nimbly demonstrated a device for tying knots in fishing line. Her boss encouraged showmanship. One time, when an elderly woman in a mobility scooter coasted up to the counter to browse, he grabbed a Liquid Caddy Ultimate Mug and Velcroed it to her prosthetic leg. Barb chimed in. "This will fit anywhere, at any time, on anything!" she exclaimed, then pointed to her boss. "He's not kidding! He doesn't pull your leg!"

The last time I saw the Stouts in Quartzsite, it was their third winter there. They were veteran nomads now. Seated at a bonfire, they performed a rite of joyful catharsis: burning their old bankruptcy papers.

CHAPTER SEVEN

The Rubber Tramp Rendezvous

THE TOWN OF NEEDLES, CALIFORNIA, is named after a range of sharp granite spires that rise up like jagged teeth. When John Steinbeck wrote about it in *The Grapes of Wrath*, he made the place just as hostile as its geography suggests. The Joad family stops to rest in Needles at a tent camp on the Colorado River, only to get hustled off by a sheriff's deputy. Calling them "Okies," he snarls, "We don't want none of you settlin' down here." Ma Joad menaces him with an iron skillet. "Mister, you got a tin button an' a gun," she retorts. "Where I come from, you keep your voice down."

Linda stopped in Needles on her way to the Rubber Tramp Rendezvous. She'd come straight from the Amazon warehouse in Fernley, eight hours away. Like the Joads, she was exhausted and hoped to sleep there. Unlike them, she planned to avoid getting rousted by police. That meant finding somewhere to park a twenty-eight-foot motorhome overnight, for free, without drawing attention. Needles didn't have a Walmart. The next-best bet would be an all-night business with an active parking lot. Pulling off Historic Route 66, Linda checked the hours of a Bashas' supermarket at the

Needles Towne Center strip mall. It closed early, but a hundred yards away stood a twenty-four-hour gym. The place didn't look especially busy, but it would have to do. She parked across from its entrance and crawled into bed.

Linda slept through the night. In the morning she woke with an errand on her mind. While working at Amazon she'd accidentally let her motorhome registration expire—"I'm such a dingbat!"—and she needed to renew it before traveling further. So she mapped directions to the local DMV. The GPS on her phone led her down the road. It told her to make a U-turn. Then it had her drive some more. When the route guidance stopped, Linda was right where she'd started. She tried again, got the same result, and pulled into a gas station for help. The attendant pointed to an office near the corner of the strip mall. "I had parked in front of it all night," Linda remembered, laughing. "I just didn't see it." Before long her motorhome was registered and cruising south on Highway 95. Quartzsite was less than two hours away.

"Come to the Rubber Tramp Rendezvous and you can take classes and learn plus make many great friends," read an invitation on Bob Wells's website. "In many ways we modern day vandwellers are just like the Mountain Men of old: We need to be alone and on the move, but we equally need to occasionally gather together and make connections with like-minded people who understand us."

That sounded wonderful to Linda, who craved companionship. When she'd set out in her RV seven months earlier, financial survival wasn't her only goal—she also dreamed about joining a larger community of people, folks who were willing to radically remake their lives in search of fulfillment and freedom. But at Amazon the graveyard shifts had been strenuous and solitary. Her days off were more about recovery than socializing, which didn't leave much time for bonding with other nomads. Once Nevada's bitter winter took hold—when temperatures dropped as low as −2 degrees—her neighbors at the Desert Rose had mostly hunkered down in their rigs, rather than hanging out in the RV park's shared outdoor spaces.

Linda was done with all that. She was ready for Quartzsite's gentler climate, with its 70-degree afternoons.

Of course, good times were not guaranteed. Linda had never been to "the Q." She didn't know her way around the vastness of the desert encircling the town. She didn't even have directions to the encampment. Unlike many newbies, who'd befriended RTR folks virtually by joining in conversations on Bob's website, Linda hadn't been a part of that dialogue. The only person she knew at the RTR was Silvianne. (Jen and Ash were off on other adventures and wouldn't make it until more than halfway through the two-week event.) As a result, Linda was like a kid walking into a new school on the first day of class. She wanted to meet people. She wanted to learn things. But what if she didn't fit in? Most of the group would be minimalist vandwellers, after all. Would they look kindly on her big, gas-guzzling RV?

She didn't spend much time worrying, though. Instead she went online for instructions. "Hi, this will be my first RTR. Is there a map to the campsite, a calendar of events? Any help would be appreciated," she posted on a Facebook page for the get-together. Someone replied with a schedule. Swankie Wheels linked what looked like a clip art treasure map, with the route to the RTR highlighted in yellow. It ended with a red "X" and the words "We are here."

And so Linda set out to find what she hoped would be her tribe. The motorhome shuddered along Dome Rock Road East on pavement that seemed increasingly post-apocalyptic the farther she got from town. In places it was so battered and cracked that drivers gave up and used the shoulder instead. On her right was Scaddan Wash, public land that offered free fourteen-day camping. Rows of giant RVs clustered at the edge, making it look more like a tailgate party than a wilderness area. Farther along what remained of the asphalt stopped at an orange-and-white striped barrier. There Linda made a hard right turn onto Mitchell Mine Road, a gravel track that rose and dipped through the chaparral, pushing south, past the crowds and into the backcountry. After a mile and a half, a yellow sign appeared

A sign points the way to the Rubber Tramp Rendezvous.

at the roadside. "Rubber Tramp Rendezvous," it said, with an arrow pointing right. (The sign made finding the campsite easy by daylight. Getting there after dark, however, was hard on the uninitiated. During my first winter in Quartzsite, I tried visiting one evening and quickly got lost. When I spotted a campfire in the distance, I drove to it expecting the RTR, only to find a tribe of Rainbows and crust punks whooping it up over whiskey and weed. I sat and listened as a guitarist belted out a rollicking Kimya Dawson song: "The beer I had for breakfast was a bottle of Mad Dog! And my twenty-twenty vision was fifty percent off!")

Linda cruised slowly into the camping area. About five dozen vehicles dotted the open desert, like tiny houses sharing the same vast backyard. Linda saw all kinds of vans—mini-vans, cargo and passenger vans, high-top conversion vans, wheelchair lift vans, box vans. One was a rental, with U-Haul graphics splashed on its sides. (This, Linda would later learn, was the temporary home of a vandweller-in-training who'd flown from Chicago to Phoenix, then picked it up for transportation and shelter during the event.) Amid the vans were some travel trailers, pickup campers and RVs, along with a few SUVs and sedans—even a Prius—set up for long-term mobile living. One bike tramp made do with even less: two wheels and a tent. There was a handful of more exotic vehicles, including a handmade wooden gypsy caravan, or vardo, that was painted seafoam green. Modeled after the traditional nineteenth-century horse-drawn wagons of the Romani, it was pulled by a pickup truck and was the home of a sixty-five-year-old shipbuilder from Oregon, who'd survived renal cell carcinoma and now kept afloat on monthly $471 Social Security checks.

In the middle of the anarchic settlement was a large campfire ring—the central gathering place. Not too far from there, Linda found a spot to park her RV near some scraggly trees. She began setting up camp.

The fleet of mobile dwellings made a striking display, and Bob later posted photos of it on his website. A reader marveled: "If I came

Lou Brochetti stands in his handmade gypsy wagon.

across your pictures without the commentary . . . one might think that this is a report on a road warrior-ish future . . . post economic collapse where everyone has taken up living in vehicles."

This was the fourth time Bob had hosted a winter Rubber Tramp Rendezvous. It wasn't easy being a guru. He'd spent months planning and spreading the word. As the event began, his work became more tangible. Along the road, he posted the RTR sign on heavy-duty stakes, which he sledgehammered into the ground to withstand desert winds. He photocopied a calendar with social occasions and a schedule of seminars he planned to teach. He set up a tipi-style tent with a five-gallon bucket, garbage bags, wet wipes, and toilet paper inside—a kind gesture for newcomers. He piled wood near the fire ring and, nearby, spread a blue tarp like a picnic blanket on the ground, weighting the corners with rocks. This would be the free pile. Vandwellers were always getting rid of things, trying to maximize limited space. New items would appear on the pile each day: blankets, books, a large straw sombrero, auto parts, flip-flops, a digital camera, tent stakes, plastic cups, *Backpacker* magazine's Yosemite issue, T-shirts, pants, and one large terracotta flowerpot, whose new owner filled it with kindling, topped it with a wire rack, and used it to boil a pot of soup. Linda would end up browsing for books there, grabbing whatever sparked her interest, and showed me one of her finds, a paperback called *The Secret Symbols of the Dollar Bill: A Closer Look at the Hidden Magic and Meaning of the Money You Use Every Day.*

Bob didn't profit off the RTR. His hospitality set a generous tone, attracting people who were just as eager to share their skills, resources, and experiences. A licensed cosmetologist gave donation-optional haircuts near the Chevy Astro van where she lived with her husband and two dogs. One RVer set up at a tiki bar with a neon sign, lawn flamingos, and a light-up palm tree, then hosted parties. Swankie demonstrated her solar oven—essentially a box with tanning mirrors for food—by baking everyone brownies, banana nut bread, and blueberry muffins. Mechanics taught basic auto repair skills. Carpenters

Bob gets his annual haircut from cosmetologist Kyndal Dimon.

hammered together bed frames and shelves to fit newly gutted vans. People with large solar panels gave away their excess power, leaving extension cords out so passersby could charge their gadgets. A deaf woman ran an impromptu class in American Sign Language. One guy demonstrated how to fix tires. He brought an old steel-belted radial that participants could practice on, letting them stab it and plug the leak, over and over again, then sharing advice on portable twelve-volt air compressors. Linda especially valued these skills and, during another stint as camp host, would put them to use rescuing some forest rangers whose fire truck had a flat.

At sunrise each morning, one vandweller, Lesa NeSmith, rose to start the first campfire and boil a pot of cowboy coffee for anyone who strolled by with a cup. That was an old tradition for Lesa. Way back when she lived in a Richmond, Virginia, high-rise, Sunday mornings were about getting up early, brewing coffee in an electric pot, and propping open her apartment door to show neighbors the coffee was on and ready to share.

There were group meals: a bring-your-own-topping baked potato night, along with chili and soup dinners where everyone added something to the colossal cooking pots, harkening back to the hobo stews of the 1930s' Great Depression. Every night after sunset, someone lit a big bonfire, though it was often abandoned by nine or ten, when sleepiness began tugging at eyelids and the evening chill set in.

There was also a pervasive feeling of pride. Almost everyone I met shared the attitude of Al Christensen, a sixty-two-year-old former advertising art director who preferred to call himself "houseless," he told me, rather than "homeless." As suits his ex-profession, Al is deft with words. He described watching advertising gigs dry up over a period of several years, with the few remaining opportunities going to younger creatives. He went from working at a "virtual agency" to being "virtually unemployed," he explained. A self-described loner, Al could only handle being around people so much. Al had to leave the RTR in the middle of a seminar on budgeting to catch up on his solitude. He came back a few days later, though. He liked the people at the RTR and felt that it put a good face on nomadic lifestyle, "made it seem very possible and respectable—it's not like I live down by the river in a van."

Linda was also delighted by the conviviality. She wanted to learn as much as she could and went to the seminars that started at ten most mornings. Many RTR old-timers were already fluent in what Bob taught—either they'd gleaned the lessons from their own lives, had attended nearly identical seminars the year before, or had read his book, which was called *How to Live in a Car, Van or RV . . . And Get Out of Debt, Travel & Find True Freedom*. While Bob's book was fairly practical, it also included some exercises for aspiring vandwellers that bordered on performance art. "Practice in your apartment," it advised. "The first step is to move into your bedroom and stop using the rest of the house." The next step, it continued, was determining the internal measurements of your future van home. If you anticipated having, say, sixty square feet, you could build a working model based on that. "Get some big cardboard boxes and use them to make a six foot by ten foot space in the corner of your bed-room," the book explained. "Now move into your cardboard 'van.' Instead of living in the bedroom you will live in your little cardboard van." (For anyone stressed about the prospects of moving into a van, it's hard to imagine that doing dry runs in a refrigerator box would boost morale.)

Still nearly everyone, old-timers included, showed up with fold-ing chairs to settle in and listen. Some took notes. Others were too busy warding off the cold morning air, stuffing hands into the pock-ets of their hoodies or sipping from mugs of steaming coffee. A few tried keeping order among the roving legions of nomads' dogs. They came in every shape—from Chihuahua to coonhound to mild-mannered half-wolf—and wandered around during the seminars, greeting each other, soliciting treats, sniffing ashes in the fire pit, peeing on creosote bushes (and once on my audio recorder), and breaking out in occasional scuffles.

One of the liveliest seminars taught the art of stealth parking. Aimed at urban vandwellers, who often dodged anti-camping laws, the lessons were about blending into one's surroundings to avoid get-ting the dreaded "knock" of a police officer tapping on the door, a drunk pounding the walls, or passersby squinting through the win-dows, asking "Is someone living in there?" Everyone knew about "the knock." It was a common enemy. Swankie even had nightmares about it. "I have this strange surreal dream of someone knocking on the van," she once wrote. "Usually happens if I am not 100% comfortable with where I am parking or boondocking. It's annoying as heck. Never anyone there. Well, sometimes someone is there, but if it is police or security, they usually SPEAK."

Bob's first piece of advice was finding a safe zone. His career in the grocery industry and his early experiences camping in the park-ing lot of his workplace made him a huge fan of twenty-four-hour supermarkets. He added that, in some cities where overnight parking at Walmart was prohibited, nomads might find refuge at other big chains including Kmart, Sam's Club, Costco, Home Depot, and

Lowe's. Retailers that catered to outdoor enthusiasts, such as Bass Pro and Cabela's, might also be a good bet. Cracker Barrel was famously tolerant of RVers. Strip malls and all-night diners like Denny's can also work well. Sometimes the best plan was positioning your rig between two businesses; each will assume you're visiting the other. Wherever you park, it's smart to back into the spot—that way the nose of your vehicle points out to the road and you can leave fast if there's trouble. And when you stay in one place for a while— particularly when you're near residential areas—it's good to have both a day camp and a night camp. The daytime location is where you can go about all your regular activities, including anything you need to do in the evening to prepare for bed. The night camp is somewhere you go after dark, strictly for the purposes of sleeping. Then you leave first thing the next morning. If you must use a light when you're already at your night camp, consider a red-tinted head-lamp, which is less glaring.

Bob also emphasized the importance of having a good story ready. If you're parked near a hospital, you're visiting a patient. If you're parked at an auto repair shop, you're getting the engine fixed. But when it came to alibis, he urged his flock to know their limits and not to overdo it with tall tales. "If you're not a good storyteller, don't try to tell stories," he said.

Another element was camouflage. That meant keeping your vehicle clean, clearing the passenger seat of laundry and other clutter, and avoiding adornments that might draw interest, from antenna toppers to window decals and bumper stickers. (This last point raised tongue-in-cheek disagreement. *What about an "Ask Me About Jesus" sticker? Wouldn't that keep people away?* One of the nomads, who was not religious, had affixed such a sticker to his pickup camper as both an experiment and an inside joke.) People living in cargo vans, Bob suggested, could go for a workman look—leave a safety vest sitting out so it's visible through the windshield, have a ladder rack on the roof. Those living in white vans could seek out local businesses—

such as plumbing or catering services—that have fleets of similar vehicles and attempt to blend with the herd. Camouflage also meant trying not to batten down your hatches too much—if your van always has the windows blocked with curtains, people will wonder what's going on in there. And it meant trying to avoid attention when going to wash up in a public restroom by being clever, such as having a hunting or outdoors-style vest with many small pockets you've stocked with toiletries, for example.

Bob also emphasized: police were not always the enemy. Some vandwellers and RVers recounted getting "the knock" from concerned officers who just wanted to ask if they were alright. There were reports from one vandweller in Ohio about a friendly cop who sometimes brought her coffee. By researching a town in advance or talking to other vandwellers, you could learn a great deal about local attitudes. In friendly places, the best choice might be going straight to the police station, telling a hard luck story, and asking where in town it would be safe to park overnight. And remember: No matter how sneaky you're being, it's quite likely the local police are aware of your presence. "Cops are pretty smart. They're going to realize something's up if you've been 'just passing through' for the past six months."

Everyone recognized, however, that it was often preferable to avoid police altogether. Some had clever ways of doing it. One vandweller online talked about installing a police scanner app on his smartphone. By listening to chatter on the local law enforcement channels, he could determine if anyone had reported him for illegal camping and get away before the cops showed up. And it had another purpose, too. If hooligans approached, he could scare them off by playing the police radio loudly, with all its static and squelches, to make his rig sound like an undercover law enforcement vehicle.

Another popular seminar was Bob's talk on budgeting, which came with a strong message in favor of minimalism and against consumer culture. Bob told people that, while they were slaves to the market economy, they could maximize their freedom by paring down material needs and spending less. "By society's standards, I'm a pauper, but by vandweller standards I live pretty well," he explained. He recommended economizing on gas by carpooling to town whenever possible, avoiding unnecessary drives, and checking smartphone apps like Gas Buddy to find the cheapest filling stations. He urged them to keep an emergency fund—$2,000 or so—even if they had to build it slowly, setting aside an envelope and adding $3 each day. He said he knew someone living on $250 a month. "How many people here are living on $500 or less a month?" he asked. A few hands went up. "How many are debt free?" The trickle of hands became a flood, prompting laughs and cheers. One guy stood to snap a picture. "You wouldn't see this anywhere else in America!" he marveled.

When someone raised the topic of making money while traveling, one vandweller revealed that he was an itinerant poker dealer. Casinos all over the country hire short-term dealers to staff tournaments and the job can easily pay $30 an hour, with free food during the workday. At his first gig, the World Series of Poker in Las Vegas, he made $11,000 in seven weeks. The hiring process appeared to be age-blind; he'd met dealers in their seventies and eighties. He could only think of two downsides. The first was that prospective dealers had to attend training classes and, while sometimes casinos offered them for free, they could otherwise cost a few hundred dollars. The second was you have to shower every day.

After the budgeting lecture, Linda told me that, while she wasn't so sure about going back to Amazon, the dealer gig sounded fantastic. It made her think back to her days working as a cigarette girl and cocktail waitress at the Riverside Casino. "I would do that in a flash!" she said. "I would go deal poker."

Other seminars offered advice on installing solar panels, workamping, cooking with a limited kitchen, and boondocking on public land. At an anonymous Q&A session, participants wrote difficult questions on slips of paper they dropped into a tin can. A moderator read them aloud. *What can I do if my family won't accept the way I live? How do I find someone to date?* There was the occasional joke, too. *How do you have sex in a van?*

Bob also explained how to get cut-rate dentistry in Los Algodones, a town in the Mexican state of Baja California nicknamed "the Molar City" because some 350 practitioners crowd into a few blocks. Linda hoped to make a trip there at some point to get her upper dentures repaired. They'd fallen out of her shirt pocket when she reached down to pat Coco and she'd accidentally stepped on them. Bob had gone to Los Algodones for the first time after he got a $2,500 quote from a Nevada dentist, which was way more than he could afford. He ended up getting the same work done for $600. Although the difference isn't always quite that dramatic, dental procedures typically cost less than half the American price.

Bob began traveling to Los Algodones each year for a $25 teeth cleaning. Since the town is also packed with cheap opticians and pharmacies, he'd stock up on medication to control his high blood pressure—no prescription required—and also pay about $100 for an eye exam and new glasses. On one such occasion, I got to join him for the annual excursion. A group of us carpooled the eighty miles from Scaddan Wash near Quartzsite down to Yuma, then drove a bit farther west to the small border community of Andrade. We parked near a casino owned by the local Quechan tribe and walked across the border, past a sign that said BIENVENIDOS in large letters and, in smaller type below, had a warning for visiting Americans. "Guns are illegal in Mexico," it said.

Bob led us to a new-looking building with a glass and marble façade. Along the right side hung a banner with photos of smiling patients—mostly white people—superimposed over an illustration of a dental implant. We walked through the mirrored front doors. Inside, the staff wore crisp, blue-gray scrubs and invited us to sit in a waiting room with diploma-covered walls. Bob tolerated my following him into an immaculate office, where his previous X-rays were loaded on a monitor. When I left to explore the town, he was leaning back in the patient's chair under a bright light, mouth agape, as his dentist peered inside.

Back on the street, I wandered past curio stands and liquor shops, signs for half-off hearing aids, and a pharmacy whose dry erase board advertised discount Viagra and diet pills. In one storefront, a pair of dental technicians sat at a workbench; one wore a face mask and was cutting into a plaster cast of teeth with a small hacksaw. White-haired tourists sat at outdoor patios, eating shrimp tacos, sipping margaritas, sometimes dancing to live music. A guitarist crooned "Desperado." Around the corner, strains of "Hotel California" drifted out of a bar. Later I read a blog post by a nomad who'd visited Los Algodones after the RTR and was treated to a soundtrack of "Take It to the Limit" and "Lyin' Eyes" on the stereo while he got his teeth cleaned and X-rayed. It seemed you couldn't walk a block without hearing the Eagles.

We waited until after the noon-to-three lunchtime rush, when it's possible to stand in line at the border station for more than an hour, then crossed back to Arizona.

LINDA WAS ENJOYING her inaugural Rubber Tramp Rendezvous when we met for the first time, after the budgeting seminar. I asked how she was finding things. "Oh my god," she said. "The other day, for the first time in years and years, I felt joy. Joy! That's better than being happy," she said, her eyes crinkling at the corners as she told me about taking a trip to town with Silvianne. "We were just driving down the street in her little bus, looking for a place to put the trash, and I was like, 'This is how we live. This is such a wonderful thing to do.'"

A few days later, Linda was still riding that surge of fine feelings. She told me about how she'd been in survival mode when she discovered Bob's website. "Now I not only survive, I thrive!" she marveled. "Which is, you know, the idea—you want to thrive in your old age, not just survive day to day."

After months of racing around the warehouse, she was finally starting to relax. Things that were usually annoying became funny, like the bill collector who kept calling, over and over, trying to reach another woman who'd been previously assigned to Linda's phone number. In the past, Linda had dutifully explained the mix-up. Now she said, "Hang on. I'll get her!" before leaving the phone on hold for twenty minutes. She cracked herself up.

Jen and Ash joined Linda at the RTR in mid-January. After finishing up at Amazon, they'd visited family in Colorado, hiked the Grand Canyon's southern rim, and toured Earthships in New Mexico. They found Linda and parked the Manatee right behind her RV. They were not surprised that, in the time they had taken to get there, she had made a bunch of new friends for them to meet.

One of them was Lois Middleton, sixty-one, camped nearby in a ten-foot 1965 Aloha trailer she'd named Home Sweet Home, or Lil' Homey for short. Like Linda, Lois had worked as a building inspector. But after more than two decades on that job in Vancouver, Washington, she got squeezed out of her job in 2010 amid looming cutbacks. Other dominoes began to fall. Her father died. Her car got repossessed. She lost her house to foreclosure. She declared bankruptcy. She had hoped to eventually move in with her son, but then his house got foreclosed on, too. When Lois set out in Lil' Homey, it was without knowing what came next. Or as she told me: "The plan is there is no plan."

Linda didn't realize it yet, but she had also met the woman who would become her best friend. (Later, they'd start calling each other "BFF." At first it sounded like tongue-in-cheek millennial-speak but, in time, the jokey veneer wore off, leaving only sincerity.) LaVonne Ellis was a sixty-seven-year-old writer who had been on the road since October. After a career in broadcast journalism that included working as a radio correspondent for ABC, she had ended up at a station in Minneapolis. A new boss came in and eliminated the news desk. She got promoted to management but it wasn't working out. They let her go. She figured she'd get a new job quickly, only to discover in her fifties how much harder the job market was. "I sort of aged out," she reflected. After moving in with her sister to hunt for work, she finally got offered a gig: reading thirty-second traffic reports for $10 an hour. She took it, working first in Los Angeles, then in San Diego. The money was tight—especially because LaVonne was a single mother whose younger son was still in the house—but she was managing alright until the migraines hit. Over time, she'd found herself increasingly sensitive to chemicals and fragrances. She'd managed to adapt at home with odor-free cleaning products, but now the hours she spent in the office left her head throbbing. Finally, she quit, going on welfare and disability. Though she managed to get piecework online, it never brought in much income. She ended up sleeping on a cot in the living room of a one-bedroom apartment she shared with her son and his wife. She hated feeling like she was cramping them, but she didn't know where else to go. Still, it wasn't working. Then she read a book on vandwelling. It gave her another idea.

In the summer of 2013, LaVonne rented a car and borrowed a tent to attend a smaller version of the Rubber Tramp Rendezvous near Flagstaff, Arizona. On her blog, The Complete Flake, she described it as a transformative experience:

> I found my people: a ragtag bunch of misfits who surrounded me with love and acceptance. By misfits I don't mean losers and dropouts. These were smart, compassionate, hardworking Americans whose scales had been lifted from their eyes. After a lifetime of chasing the American Dream, they had come to the conclusion that it was all nothing but a big con.

She liked it so much that she bought a van. It was a 2003 maroon GMC Safari with 129,000 miles on the odometer. She picked it up for $4,995 in a used car lot in El Cajon and named it LaVanne. The rear seats became her couch and bed. She set up a kitchen on the tailgate. Her goal was to get out of debt, pay off the van, and build an emergency fund while living within the means of her Social Security and trying to write a memoir. Two months before she met Linda, she moved into LaVanne and went to see Bob. Making the shift was hard at first, with many cold nights. Bob lent her a warm sleeping bag and then insisted she keep it, telling her "I don't like it." Now LaVonne was enjoying her first RTR as a full-fledged vandweller. Two new friends had helped her install a solar panel on the roof of LaVanne. She had volunteered to lead the group's daily walks, which left at 8:30 each morning from the fire ring. Once she issued an open invitation to her campsite for a scrambled-egg-and-potato breakfast. I showed up with orange juice and eggs. LaVonne shot me a skeptical look. Folks weren't sure how they felt about a journalist hanging around, she said. They worried I'd make them look like "a bunch of homeless vagabonds." I told her that wasn't my agenda and retreated to chat with some of the other diners.

Around that time, LaVonne and many others in camp were looking forward to an event that overlapped with the RTR and attracts thousands of nomads each year: the Quartzsite Sports, Vacation & RV Show. That name was too long, so everyone just called it "the Big Tent." With more than two hundred exhibitors, it felt like a giant infomercial. Barkers in headsets demonstrated Vitamix blenders and rubber mops. Booths peddled cures for an alphabet of ills, from anxiety and arthritis to backache and bunions, gout and heel spurs to sore muscles and sciatica. One vendor promised to help owners of upside-down motorhomes, with signs reading "We're the solution for getting you out of your RV payment." There were tables for the American Association for Nude Recreation, Twin Peaks RV Insurance, and America's Mailbox, a business that offered "mail forwarding and home base services" for itinerants who needed a South Dakota address, fast. Other stands offered lint rollers, super glue, pet ID tags, firearms training, and massage pillows.

There were also recruitment tables for workampers. Amazon had sent representatives who took down names and gave out souvenir pads of sticky notes with CamperForce's smiling RV logo. Concessionaires for the Forest Service were there, urging passersby to apply for jobs as campground hosts. Some were interviewing candidates and making site assignments on the spot. One representative had uniforms to give new employees. A temp firm called Express Employment Professionals sought laborers for the annual sugar beet harvest. "If you're willing to fill out an application, then you're hired for the coming season," the recruiter told me. "We would hire you today."

One of the more eye-catching tables had a backlit sign that said "Adventureland." A three-panel display below it showed photos of gray-haired amusement park employees wearing blue polo shirts and plastic name tags. Smiling workers sat in the front car of the Tornado rollercoaster, rode an old-time locomotive, hung out at the Chicken Shack fast-food station, and held giant plush carnival prizes. Scattered among these snapshots were cartoons—yellow smiley faces, a dog mascot with a lolling tongue—and printed slogans:

Feel Like a Kid Again!

Hey Workamper, It's Time for Fun!

Camping + Working + Smiles = Fun!!!

Based in Altoona, Iowa, Adventureland had sent recruiters to hire around three hundred workampers to run its rides, games, and concessions for wages ranging from $7.25 to $7.50 an hour. The park owns a neighboring mobile home park where laborers were encouraged to stay, for a fee. From June to September, the rate was $160 a month; employees who stayed until the season ended would get their August and September rent waived.

Adventureland's managers had been hiring transient older workers for nearly two decades and appreciated their upbeat attitude. "I think some workampers could carry on a conversation with a telephone pole because they have the gift of gab," gushed the park's human resources director, Gary Pardekooper, in a 2012 video interview with *Workamper News*. "We like it, and our guests like it."

I'd only ever met one former Adventureland workamper; I spoke with her when she was working for Amazon in Fernley. She was not a fan. "The management was horrid and the public was really really bad and the weather was brutal and it was Iowa and it was hot," the sixty-two-year-old woman blurted, adding that many of her coworkers felt mistreated and quit. "There was a dude that was so pissed he jumped into his motorhome. His awning was out and staked down but he just drove," she added, cracking up as she described how the canopy flapped in the wind.

I didn't know it then, but the next year I'd get a chance to stop at Adventureland during a cross-country road trip in mid-July. The afternoon was humid, with temperatures in the nineties, and the air shimmered with heat. The theme park looked like a candy-colored mirage between green cornfields and Prairie Meadows. (That was the name of a racetrack casino complex next door.) The employee campground was planted with ash trees. Many of the RVs there sported American flags and displayed license plates from around the heartland—Iowa, Nebraska, Minnesota, and South Dakota. A couple of camping tents were set up in the back. There seemed to be a handful of long-term inhabitants among the nomads—you could tell by the weeds that had grown up around their tires and the mature tomato plants thriving in five-gallon buckets.

Inside the park the staff seemed evenly split between local high school students and the elderly. There were numerous souvenir shops. One sold T-shirts that said, "Wanna Taco 'Bout Jesus? Lettuce Pray" and "God Is Greater Than Any Failed Plan Debt Disease Army or Mountain Standing in Your Way." At another one, a sixty-something clerk spoke excitedly about a recent wage increase that had taken everyone by surprise. They were now getting $8.50 an hour. She and her coworkers speculated that it came from peer pressure, since Walmart had just started paying $9 an hour. Though she'd come here for part-time work, she added, the company was understaffed and had her on a full-time schedule. (That explained why, in the middle of the season, there were still signs up around the park reading "Now Hiring! Fun-Filled Summer Job. Work with All

Your Friends!") Changing the subject, I asked if she had a favorite ride. "My favorite ride is if someone gives me a ride on a golf cart home," she quipped.

Another clerk, seventy-seven, said she used to be an Adventureland recruiter. She was proud that advanced years and age-related disabilities didn't seem to hold back her fellow employees, adding that she currently had a close coworker who was eighty. "I had someone who was eighty-six in my department at one time," she said. "We had a man in a wheelchair, who was capable of counting using the clicker, so they had him stationed at the water park. We had a one-armed man who was a supervisor of all the rides." Over at the Tornado rollercoaster, the ride operator wore wire-rimmed bifocals and a broad-brimmed straw hat. He told me he was eighty-one.

Not even the most upbeat attitude, however, could ward off tragedy. Less than a year after I visited Adventureland, a workamper died from an on-the-job accident there. Retired postal carrier and pastor Steve Booher, sixty-eight, was helping passengers disembark from the Raging River ride when the conveyor belt carrying the rafts started up prematurely. With one foot still on a raft as it lurched forward, he fell from the concrete loading platform onto the conveyor belt, fracturing his skull.

Adventureland reopened the Raging River the next day. Following an investigation, state workplace regulators sent the park a violation notice two months later. It called for safety upgrades and a $4,500 fine.

———

AFTER THE BIG TENT OPENED, the mood at the Rubber Tramp Rendezvous shifted. Until then the days had passed languidly. Now they sped by. More people started disappearing on day trips to town. When they were in camp, questions hung in the air. *Where are you going next? When will I see you again? Did you find a job?* The fourteen-day limit for free camping would end soon and, this year, there was no getting around that. On the first day of the rendezvous, a BLM ranger had showed up to issue permits and take down everyone's license plate numbers. Soon campers would have to move at least twenty-five miles away.

The diaspora was about to begin. A few folks would leave by themselves. Others banded together in small, traveling groups. In some years, the beaches of Baja were a favorite among those fortunate enough to have passports and gas money. Often a delegation would visit Slab City, an encampment of squatters, outsider artists, and snowbirds on the site of a former military base near the Salton Sea that calls itself "The Last Free Place." (The RTR outpost there got nicknamed "Friends of Bob.") Others would go toward the Yuma area. One popular camping spot there was Fortuna Pond, which was tranquil by day but felt like something out of *The Twilight Zone* after dark, when the fields glowed lurid green under the bright lights of crop dusters that droned loudly all through the night.

When the RTR ended, Bob took down the official sign. Silvianne boxed up the leftovers on the free pile—including the large straw sombrero, which no one wanted—for a local thrift shop. Linda made coffee and I drank a cup with her. She showed me a new solenoid a friend had helped her install. It would allow her to charge the RV's house power off the overflow from her car battery when she was driving. Soon word came that Bob had left for his next encampment in Ehrenberg. He'd invited anyone who wanted to follow him there. Linda hustled to break down camp. She hugged Jen and Ash goodbye. The girls planned to wander the Southwest until their next gig, working at Rocking 7 Ranch in the mountains just east of the Salinas Valley or, as Ash referred to it, "Steinbeck Country." The ranch was part of an international network called WWOOF (World Wide Opportunities on Organic Farms), whose members trade food, lodging, and training for labor from volunteers, who called themselves WWOOFers. After that they'd drive farther inland to their next paid job, camp hosting in Sequoia National Forest.

Linda followed Interstate 10 west toward the Colorado River, exiting just before the California border near a Flying J truck stop. She turned onto the frontage road, continued past a Dead End sign.

Here the landscape was stark and echoingly empty. The ground was covered with gravel. Vegetation was sparse; the deserts around Quartzsite had been a Garden of Eden by comparison. Tucked away from the unpaved entry road were ancient weather-beaten RVs. Flat tires and general disrepair suggested they'd rolled in years ago and never left, their inhabitants settling down to stay year-round. Technically the Bureau of Land Management had a fourteen-day limit on camping here. But that rule—and the area in general—went largely overlooked by both visitors and patrols, probably due to its conspicuous lack of charm. Not many campers found the location desirable, which benefitted the few solitude seekers who did. In dozens of visits, I never saw a ranger or heard of anyone getting asked to leave.

Rigs were parked further apart here than at the RTR. Introverts were recovering from their two weeks of intense socialization. Some of them still got together for morning coffee meetings. After one of those, I found Silvianne, hanging out in her rig with Layla the cat, reading a book called *Hamlet's Mill: An Essay Investigating the Origins of Human Knowledge and Its Transmission Through Myth.*

"How many people do you think are here?" I asked.

"No one knows!" she replied cheerfully. "That's the whole point. It's off-the-radar America." Though campers were widely dispersed, coming and going regularly, the number seemed to hover around fifteen. I also bumped into LaVonne. She was warmer than at the RTR, more relaxed. She laughed and shrugged at her earlier suggestion that an outsider might size up the group as "a bunch of homeless vagabonds."

"What is it about the idea of homelessness that is so emotional?" she mused. "Some people would consider me homeless. I don't. I have shelter." At the same time, she explained, she felt guilty about putting herself in a different category, as if it might reinforce the larger social stigma.

By now LaVonne and Linda had hit it off so well that they'd decided to try working together. Linda's next job camp hosting would start in the spring at the Sherwin Creek Campground in Mammoth Lakes. Meanwhile the Big Tent was still happening and had a table with recruiters from California Land Management. On Linda's advice, LaVonne and another job-seeking nomad—Trish Hay, a fifty-nine-year-old living in a Nissan Sentra—planned to apply there for work.

That afternoon I sat with Linda as she heated dishwater in a tea kettle. She should have had on-demand hot water, she explained, but someone in Nevada had sold her the wrong kind of battery—an engine-starting battery instead of a deep-cycle one—to run the house power for her RV, which meant there wasn't enough juice to pump water from the storage tank under the couch to the sink. She was glad to be in Ehrenberg but didn't want to stick around as long as LaVonne, who planned to follow Bob with what remained of the RTR crew. Meanwhile Bob was sticking to his regular routine—staying in Ehrenberg until the heat came and the rattlesnakes woke up, then moving to the higher elevations of Cottonwood and Flagstaff. Linda had some important errands to accomplish before her next job, including searching for land and emptying an old storage unit. So before too long, she said good-bye.

After her departure, LaVonne posted a photograph of Linda on her blog and wrote:

> Another new friend has moved on, and I am sad all over again. One by one, they are leaving for other places. I will see some of them again, I'm sure, but this sadness is an inevitable consequence of nomadic living. People come and go in your life. You don't get to hang onto them forever.
>
> Here is Linda May, everyone's surrogate mother, who fed us French toast and made us laugh. There is no one who doesn't love Linda. She is off to find a piece of land where she plans to build a sustainable, off-grid Earthship home. I have promised to help build it (i.e., pound dirt into lots of tires), just so I can spend time with her again.

———

AFTER LEAVING HER FRIENDS, Linda traveled 380 miles southeast to the deserts of Cochise County, Arizona, where building codes were loose and land was cheap. She hoped to find a few acres for her Earthship but, after hours of exploring, felt disappointed. The area was too isolated. Coming off the high of the Rubber Tramp Rendezvous—all those warm feelings of community and connectedness—she was not interested in a hermit's life. "Nobody's going to come visit me here," she thought. "I'd better find land where family can come, because that would be the idea of the whole thing, so that it's accessible and we can have gatherings." She spent one night stationed in a parking lot near the Mexican border. Then she got back on the road.

Next Linda went to clear out a storage unit she'd been renting for four years in the Phoenix suburbs. ("I would like to just throw a match in there, I think," she'd reflected earlier.) She loaded a moving truck with the contents and went to a friend's five-acre property in New River, Arizona. She set aside mementos—a kindergarten watercolor of a catlike creature from her grandson Julian, a birthday card from her younger daughter Valerie with a pinup girl in a cactus bikini. "You're still looking sharp!" it quipped. But everything else—the old record player, the matching glass lamps with tufted shades, the piles of cookware—had to go. She held yard sales. After deducting the cost of trucking everything to New River, her take for the first weekend was $99.75. "I will never rent a storage unit again," Linda vowed. Not long after, she wrote to me, sharing a quote she'd seen online and found poetic: "Inevitably bouts with obstacles offer discouragement as you cut every tether holding you from freedom."

Meanwhile the Rubber Tramp tribe had migrated from Ehrenberg, where it was getting uncomfortably hot, to the Prescott National Forest near Cottonwood, which was three thousand feet higher and around ten degrees cooler. There the vandwellers spread out. Some parked in the open, on a hill with views of sun-dappled mesas. Others nestled more stealthily below, in a wooded patch out of the wind. Bob,

Lavonne, and Silvianne were there, along with some of Linda's other new friends. They included Atli Pommer, thirty-four, a former transit bus driver living in a Chevy Astro named after the 1960s' singer Donovan, and Sameer Ali, sixty-five, who had lost his halal goat farm amid rising hay prices from the western drought and now lived in a van with his Chihuahua, Mr. Pico. (A practicing Muslim, Sameer made his faith portable with an iPhone app that issued calls to prayer five times a day. It also displayed a Mecca-facing compass that he used while parking, so his van was always oriented in the proper direction for worship. "There's an app for everything," he marveled.)

When the yard sales were done, it was already late March. Linda went to Cottonwood, showing up just in time for a pizza party. Bob managed to feed eleven people on $28 with pies from Little Caesars. Afterwards, they walked off the meal with a hike under sunset-pink skies. The group of nomads was mostly female—seven women to three men and a teenage boy—and Bob later remarked that, in a culture that had long discouraged female independence, this seemed like a good thing.

A forest ranger appeared in camp the next day. Puzzled, he inquired whether the group was a club—"I guess we are!" Sameer replied—and asked the length of their stay. Bob told a white lie: They'd only been there four days. (In truth it had been just over two weeks.) The ranger noted their license plate numbers and left. This meant the clock would start ticking on the fourteen-day limit for free camping, so now the tribe had to decide where to wander next. They settled on the Kaibab National Forest near Flagstaff. At an elevation of seven thousand feet, it would be much cooler there. Meanwhile the roof of Linda's RV was in poor condition. She hoped to patch and reseal it before the move, since liquid rubber cures faster in warmer temperatures. Another member of the RTR tribe, a professional painter named Wayne, clambered up on the roof and applied the sealant with a long-handled roller. The job was done just in time.

In Flagstaff, they parked in a grove of tall pines. Linda posted pictures on Facebook so friends and family could see. "The dogs and

I love it here," she wrote. "What would you pay for a yard like this? It's free." Linda thanked Wayne for his help with a home-cooked dinner: Salisbury steak, mashed potatoes, and gravy, served on Kansas City Railroad china from the 1930s that she'd picked up at an estate sale. Since the plates had lasted three-quarters of a century without chipping, she figured they were rugged enough to clatter around in her RV. Linda also got to hang out with Lori Hicks, a single mother with a heart condition who lived with her thirteen-year-old son, Russell, and their dog, Kaylee, in a 1995 blue Chevy Tahoe nicknamed "Babe," after Paul Bunyan's ox. Together they explored their new surroundings. While visiting Linda's campsite, Russell and Kaylee found a giant elk skull. Meanwhile, Linda had given Lori a copy of *Travels with Charley*, which Lori was devouring. John Steinbeck's tale of road-tripping in a pickup camper with his French poodle was popular among the nomads, and dog-eared copies passed from hand to hand.*

A few days later, Linda had to move on again. Her next job, camp hosting at Mammoth Lakes in the Eastern Sierra, was about to begin. She drove ten hours the first day and stopped for the night at a Texaco in Tonopah, Nevada. Linda took the dogs out for a walk. Back in the RV Coco had a sudden seizure. The dog stiffened and shrieked, then fell limp and stopped breathing. Frantic, Linda pressed her mouth to the dog's jaws and exhaled deeply. Soon Coco was conscious again, rigid but breathing. Linda pressed a bag of frozen vegetables to the dog's back—she'd heard using an ice pack that way could alleviate canine seizures—and called her daughter. Audra had studied essential oils and recommended frankincense. Linda dabbed some on Coco's paws. The dog's muscles relaxed. Soon she was snoring. Linda

---

* One guy at a Rubber Tramp Rendezvous campfire was horrified to learn I hadn't yet read *Travels with Charley*; the next day he arrived at the van to lend me a paperback. Other entries in the literary canon of this subculture included *Blue Highways* by William Least Heat-Moon, *Desert Solitaire* by Edward Abbey, *Into the Wild* by Jon Krakauer, *Walden* by Henry David Thoreau, and *Wild* by Cheryl Strayed.

kept watch for hours, monitoring the gentle rise and fall of her chest. The next morning Coco looked normal. Shaken, Linda began driving the final 150 miles to Mammoth.

Sherwin Creek Campground was quiet when Linda arrived in mid-April. Her only visitors were deer and a truck transporting sled dogs to a film shoot. Within a week, wintry weather struck. Footlong icicles dangled from the cab of her motorhome and heavy snow piled on top, more than Linda had ever encountered in the RV. But inside she was warm and dry—the newly repaired roof wasn't leaking. Coco seemed healthy. All things considered, Linda reflected, life was good. On April 28, she celebrated her AA birthday—twenty-four years clean and sober. "Tears of gratitude fill my eyes as I write," she posted on Facebook. "My oldest grandchild is twenty-one years old and has always had the miracle of a sober, loving grandmother. Prayers were answered . . . I am happy, joyous, and free."

Linda had once wisecracked that congratulating an alcoholic for not drinking was like praising a cowboy with hemorrhoids for not riding his horse. Still her page was flooded with affectionate comments from family and friends, celebrating the milestone. "Thank you for standing up against addiction and bringing light and awareness to a disease that has plagued our family for generations," wrote Audra. "I love you very much."

Cash was tight but nothing could dampen Linda's upbeat mood. She stretched her dwindling food supply, making stale tortillas into chilaquiles and old bread into a French toast casserole. Her nonperishables were mostly gone. Her fridge was down to four eggs, a half-gallon of milk and some condiments—ketchup, mayonnaise, mustard, and jelly—that she jokingly called "food to put on food." Then her paycheck came and she stocked it up again.

Linda and I spoke by phone in late May. "It's a lovely day! My campground is full," she said cheerfully. I asked how her hunt for land was going. The last scouting trip had been a bust, Linda explained. She'd shifted her focus to the area around Julian, California, an hour east of San Diego. "That's out in the mountains, an old gold-mining town, and it's beautiful out there," she told me. "And in case the shit hits the fan, like all these preppers are thinking, it's close to water. If we go to extreme droughts, water can be brought in. We never know about our weather." Linda also expected to have more money for the project soon—she'd be camp hosting through early fall and then rejoining CamperForce. The wrist injury from her last stint at Amazon still hadn't healed but, with her start date still months away, Linda was optimistic. A few weeks earlier, she'd helped rally a vandweller friend who wanted to join CamperForce but was fretting over whether she could handle the strenuous labor. "Don't worry," Linda had replied. "We'll hold each other up."

Meanwhile Linda told me she was doing fabulously. "My whole life has been ups and downs," she explained. "The happiest I've been is when I have very little." We talked about her dogs, about how she hoped to refurbish her RV. Before long, though, she had to excuse herself ("Looks like I've got a camper coming to my door!") and get back to work.

CHAPTER EIGHT

Halen

WHEN LINDA STARTED HER JOB at Sherwin Creek Campground, I'd been interviewing workampers for about six months. In that time, I'd also scoured the media—online, print, and broadcast—for anything about the subculture. Much of what I found made workamping sound like a sunny lifestyle, or even a quirky hobby, rather than a survival strategy in an era when Americans were getting priced out of traditional housing and struggling to make a living wage.

One segment on NPR's *All Things Considered* began with a correspondent's voiceover: "Santa, of course, needs elves to make sure he delivers his presents on time. Amazon.com needs workampers!" The reporter introduced one CamperForce worker living at the Big Chief RV Park in Coffeyville, Kansas. They spent most of the three-minute segment chatting about the joys of traveling cross-country and making new friends. The conversation was punctuated four times with peals of laughter.

Other stories were less chirpy, but still they emphasized the thrill and camaraderie of the open road, sidestepping the challenges that had driven so many people to radically reimagine their lives. In a way,

I couldn't blame reporters for accepting what I also had found in my early interviews. A journalist who parachutes in for an afternoon to cover a story seldom gets close enough to hear any kind of truth. When I reached out to workampers for the first time, I was met with cheery platitudes. I got warnings, too. One CamperForce RVer agreed to meet me, but added that I'd better not portray him and his comrades as Americans in crisis. "There are plenty of indolent whiners, slackbodies, and layabouts who are happy to complain about nearly anything, and they are easy to find," he wrote proudly. "I'm not one of those."

I saw a similar "no whiners" sentiment in *Workamper News*, a bimonthly magazine that targets nomads. "Do you need an attitude adjustment?" asked one headline. The column below it urged unhappy workampers with on-the-job problems to seek solutions by turning inward. "See if you can change your attitude and not let it get to you by soothing yourself with some of these statements," the writer suggested. "'We won't be here forever. It's a means to an end. We're getting to travel, spend time in this area exploring (or visiting family), and living our dream.'"

That pep talk was surreal, but not entirely surprising. Positive thinking, after all, is an all-American coping mechanism, practically a national pastime. Author James Rorty noted this during the Great Depression, when he traveled America talking with people forced to seek work on the road. In his 1936 book, *Where Life Is Better*, he was dismayed that so many of his interview subjects seemed so unshakably cheerful. "I encountered nothing in 15,000 miles of travel that disgusted and appalled me so much as this American addiction to make-believe," he wrote.

I'm not that cynical. While it's human nature to put on a good face in turbulent times—and to present that face to strangers— something else was also happening among the nomads. The truth as I see it is that people can both struggle and remain upbeat simultaneously, through even the most soul-testing of challenges. This doesn't mean they're in denial. Rather, it testifies to the remarkable ability of humankind to adapt, to seek meaning and kinship when confronted with adversity. As Rebecca Solnit points out in her book *A Paradise Built in Hell: The Extraordinary Communities That Arise in Disaster*, people not only buck up in times of crisis, but do so with a "startling, sharp joy." It's possible to undergo hardships that shake our will to endure, while also finding happiness in shared moments, such as sitting around a bonfire with fellow workampers under a vast starry sky.

In other words, the nomads I'd been interviewing for months were neither powerless victims nor carefree adventurers. The truth was much more nuanced, but how could I access it? At this point, I was no longer a day-tripper. I'd spent many weeks up close with the workampers, documenting their stories across five states and then staying in a tent in Quartzsite as nighttime temperatures dropped into the thirties during their winter gatherings. Still I wasn't understanding the story on the level I'd hoped for just yet—I hadn't gotten close enough to truly grasp their lives. Doing that would require a fuller immersion, spending months among them, day in and day out, becoming a regular at some of their encampments.

With my tent, I'd been able to live off-grid in the desert, but not out in the backcountry where most of the people I was writing about were boondocking. Tent campers were only allowed in areas near outhouses. That meant I ended up sleeping four miles away from the site of the Rubber Tramp Rendezvous, then commuting over to visit. To actually join the nomads I would need a more robust portable shelter—something that I could sleep, cook, and write inside, with at least a rudimentary toilet setup. In the parlance of RVers, my rig would have to be "self-contained."

For months I scoured Craigslist ads for old vans. Many looked great at first but turned out to be rusty or rotting, including one ancient RoadTrek whose seller told me he'd had years of fun in the rig he'd nicknamed "Porta Party." At last something caught my eye: a white 1995 GMC Vandura with a jaunty teal stripe. (A friend later pointed out it was the same model as Mr. T's van in *The A-Team*, so nostalgia may have exerted some influence.) For a decades-old vehicle, it was in fine condition, with just 64,000 miles on the odometer. Parked mostly on the California coast, it had not seen hard winters, and the interior had been converted for camping.

The first time I stepped inside the van, it felt larger than the exterior suggested, as if it were somehow exempt from physics like the tardis in *Doctor Who*. The walls were upholstered in powder-blue velour. At the rear, a tiny dinette folded into a bed. The cabin contained a twelve-volt mini-fridge, small propane stove, and portable chemical toilet, useful amenities for boondocking. Overhead was a pop-top roof. When I undid the latches and raised the lid, I could stand upright, but any pretense of stealth evaporated—from the outside it looked like a canvas safari tent was riding piggyback.

The van needed a name. In my encounters with vandwellers I'd already met Vansion, Van Go, DonoVan, Vantucket, and Vanna White—this was a pun-happy subculture. A friend suggested "Beethoven," referring to the band Camper Van Beethoven. But that made me think of "Roll Over Beethoven," a disastrous portent for driving. I named the van Halen instead. I was born in the late 1970s, when the rock group's first albums hit, and tried to decorate with appropriate talismans, including a black velvet painting of Ernest Hemingway from a Quartzsite swap meet and a squirrel skull Linda found while camp hosting. A strand of blue glass "evil eye" beads I'd received as a gift dangled from the rearview mirror, the closest I'd get to a burglar alarm.

Halen had come from a seller in California. My best friend, the journalist Dale Maharidge, met up with me to collect it. Together we traveled to his uncle's homestead in the canyons of northern San Diego County. I drove Halen, struggling to acclimate to the nineteen-foot, two-ton behemoth. It handled like a boat, drifting sideways, demanding constant correction. (Staying on course made me so tense that my shoulders ached for hours after the first few times I drove it.)

When we arrived, we parked Halen beside a citrus orchard and got to work. The easiest part was cleaning it up—scrubbing out hard-

Halen the van in the desert near Ehrenberg.

ened maple syrup that had drooled down the inside of a cabinet and removing minor surface rust with a wire wheel. The hardest work was putting in a hundred-watt solar panel. Many nomads mount solar panels on their rigs using rooftop cargo racks with side brackets. That wouldn't work with Halen's pop-top, so we had to do something that made me cringe: drill two holes through the pristine rear portion of the roof. The holes were necessary to install an aluminum frame, which would hold the solar panel and could tilt up at an angle to catch more sunlight when Halen was parked. After tightening down the bolts, I slathered the area where the holes had been with a tough waterproofing compound, praying it wouldn't leak. Next Dale and I mounted a charge controller inside the van. We wired the solar panel to run through it, then into a pair of six-volt golf cart batteries we'd stowed under the dinette. These would provide power when I was boondocking. Last we installed an inverter, also under the dinette, to create the 110-volt power I would need to charge my laptop and camera.

Briefly I worried all this preparation would prove excessive, but it didn't when I found myself living in Halen episodically over the following two years of reporting, taking trips that lasted up to two months at a time. The journey spanned more than 15,000 miles, from border to border—Halen touched both Mexico and Canada—and from coast to coast.

The first thing I would realize on the road was that, despite having interviewed many dozens of nomads, I didn't know a damn thing about living in a van. The learning curve was steep and it never really tapered off, since the circumstances kept changing. Driving in the desert, I got Halen stuck twice, spinning the tires in soft silt each time until a passing Samaritan with a Jeep winched it out. High in the mountains, the van got stuck in a blizzard and its toilet and water tanks froze solid. Late at night on an empty Kansas highway, the alternator blew. The instrument panel dimmed as Halen lost power, coasting to a halt in front of a rest stop.

Once near Fort Worth, Texas, I'd parked to get coffee when the sky turned green and tornado sirens began wailing. The barista gave advice: If you see a tornado, go hide in your basement. I pointed out the window to Halen—no basement—and we laughed. Later that day, I took shelter in Halen during torrential rains and watched with horror as water penetrated the seal above the rear doors and cascaded inside, swamping my bed and frying part of the electrical system I'd built. On another occasion, after a break back home, I returned to a long-term parking lot to find Halen ransacked. Someone had put a rock the size of a large potato through the driver's side window, littering the cab with broken glass. Fortunately, there was nothing to steal but the black velvet painting of Ernest Hemingway and a bottle of really good hot sauce. Neither was missing.

I inflicted many indignities on Halen: backing into a boulder, pulling out of a campsite with the pop-top still raised, and driving a couple blocks without realizing I'd pinned a large traffic cone under the chassis that dragged on the pavement. One time, parked near a Starbucks for WiFi, I tried installing a combination fire and carbon monoxide alarm. (Nomad Safety 101: Any live-in vehicle should have both a fire extinguisher and a carbon monoxide alarm.) But whenever I tried to mount it on the wall, a robotic female voice blared, "FIRE! FIRE! EVACUATE! EVACUATE!" My cover was blown; strangers stopped sipping lattes to stare.

During one long reporting trip, I had to get a prescription refilled. My doctor called a drugstore. Later he told me that, when the pharmacist demanded my home address, he didn't know how to answer and blurted out, "She's living in a van!" The pharmacist let it slide, but the episode made me think. *In America, if you don't have an address, you're not a real person.*

When I was in Halen, my address was everywhere. I slept at Flying J truck stops, Walmart Supercenters, a casino called Whiskey Pete's, and an abandoned gas station; in barren deserts, mountain wildernesses, and suburban streets. Residential areas were the worst, because curious neighbors could bring trouble. After one night stealth camping in Mission Viejo, I awoke to the whine of an electric hedge trimmer. A landscaper was working a couple feet away. I lay in my sleeping bag, silent and motionless inside Halen, until his job was done. Later that day Linda and LaVonne teased me for being paranoid.

Experiences like these were the background music to my reporting this book. Without living in Halen, I don't think I would have gotten close enough to people to really hear their stories. But it's fair to say that, in the beginning, I anticipated very little of this. I had no idea what I was getting into, though I did have the good sense to feel a little freaked out at first.

It took a couple of days wrestling with the solar power system on the van before Dale and I finally got it to work. When everything was functional, there was nothing left to do but head out. It was already dark when Dale hugged me good-bye. I climbed into the driver's seat and inched Halen away from his uncle's homestead, past the dim shapes of citrus trees. The driveway was steep. Suddenly, the two-ton van felt staggeringly heavy. I clutched the wheel and rode the brake all the way down. At the bottom, my eyes blurred with unexpected tears and I wiped them on my sleeve, wondering if I'd ever feel comfortable piloting Halen, let alone living in it.

All you have to do now is focus on the road, I told myself. *You've got a full mug of coffee, GPS on your smartphone, and a destination you've been excited about for months.* And so the van wound slowly back through the canyons, on the way to visit Linda.

JUST BEFORE CHRISTMAS IN 2014, Linda was couch-surfing at a small apartment her daughter and son-in-law had rented in San Clemente with her teenage grandchildren. The rear window looked onto Camp Pendleton, the Marine Corps base. Strains of "Taps" could be heard at sunset and sometimes live-fire artillery drills ran through the night. (The family hadn't yet gone to their next rental, the house in Mission Viejo where Linda was staying when she bought—and moved into—the Squeeze Inn.)

Linda's RV was street-parked and gathering tickets. Raccoons had chewed a hole in the fuel line. She had discovered this while pumping gas—startled, she'd looked down and seen a puddle growing around her feet. Linda had expected to be back working at Amazon's Fernley warehouse this season, but her wrist was still a mess from the year before, so she had to cancel. Cash was tight again.

The evening I arrived, over my protests, Linda treated me to dinner with her family at a Mexican restaurant. As we left, a busker outside was playing the pop hit "Royals" by Lorde. Her violin case lay open on the curb, and Linda handed each of her two granddaughters a dollar bill to drop inside. Back at the apartment, the family said I was welcome to bunk indoors. Linda was already sleeping on the couch, though. One of her granddaughters occupied a walk-in closet. As if I'd done it a thousand times before, I said I'd sleep in the van, which was parked in a lot beside the apartment building. Linda leashed her two dogs and the family's Chihuahua, Gizmo, for their last walk of the night. Together we strolled across the parking lot. As we neared Halen, I grew anxious. At that point I'd only slept one night in the van—on the homestead in San Diego County—with no strangers or traffic around. This was my first night parked in the open. *What if neighbors called the cops? What if someone tried to break in while I slept?*

A searing pain jolted me from those thoughts. Gizmo had sunk his teeth into the back of my right thigh. I tried laughing it off. Earlier Audra had called him an "ankle biter," but I'd taken that as an endearment, not a warning. The wound stung badly. I tried to make light of it but, inside, my worries curdled into panic. *Was the dog up to date on his shots?* I didn't want to offend anyone by asking.

I said goodnight, slunk into the van, and closed the shades before digging into a care package from a friend in Los Angeles. Tucked under a small American flag and Irish Spring soap were Band-Aids and a half-used packet of Neosporin. I shucked off my jeans, expecting a bloody puncture wound. There was no broken skin, though—just a nasty bruise. That should have comforted me, but it didn't. I brushed my teeth and curled up in my sleeping bag, thinking about something Bob Wells had written in his book. "For most people, their first night sleeping in a van is so far out of their comfort zone, it can be very difficult," he'd explained. "Your fear will magnify every sound (and there are a lot of them) and you may not get much sleep. When you wake up in the morning, you will be disoriented and wonder where you are."

I hadn't thought those words would apply to me. After all, I was just a writer with a digital camera, recorder, and notebook, not someone making a radical lifestyle change. I planned to live in my van for months, not years.

Cars swung through the parking lot, strafing Halen with their headlights. The shades glowed bright white as each approached, dimming to red as the vehicles passed. Shadows wheeled around inside the van. *Was that driver slowing down? Was this one parking too close? Did they know I was in here?* I closed my eyes and tried to relax, but it was hours before sleep came.

A TAP ON THE WINDOW startled me awake. It was morning. A familiar voice called, "Hell-ooo-ooo!" Linda was walking the dogs again. She had coffee brewing upstairs. Groggily I pulled on some clothes and followed her to the apartment. She pointed out the shower and handed me a pink patterned towel. "Here, just out of the dryer," she said. "Polka dots, because polka dots make you happy."

We took Halen for a drive. Linda let me buy us breakfast burritos at her favorite take-out place. We brought them to the beach, where we ate and chatted while watching surfers bob on the swells. Back at the van she gave me a brief parking lesson. While piloting a nineteen-foot cargo van was elementary for Linda, thanks to her six months as a professional trucker, she could tell it still freaked me out. Next she directed me to a thrift store to outfit the van with cooking supplies. I rummaged through a bin of mismatched flatware, while Linda found me a bargain on a Dutch oven and a percolator. Later that afternoon, we said our good-byes.

My next stop was Quartzsite, where I planned to boondock in the desert for a couple months, which would include the Rubber Tramp Rendezvous. That gathering was still weeks away, though. I had no idea where to park until it began.

Then a potluck dinner invitation arrived via Facebook. It was from Charlene Swankie, the seventy-year-old vandwelling guru better known as Swankie Wheels. We'd met briefly the year before and I'd read about her adventures on Bob Wells's website. I was thrilled. Swankie's camp would be a soft place to land. Plus she was a boondocking expert, someone to learn from.

"Kidnap Linda and bring her with you," Swankie joked. I explained that wasn't possible—Linda was broke, without a functional vehicle, and had politely declined my offer to drive her there. So Swankie asked me to pick up some hot dogs instead.

Arriving at her camp, I saw Swankie was no stranger to mentoring first-time vandwellers. She'd already adopted a protégé this season, a twenty-seven-year-old named Vincent Mosemann. Before long, he was telling his story.

Until two months earlier, Vincent had been living with his mother in Billings, Montana. Though he yearned to be on his own, renting an apartment didn't seem realistic. He had more than $25,000 in student loans from an unfinished degree, despite working two jobs during college—as a lab monitor and a barista—to stay afloat and making a foot-long Subway sandwich last for two days' worth of meals when cash got tight. Three years into his studies his parents had divorced. When Vincent went to reapply for financial aid, he had to get a signature from his father, who was nowhere to be found. So Vincent dropped out. After moving back home, he took a job at a group home for autistic adults, but it didn't pay much. He figured there was only one way he could live independently. So he bought his mother's minivan, a 1995 Plymouth Grand Voyager LE. He gutted the interior, added linoleum flooring, curtains, shelves, and a sleeping bunk. He named it "Tillie," after the train in *The Little Engine That Could* that says, "I think I can, I think I can." Then Vincent set off on a journey.

"I hit the road to learn how to stand on my own two feet," he explained.

Vincent was bound for Quartzsite. There he planned to meet Swankie, whom he'd befriended in a Facebook group for nomads. She had invited him to camp *near* her—but not *with* her—at the La Posa Long Term Visitor Area in the desert south of Quartzsite, which is where I later joined them.

After making him that offer, she was flooded with worry and regret. Swankie cherished her solitude, so much that she had bought a skull and crossbones flag to fly when she didn't want visitors. Vincent, on the other hand, was hypersocial. He described himself as having "LPS," or Lost Puppy Syndrome.

Vincent arrived the day before Halloween and parked next to an arroyo. It was right across from Swankie's campsite, which looked like an outdoor living room, with a weatherproof rug, chairs, cargo trailer, and shade canopy. Alongside it was her van, furnished with a bed, a computer desk, a freezer, and a microwave she could run from an inverter while running the van's engine. The roof held a kayak and a solar panel. On the rear door was a sticker from Planet Fitness, the gym chain she'd joined for access to showers.

Swankie gave Vincent a spare tent to store his food and supplies. He helped her install a cabinet in her cargo trailer to use as a pantry. She coached him through setting up a solar panel. When Vincent bolted it to his roof, he used drilled-out pennies—they were cheaper than washers. Swankie also let Vincent use her rented post office box. That gesture meant a lot. Her own family would no longer accept her mail, she said. For Vincent, who is a transman, a mailing address was crucial. His therapy required a shot of testosterone in the thigh every two weeks. Refills came by post. Other good things showed up in the box, too, including a Christmas care package from his mother: a batch of homemade snickerdoodles and a tiny replica of a red-brick fireplace crafted from a Saltines box, with a dollhouse-sized fir tree perched on top.

Swankie and Vincent were quite the pair. The vibrant, gray-haired vandweller stood at least a head taller than her bearded young apprentice, who had a testosterone molecule tattooed to his wrist, and a mischievous smile with a gap on the upper-right-hand side. Pulling that tooth had cost $250, Vincent told me, while a crown would have been $1,000. For many nomads I met, missing teeth were the badge of poverty of which they were most ashamed. Some tried to avoid smiling when my camera came out, or asked me not to share pictures that revealed empty sockets. (It's sad—but not surprising—that teeth have become a status symbol in a country where more than one in three citizens lack dental coverage, which isn't included with

Vincent and Swankie enjoy a campfire in Quartzsite.

standard medical insurance.) But Vincent called the gap his straw holder. He flashed it with pride. "Anyone who has a problem with it isn't someone I'd want to hang out with anyway," he explained.

Vincent and Swankie shared a defining trait—neither abided snobs. Swankie recalled one desert evening when she was enjoying a conversation with folks who lived in luxury motorhomes. They asked about her RV. She said it was a van. Pleasantries ended abruptly. "They got up and left their own campfire," she said, shaking her head. On another occasion, Swankie joined the Wandering Individuals Network, only to learn that the group wouldn't add her blog to its online roster of members' websites. The reason? Her blog included a detailed tutorial on using a five-gallon bucket as a toilet. So she quit.

Just like Vincent, Swankie didn't need friends like that. Her encampment was growing. After dinner that first night, I wound up staying there in my van. So did Kat and Mike Valentino, both forty-seven, who lived in a blue 1991 Ford Econoline named Katvandu with their nine-year-old son, Alex, and a pet ferret named Ronnie. Months earlier, they had been living in Washington when Kat, an Army veteran, got rushed off her job as an Albertson's manager in an ambulance with what was diagnosed as multiple sclerosis. She was still trying to get on disability, a process that would end up taking three years. Meanwhile, Mike had been working for $9.40 an hour at a frozen vegetable processing plant, but his contract was nearly up. They feared for the future.

For a long time, Kat had been checking out RVing and vandwelling online. She'd written on Facebook, "I can't decide if it's sad or hopeful that SO MANY of the folks I talk to in my various RV groups are going full-time because of financial hardship. I suppose it's bittersweet. The new freedom . . . able to live while reinventing oneself. Thank goodness for the deep and varied Tribes out there that offer so much guidance, advice, stuff, and willing ears. Is this the evolution of the former middle class? Are we seeing the emergence of a modern hunter-gatherer class?"

The Valentinos ended up in a couple of filthy short-stay motels. Some of the neighbors sold drugs and turned tricks. It was no place for a family. So they bought the van and took off a couple weeks before Vincent began his own odyssey. So far things seemed to be going alright. Kat explained to me that Alex was being "roadschooled," the nomadic equivalent of homeschooled. He was a brilliant, inquisitive kid with a precocious sense of humor but grappled with social issues related to Asperger's and had been bullied in public school. Now he was telling everyone he wanted to start his own democratic nation. The capital would be called "Vandweller City."

One of the hardest moments came in Quartzsite, when temperatures dropped into the twenties overnight. Kat and Mike ran out of gas from running their van to stay warm; the fuel gauge was broken, so they couldn't tell how fast the tank was emptying. At this point they were camped near Swankie and Vincent, who'd been doing the same thing. I copied the strategy, idling Halen's engine while blasting the heat, then crawling into my sleeping bag. I'd sleep for a few hours, wake up freezing, and repeat the processes. Throughout the night, I heard the chorus of vans, intermittently sputtering to life and then going quiet again.

Later I ended up buying a Buddy propane heater—a popular choice among vandwellers—but it didn't help much overnight because it isn't safe to run a standalone propane heater while sleeping. In small living spaces, incomplete combustion from heating or cooking—combined with limited ventilation—can create a lethal buildup of odorless carbon monoxide. This can happen unnervingly fast in a van. One time, when I'd just extinguished my Buddy and began drifting off, a high-pitched screeching split the night. It was the carbon monoxide alarm. I hadn't been venting the heater well enough. I flung open the doors and windows and stood outside in the desert, shivering in my pajamas, until I figured it had aired out enough and was safe to reenter.

The morning after the Valentinos ran out of gas trying to stay warm, Vincent drove them to town to fill a fuel jug. They returned with more than they'd planned—spoils from the Quartzsite food bank, including apples, sausages, and a bag of spring mix salad the size of a pillow.

Two days after Christmas was Alex's tenth birthday. Swankie threw him an ice cream party. Around the same time, Vincent landed a part-time job at Dollar General for $9 an hour. On the side, he'd been selling aprons and reusable grocery bags he made on his sewing machine, which he'd converted to run on a treadle instead of electricity. He gave one of the aprons to Alex as a birthday present, along with a copy of *The Lord of the Rings*. Alex was ecstatic. And suddenly, Vincent seemed like less of a kid.

Later Kat wrote to thank everyone for "thoughtful gifts and lots of laughter. From people I hadn't met until a couple of months ago. I am touched, humbled, and overwhelmed. This is what a family looks like. . . ."

It echoed something Swankie had said earlier. "Once you stay in Swankie's camp for more than twelve hours," she'd told me, "you're family." She did have a way of making newcomers feel included. One day, she led a bunch of us in our vans to visit petroglyphs carved into a nearby rock face. There was something exhilarating about that trip, our caravan fanning out behind her. Driving Halen, watching dust rise from the tires ahead of me, felt like being part of a posse riding horseback into the open desert. Later that day, when a member of our party got stuck in a ditch, Swankie hauled his vehicle out using her own van and a strap of nylon webbing.

When it was time for the Rubber Tramp Rendezvous, we all drove over to the backcountry behind Scaddan Wash. This was my second time at the gathering. I found myself noticing things that hadn't grabbed my attention the year before—in particular what I referred to, tongue-in-cheek, as "the unbearable whiteness of vanning."

Swankie had joked earlier that RTR felt like a "white van convention" and, in a literal sense, this was true. Most of the vans were painted white, glinting in the bright desert glare. Since commercial fleets often use white vans, the vehicles are ubiquitous. They are easy to buy secondhand and blend in just about everywhere, making them a popular choice for vandwellers. Living in a white van comes with its own set of challenges, though—what one guy at the RTR called the "creepy factor," the cultural stereotype that connects them with child molesters and other noxious predators. A fifty-three-year-old contractor from Salem, Oregon, told me that, after his business collapsed and he moved into a white Ford E150, his friends nicknamed him "Rape-O Van Dan" and started asking him for candy. The friends meant well, but their jokes stung.

It's also common for vandwellers—regardless of vehicle color—to get harassed by passersby who assume they're up to no good. As I write this, one guy in an online forum just recounted waking up after midnight to harrassment from strangers who had no reason to bother him. They were shaking his van and yelling "Come on out, you fucking pervert!" and "We're gonna kick the shit outta you!"

But white vans weren't the only thing on my mind. I'd been noticing something else, which I'd continue to think about long after the

RTR. It would also come up much later, when I showed my snapshots from the event to a friend, an African-American photographer whose work deals with race and colonialism. He observed, "Almost all the people in these pictures are white." He wanted to know why.

I did, too. By then I'd met hundreds of folks living this way—workampers and rubber tramps and RVers from coast to coast. And while a handful were people of color, they clearly represented a micro-minority in the subculture.

So why was the crowd so white? Members of the nomadic community have wondered the same thing. On Amazon's official CamperForce Facebook page, photos of laborers show mostly white faces, prompting one black RVer to post a comment. "I'm sure Afro-Americans have applied for these positions," he wrote. "I don't see any in Amazon's pictures of employees."

I wondered if the lack of racial diversity had something to do with the fact that camping attracts a disproportionately white audience, a trend borne out by studies from the U.S. Forest Service. Perhaps it takes a certain kind of privilege to regard "roughing it" outdoors as a vacation. The satirical website "Stuff White People Like" sums it up like this:

> If you find yourself trapped in the middle of the woods
> without electricity, running water, or a car you would likely
> describe that situation as a "nightmare" or "a worst-case
> scenario like after a plane crash or something." White people
> refer to it as "camping."

Or perhaps the problem was racism? I asked some nomads if they'd seen examples of it in their community. Most said they hadn't observed anything overt. One vandweller, however, recalled when a longtime RTR attendee insulted a black friend of hers, calling the woman a "darkie." Other nomads stepped up to condemn the bigot, but the damage was done and the woman left camp. Concern over that episode lingered, sowing seeds of unease. A cardinal rule at the forum on Bob Wells's website was "Don't ever attack, belittle, or denigrate anyone." What if the nomads couldn't manage that in the temporary community they'd created together offline, in the real world?

Ash, Linda's friend from Amazon, mused on Facebook that "a vast majority of us vandwellers are white. The reasons range from obvious to duh, but then there's this." Linked below the post was an article about the experience of "traveling while black." That made me think: America makes it hard enough for people to live nomadically, regardless of race. Stealth camping in residential areas, in particular, is way outside the mainstream. Often it involves breaking local ordinances against sleeping in cars. Avoiding trouble—hassles with cops and suspicious passersby—can be challenging, even with the Get Out of Jail Free card of white privilege. And in an era when unarmed African Americans are getting shot by police during traffic stops, living in a vehicle seems like an especially dangerous gambit for anyone who might become a victim of racial profiling.

All that made me think about the instances when I could have gotten in trouble and didn't. One time I got pulled over at night while reporting in North Dakota. The cops asked where I was from and recommended some local tourist attractions before letting me off with a warning. In general, people didn't give me grief when I was driving Halen. I wish I could chalk that up to good karma or some kind of cosmic benevolence, but the fact remains: I am white. Surely privilege played a role.

After the Rubber Tramp Rendezvous, I followed the tribe over to Ehrenberg. One night, sharing supper in a neighbor's van, I realized we were using her toilet bucket—which was covered and sealed—to support the tray that held our food. Back home, an impromptu table like that might have bothered me. Here it was a detail that dissolved into the background. We were in a tight space, using what we had.

A couple weeks later, after making arrangements to store Halen at a long-term parking lot, I flew home to New York. Reoccupying my Brooklyn apartment felt weird. When you're living in a space as small as a van, claustrophobia eventually gives way to a den-like coziness. The walls are close, the windows are covered, almost everything you need is within arm's reach. It's womblike. Waking up in the morning brings a sense of security, even if you don't immediately remember where you parked the night before.

All that made my homecoming more jarring than expected. For a few days I awoke in my bed profoundly disoriented. The full-sized mattress seemed too wide. The walls were too far away, the ceiling too tall. All that empty space made me feel anxious, exposed. The sunlight streaming into the bedroom felt too bright. One time, still half-asleep, I briefly mistook my window for the rear windshield of the van.

After the first week home that confusion faded. Then something else took its place: I missed Halen and the nomads. I wanted to get back on the road.

CHAPTER NINE

Some Unbeetable Experiences

BACKCOUNTRY CAMPING WAS JUST THE BEGINNING. Soon the van opened up other territories to explore. During my last trip to the desert, I'd gone back to visit the "Big Tent"—the RV show where recruiters sought workcampers for jobs all over the country. There a smiling woman handed me a flyer that said "Be Part of an 'Unbeetable' Experience!"

The annual sugar beet harvest had baffled me for a long time. It sounded like tough work for aging bodies, incongruous with the gray- and white-haired wanderers who were drawn to this RV show. I took a closer look at the flyer, which included a quote from an unnamed worker describing the job as "a little strenuous, but not really hard." That didn't tell me much. Most of what I knew about the job came from talking to people around Quartzsite.

"It was cold. It was snowy. It was wet," Gretchen Erb said as we sat together in her 1999 Fleetwood Bounder RV. On the overnight shift in Minnesota, she'd stood outdoors in subfreezing temperatures to collect paperwork from truck drivers and "take samples"—

Recruiters at the Big Tent seek workampers for the annual sugar beet harvest.

that is, fill heavy-duty vinyl sacks with thirty-pound loads of beets, then haul them to a workstation, where they would later be collected and shuttled to a lab for testing to assess their sugar content. Another worker, sixty-two-year-old Brian Gore, told me about the harvest in Montana, where he drove a Bobcat loader with a broken-off door. Through the opening, he got pelted with sugar beets—including one the size of a grapefruit—that flew off a malfunctioning conveyor belt. "I was taking a beating from all those beets!" he exclaimed. He compared it to being strafed by "an automatic potato gun." Still, he continued, he'd probably do it again because he needed the money. "The short time frame makes it tolerable," he added. "I think if you look to the far distant future and you're still slinging beets, that would rot your brain."

So I took an application from the recruiter. *Why not?* I figured. I'd spent countless hours talking to nomads about their seasonal jobs but had yet to see any of the worksites firsthand. I had no illusions:

Sampling this kind of labor wasn't going to magically turn me into a workamper. But at the very least, immersion might help me understand more deeply the lives I'd heard so much about.

Months later, my application was accepted by Express Employment Professionals, the temp agency that hires workers on behalf of American Crystal Sugar. So I began reading up on the industry. The United States is one of the world's largest producers of manufactured sugar, and sugar beets account for 55 percent of that yield. (The rest comes from sugarcane.) More than half of the country's sugar beet fields—some 680,000 planted acres—lie in the Red River Valley, which spans western Minnesota and eastern North Dakota. That region is home to American Crystal Sugar, the nation's biggest beet sugar company. This region is a national anomaly, boasting nearly full employment, which makes hiring workers very difficult. (The challenge had been even greater when the Bakken oil fields were booming.) For this reason, American Crystal seeks itinerant workers who can come—bringing their own homes—from far away to work the autumn harvest.

Equipped with that information and two pairs of heavy-duty work gloves, I arrived during the last week of September at Drayton Yard, a massive sugar beet storage and processing facility in North Dakota near the Canadian border. For beet producers throughout the Red River Valley, the first two weeks of October are a race against the weather. Borrowing military jargon, they call it a "campaign." The battle starts at midnight on October 1. Farmers rush to pull beets from the fields before the ground freezes, hoping temperatures stay cool enough to stave off rot. Twenty-four hours a day, semitrucks bearing several tons of cargo apiece speed along local highways to storage facilities. Haulers are heaped above the brim. Spilled beets litter the roadside for miles in every direction. Haggard drivers chain-smoke to stay awake. Traffic snarls. Accidents happen. Some locals blame the crashes on state regulations that allow inexperienced farm workers to haul multi-ton loads of produce without the commercial driver's licenses required of most truckers. At peak, American Crystal's more than three dozen receiving stations get some fifty thousand truckloads a day.

I was assigned twelve-hour shifts on the ground crew at "Piler Number One." Our station was inside "the shed," a colossal refrigeration facility that resembled an open-ended airplane hangar with a concrete floor. Already a pile of beets towered toward the ceiling; our orientation trainer estimated it was about twenty thousand tons, brought in as part of a smaller "pre-pile" crop before the main harvest. This season's beets, he added, were coming in larger than the year before; they were seeing beets the size of basketballs.

Many of the other stations were outdoors. We were told we were lucky because we'd be protected from rain or snow, but there was a trade-off: The noise and fumes were worse. Inside, the cloying smell of muddy beets mixed with dust and diesel.

When trucks arrived at Drayton Yard, they got weighed at a shack called the scale house and then lined up at our station. We waved them in one by one to pull up beside the piler, a giant clanking contraption that looked like a small factory mounted on tank treads. A huge hopper locked into place behind each truck to receive its load of beets. From there, the beets rode a conveyor belt into a tumbler that knocked off excess dirt, dumping it back into the truck. They continued along yet another conveyor belt, traveling up and away from the piler on a long boom that resembled the arm of a construction crane, flying out its open end onto the top of a three-story beet mountain. Over the course of the harvest, that mountain would get much longer. To give it room to grow, the piler occasionally inched backward on its treads. By the end of the harvest, the heap of beets would be the length of two Boeing 747s parked end to end and roughly as wide as the planes' wingspan. A forced-air ventilation system would help keep the pile near freezing as the beets awaited trips to the refinery.

The process was thunderously loud, rushed, and messy as hell. Our job involved constant cleanup: shoveling masses of spilled beets—some the size of frozen turkeys—back into the hoppers with pitchforks and agricultural scoops. (Standing around was discouraged: "If you can lean, you can clean!" was one manager's favorite slogan.) When the repeated lifting got too hard, we'd give up on the shovels and scoop smaller loads with our hands. If we didn't move fast enough, our overseer—who wore pink cowboy boots and a full face of makeup to work—would blare a WWII-submarine-sounding horn from the elevated control booth, as if she were arming the torpedoes, and then make frantic shoveling gestures through the window in our direction. Meanwhile the conveyor belts that churned over our heads shot beet bits and clods of dirt at everything in range, spattering our yellow safety vests and green hard hats. When I raised my left hand to signal a coworker about an oncoming truck—it was hard to hear even when we shouted over the din of the machine—an apple-sized beet pocked me hard on my wrist. Another part of our job was keeping the floors free of dense and slippery mud using snow shovels, which constantly got stuck in it and took a full-body shove to dislodge. We also had to take samples, the task Gretchen had told me about. What she hadn't mentioned was that it involved holding each vinyl sack open below a vertical chute coming off the piler; the beets rocketed down into the bag and keeping it steady meant bracing yourself for impact. It felt like catching bowling balls in a pillowcase.

The hardest bit was cleaning the piler. Our supervisor powered down the giant machine so we could all climb inside and scrape out the main chute with our shovels. The mud was intractable and, when it finally budged, it peeled off in leathery strips as thick as tire tread. Our overseer yelled at us to "put some muscle in" and explained that we only had fifteen minutes. Downtime was expensive.

After two days of orientation came a twelve-hour work shift. When it was over, I drove back to my campsite in the dark, past an "UNBEETABLE EXPERIENCE" harvest recruitment sign. My whole body hurt, especially my back and shoulders; old injuries and strains I'd long forgotten about had been newly invigorated. This surprised me, since I was thirty-seven and in reasonably good shape, and there were retirement-aged people working at some of the stations. I hoped for a hot shower—we'd been promised access to bathing facilities—but that part of the campground was still under construction. I cooked dinner in the van and fell asleep in my clothes with a splitting headache. I woke up at dawn the next day to begin what would be an even more eventful shift. A seven-foot metal pole from a broken harvester arrived hidden in a load of beets. It got sucked into the piler. By the time our overseer called an emergency shutdown, the pole had traveled partway up the first conveyor and was nearing the giant tumbler that shakes dirt off the beets. If it had gotten there, it could have done serious damage to the machine—and quite possibly to those of us standing on the ground nearby. Later that day, a coworker fell on the slippery concrete and had to file an accident report because his knee swelled up.

My working neighbors at the campsite included Dan, sixty-nine, who left his job as a Walmart truck driver in 2006 due to medical problems. Dan told me he had to plead with the foreman to get off the night shift, since he was going blind in his right eye and needed daylight to get around. His wife, Alice, also lived in their motorhome, but she had been diagnosed with ALS in January and could not work. There were other older people in the campground but also fiftysomethings and workers my age and younger. To the immediate right of my van a twentysomething couple of crust punks were living in a matte black pickup truck with New Jersey plates, eating cups of ramen noodles, and sleeping in the cab. I also met a goateed worker who was riding his bike through the RV camp and called himself Overdrive. He talked a bit about his philosophy. "In the morning if it's raining you can wake up and say this is a shitty day or you can say this is a great day," he said. "I choose to say, 'This is a great day.'"

Stressed, sore, and covered in dirt, part of me felt obligated to the people I'd met and wanted to tough it out through the end of the campaign. But no matter how long I stayed, the experience wasn't going to initiate me into the ranks of real workampers—I'd be going home at the end to write. By now I'd seen—and especially felt—enough to know that the workers I'd met had not exaggerated their experiences. So one night after my shift, I told the foreman I wouldn't be back. She didn't seem surprised; attrition was common. A few days later, I would learn that most of the coworkers at my piling station had also quit. I would also hear about a woman at another station who'd broken her wrist. With a twinge of guilt, I'd feel relieved that hadn't been me.

I drove away from Drayton Yard in the dark, past a stream of semitrucks heading the other direction. In the rearview mirror, the refinery's red neon sign read "American Crystal Sugar." It glowed through the steam billowing up from the plant. That night I sprung for a hotel in Grand Forks. There I enjoyed a hot shower, smoked a joint, and dozed off while trying to watch a movie. One of those things turned out to be a mistake.

I'D SENT OFF AN APPLICATION for CamperForce around the same time I'd submitted one for the sugar beet harvest. Getting the Amazon job required a pre-employment drug screening, a practice that has always struck me as invasive and degrading. The whole thing seemed even more absurd when I envisioned aging RVers across the country submitting bodily fluids or tissues for analysis in order to get precarious, low-wage, temporary work.

I had already researched Amazon's testing policy online and found employees talking about a "cheek scrape" test. In this kind of screening method, most drugs, including marijuana, are only detectable for a matter of days. I figured I'd be fine, since I had told Amazon I could report for work beginning in November.

Back home, I got an email from CamperForce setting my start date: November 4 at the Amazon warehouse in Haslet, Texas, near Fort Worth. A couple days later, after passing the criminal background check, I received another message giving me seventy-two hours to complete a drug test at a lab on Atlantic Avenue, close to my apartment. No problem, I thought. But the email also revealed an unpleasant surprise: I was getting a urine test.

Marijuana can show up in urine more than a month after smoking, since the metabolites lurk in your fat tissues. My test was scheduled for a week and a half after I'd smoked in North Dakota. For a cheek scrape, that would have been fine. For a urine test, it was shaky. I ordered a ten-pack of THC test strips from Amazon and gave one a try. The line signifying a drug-negative result appeared, but it was dishearteningly faint. The instructions said any stripe at all—no matter its shade—was grounds for passing the test. Mine was barely visible, though. I didn't want to risk it.

There was only one foolproof way to pass: smuggling clean urine in. Luckily, I still had nine unused THC test strips. I distributed them to friends and loved ones. Soon I found a donor, who provided a clean sample. I stored it in a tiny travel shampoo bottle. On the day of the test, I stashed the bottle in my underwear and put on skinny jeans to hold it in place. When the deed was done, a technician said I would receive the results in forty-eight hours.

I never heard back from the lab, but days later an email came from CamperForce: I was clear to work. Soon, I was back in the van and bound for Haslet, Texas.

⸻

ORIENTATION BEGAN on a Wednesday morning, with our thirty-one-person group gathered in a classroom at the Amazon warehouse. "You're going to be doing really physical work here," warned our instructor. "You're probably going to do a thousand squats a day, and that's not an exaggeration. Buns of steel, here we come! Right?"

A few trainees chuckled. We sat at long tables in alphabetical order, like schoolchildren. Most of the crowd was north of sixty. I was the only person under fifty, one of three workers without gray hair. Managers at the Haslet warehouse, we were told, had requested eight hundred CamperForce workers and got more than nine hundred applicants. Nearby trailer parks, however, didn't have enough space to accommodate the army of nomads. Another idea—renting a local cow pasture—had been summarily rejected. (Can you imagine that field, frozen in one of Texas's famous winter ice storms, with hundreds of elderly workers lacking electric, water, and sewage connections? A PR nightmare!)

In the end, managers scrounged up a limited number of RV spots at a dozen trailer parks within a forty-mile radius. They hired 251 CamperForce workers, as many as they could fit. Some new hires got stuck commuting ninety minutes a day, on top of their ten-hour work shifts. One woman living in a white Ford van told me she planned to "stealth camp" in Amazon's parking lot twice a week, saving gas and time.

Our trainer—herself an RVer and CamperForce veteran—apologized for the hassle. She said Amazon was thrilled to welcome us. "Campers are known for their integrity, attendance, and quality," she explained. "We know what it's like to put in a hard day's work. That's what Amazon is banking on. They're getting this experienced group to come in and kick booty!" Our cohort, she added, was known for "the CamperForce effect": a can-do, Eisenhower-era work ethic that rubbed off on younger, less-experienced laborers. In the days that followed, however, our team seemed to have little effect on our disaffected millennial coworkers. Like the twentysomethings, we mostly gave off vibes of "tired" and "bored.")

At least we brought a wide range of experience. Keith, sitting to my left, was a sixtysomething minister with ten children (five were adults and the others lived in his RV). Charlie, seventy-seven, told me his knees were shot from years of working as a mechanic for a copper mining concern. Ed and Patricia, married for more than forty years, had retired in the late 1990s from jobs as a motorcycle cop and a mail carrier.

Together, we trained to work in a department called Inventory Control Quality Assurance, or ICQA. The job sounded benign: scanning merchandise so it could be matched against digital inventory records. But we quickly learned that our warehouse—the largest in Amazon's network, according to our trainer, and comparable in size to more than nineteen football fields—was a maze of hazards.

Over twenty-two miles of conveyor belts shuttled boxes around the interior. They sounded like a freight train and jammed easily. We were told to keep our hair pinned up and to avoid tying sweatshirts around our waists, lest they get caught in the rollers, and the ID badges that dangled from our necks were on breakaway lanyards to avoid strangulation. A horn kept blaring over the din. When I asked what it meant, a coworker said a jammed belt had just been fixed and was starting up again.

Barb and Chuck Stout, whom I'd last seen in Quartzsite burning their bankruptcy papers, were working in Haslet, too. Chuck was stationed near one of the conveyor belts when a cardboard box flew off, knocking him flat. His head hit the concrete floor. Soon medics from AmCare, the in-house medical service, were hovering over him. They said he didn't have a concussion, so he could return to his job in the receiving department, walking fifteen miles a day. (Chuck, Barb, and I later reconnected at a Buffalo Wild Wings between shifts. They said that, before I arrived in Texas, union organizers had been campaigning in the warehouse parking lot. For about two weeks, managers gave twice-daily lectures warning workers to stay away from them and, above all, not to sign anything. Information about employees who engaged with organizers would end up in the union's database and be used to "track" and contact them, Chuck remembered the managers saying.)

During orientation, we also learned that our facility was one of ten distribution centers where Amazon was using robot "sherpas." The 350-pound orange contraptions look like giant Roomba vacuum cleaners. They're technically "drive units," but most people call them "Kivas," after the name of the manufacturer printed on their sides. They scoot around inside a dim cage—after all, robots don't need light to see—on a floor nicknamed the "Kiva field." Their job: ferrying open-faced shelving columns full of merchandise to stations operated by humans along the perimeter. No one, except for members of a labor unit called "Amnesty," was allowed to enter the

Kiva field, even when products tumbled off the shelves there. Regular workers were allowed to fish for such items from outside the cage using an "Amnesty Retrieval Tool." (Despite the highfalutin name, this was just a paint roller on a five-foot pole. Every station was equipped with one.) When I expressed interest in trying my hand at it, I was told that I would have to wait: Wielding the Amnesty Retrieval Tool took special training.

I'd heard a lot of hype about the Kivas. They were either an efficiency expert's wet dream, an innovation to free humankind from mindless toil, or they were the harbingers of a jobless dystopia where manual labor became obsolete as the wedge between rich and poor grew into a wall.

The reality was less polemic, more slapstick, like an updated version of Charlie Chaplin's film *Modern Times*. Our trainers regaled us with tales of unruly robots. Kivas had gone AWOL, escaping through a gap in the fence. They had tried to drag a stepladder away from a station while a worker was still standing on it. On rare occasions, two Kivas collided—each carrying up to 750 pounds of merchandise—like drunken European soccer fans bumping chests. Sometimes the Kivas dropped items. Sometimes they ran those items over. In April, a can of "bear mace" (basically industrial-grade pepper spray) fell off one robot's payload and got crushed by another. The warehouse had to be evacuated. Paramedics treated seven workers outside. Another was rushed to the hospital with respiratory problems.

Apart from marauding robots, we were told to beware overexertion. "Prepare to be sore!" a poster warned. One of our trainers joked that you could call it a good day if "you didn't have to take more than two Tylenols the night before." Wall-mounted dispensers labeled "Lil' Medic" offered free generic pain relievers. If you wanted the brand-name stuff—or, say, a bottle of Five-Hour Energy—you could buy it in the break room.

We got a tour of the building. The walls featured murals of Amazon's warehouse mascot—a blob-like orange cartoon called "Pecy:

Peculiar Guy"—and Orwellian slogans, including "Problems Are Treasures" and "Variation Is the Enemy, Takt Time Is Key." ("Takt" is business jargon. Defined as "the desired time that it takes to make one unit of production output," it is used to regulate the pace of work.) A large calendar revealed that, so far in November, there had been at least one safety-related "incident" each day. Our guide pointed out a "wall of shame" with anonymous profiles of disgraced workers. Each was illustrated with clip art: the black silhouette of a head over-laid with red block letters that read "ARRESTED" or "TERMI-NATED." One worker had stolen iPhones, smuggling them out in his steel-toed boots. Another got caught eating merchandise instead of putting it on the shelves (exactly $17.46 worth of food products, the profile helpfully revealed). Regimentation was the rule. We were told to walk in paths that were marked with green tape on the floor; when someone cut a corner, our guide scolded him. When I stopped to use the restroom, the inside of my stall had a chart with a color palette ranging from pale yellow to terrifying puce. It instructed me to find the shade that matched my urine and suggested that I should be drinking more water.

I spent a week at the warehouse. The cognitive dissonance was intense. At the start of each shift, a blonde, ponytailed manager in her twenties chirped "Hellllloooo, *campers!*" to our cohort of mostly elderly workers, while her assistant coached us through stretches. Afterward, I scanned barcodes on everything from dildos (manufac-turer: "Cloud 9" model "Delightful Dong"), to Smith & Wesson Gun Wraps (available in granular and rubberized textures) and $25 AMC gift cards (there were 146 of them, and they had to be scanned individually).

On one occasion, a Kiva robot carrying a column of shelves rolled toward my workstation. There was a whiff of nauseating per-fume, and then a cloud of it, growing denser as the robot drew nearer. For some reason, the smell reminded me of . . . college? When the shelves parked in front of me, I found eighteen boxes of patchouli incense waiting to be scanned. The odor stuck to my hands. I gagged,

I remove the contents of a robot-borne shelf to scan the barcodes.

finished the job, and pushed a button to send the robot away. Three other robots had been waiting in line to the right of it, like patient Labrador retrievers. As the stinky shelf departed, a new, much fresher one slid into place. But five minutes later, the patchouli-bearing robot returned. I re-scanned everything quickly and it left again. Five minutes later, it was back. I couldn't decide: Was this proof that humans are smarter than robots? Or was the robot patronizing me with round after round of redundant object counting—perhaps it would take the best two results out of three? After I dispatched the shelf for the third time, my shift was over. I joined my coworkers to leave. They could smell the incense. "Saturday Night Fever!" Keith, the minister, pronounced.

The following night's shift would be my last. For a few hours I worked with the Kivas again. I tried to lull myself into a meditative state. Another CamperForce worker, a white-haired septuagenarian, had told me earlier that she was on the verge of quitting because she found the robots so maddening. The Kivas kept bringing her the same shelf to scan. The situation resembled my patchouli problem. After it happened to her three times, the shelf began going to her husband, who was working at a station twenty-five feet away. He got it six times in total. She told me this outside the break room, as we walked past a cheerful-looking member of the cleaning crew dusting lockers. Trailing off from her story, she stared at the worker and demanded, "How'd she get that job? I'd rather do that! I'd rather clean toilets!"

Toward the end of the night, a manager asked me to scan items in "Damageland," where all the broken merchandise gets exiled. But the readout on my handheld scanner insisted I was supposed to be driving a forklift. (I do not know how to drive a forklift.) The manager didn't know what to do. We kept rebooting the scanner. Finally I made it to Damageland. After a few hours taking stock of dented cans, broken boxes, and a novelty gift called a BUTT/FACE towel, my shift was over.

I walked past three other CamperForce workers who had given up altogether on the scanners' erratic commands. They sat listlessly outside the bank of shelves, with their backs to the wall. It was time to quit, but I hadn't decided how to do it yet. Now a perverse urge arose. There was one act, we'd all been told, that led to instant termination. What if I ran headlong, heedless and free, onto the Kiva field? I'd fantasized about it earlier that week. What would it feel like to dash down those dim aisles, dodging busy Kivas, like I was doing some kind of proletarian parkour routine? How long would the Amnesty team take to catch up with me? What would happen when they did? (Stranger things had occurred. Later on, I'd hear about two amorous workers who got fired after attempting a tryst on the Kiva floor.)

But I'd come here to gather stories, not to enact a scene from *Braveheart*. And I didn't want to lose my notes. These had been carefully collected on a pad in my back pocket. I'd also dictated observations, *sotto voce*, to an audio recorder concealed in a pen and shot video with a camera that looked like a key fob. Both devices hung on the lanyard with my worker ID badge.

I walked to the security station at the warehouse exit. After putting the lanyard—and its cargo—in a TSA-style basket for keys and loose change, I slid it down a ramp to the guard while stepping through a metal detector. I paused nervously, looking back and forth between the guard and the basket, but she barely glanced at the items. Instead she looked at me, eyebrows raised, as if to say, "What are you waiting for?" So I told her "goodnight" and left.

Part Three

CHAPTER TEN

The H Word

A FEW WEEKS after Linda moved into the Squeeze Inn, LaVonne was parked alone in San Diego. She'd been stealth camping there. Her morale was low after a hard few months. Her former home—the maroon 2003 GMC Safari named LaVanne—had broken down after the last Rubber Tramp Rendezvous, leaving her stranded in Ehrenberg with no money for repairs. Making matters worse, she still owed a few thousand dollars in payments on her now-worthless van, which had died several times before. She decided to stay put and wait on her Social Security checks. Lori, the woman who lived with her son in a Chevy Tahoe, took LaVonne on grocery runs. LaVonne also found solace snuggling a new travel buddy: a rambunctious puppy named Scout, from a litter recently whelped by Lori's dog.

LaVonne ended up living in the dead van for nearly a month and a half, as temperatures rose and the tribe thinned around her. Finally she could afford a tow to the repair shop, where she was quoted $3,000 to fix the engine. That was more than she could pay. Walking Scout nearby, she spotted a nearly new twelve-person Chevy Express on a used car lot. A salesman emerged from the office. He said he could help her get a loan even though she had bad credit. This is not surprising—subprime auto loans have surged in recent years.

LaVonne wasn't sure about the terms, but what choice did she have? "If I didn't get it, I was going to be homeless," she later told me. She named the vehicle LaVanne Two.

That experience had been an unwelcome brush with the dreaded H word: *Homeless*. Most nomads avoid the label like a contagion. They are "houseless," after all. "Homeless" is other people.

But even after she escaped Ehrenberg and returned to familiar San Diego, Lavonne felt haunted by the word. On her blog, The Complete Flake, she wrote:

-When you live in a van in the city, people think you're homeless.

-When people think you're homeless, you start to feel homeless.

-So you start hiding in plain sight . . . doing everything you can to appear "normal" . . .

-So when the obviously homeless old man you have observed hiding his trash bag of stuff in a bush near your van every morning smiles and says hello like he knows you, it is unnerving to say the least.

-Because you realize you have joined the growing club of people who live on the streets, and there is not so much difference between the two of you after all.

A few days later, LaVonne followed up with a guilt-wracked confession. She explained in a new post that she'd been relying on payday loans to survive the month and, at $255 each, they were due in a week with $45 interest apiece. She was upset and ashamed. Her RTR friend Sameer, who was traveling with Mr. Pico the chihuahua, wrote back quickly:

I wish I was in your vicinity so I could give you, my sister, a hug. I would like to let you know that you are not alone in this situation. I can remember myself and Mr. Pico sitting in the forest in Dolores, Colorado, eight days before payday with the needle on the gasoline tank reading almost empty, five days' worth of food and two days' worth of water . . .

. . . Accepting poverty and the fact that you are probably considered poor, it's a hard thing. We were presented with this lifestyle as being exciting and innovative and it is. However, the truth of the matter is most of us are doing this because of our financial situation . . . Here are some words of advice from your brother Sameer's point of view . . . Leave California and the streets of San Diego where you are considered homeless. Remember in the desert or the forest you are camping. . . . Come to the desert or the forest and live with your own people who love and care about you.

From your brother, Sameer

Sameer and LaVonne were not naive. They know that, in the eyes of the law, they are homeless. But who can live under the weight of that word? The term "homeless" has metastasized beyond its literal definition, becoming a terrible threat. It whispers: *Exiles. The Fallen. The Other. Those Who Have Nothing Left.* "Our society's untouchables," LaVonne suggested on her blog.

"In the beginning, I worried about people's perception of me living in a van," Sameer told me once in an interview. "I didn't want to be defined as 'homeless.'" That word gave him trouble. One time he drove the van to visit his sister for Ramadan. She ended up throwing him out, deciding he was a "homeless bum" who didn't set a good example for his nieces and nephews. "I thought my family might be kinder." He trailed off, then continued: "How we define ourselves is really important. If you're driving down the road calling yourself

Sameer sits in his van with Mr. Pico.

homeless, or any other negative label, you're in trouble. Paul Bowles wrote a book called *The Sheltering Sky*. He described the difference between tourists and travelers." There he paused. "I'm a traveler." In his book, Bob Wells draws a bright line between vandwellers and the homeless. He suggests vandwellers are conscientious objectors from a broken, corrupting social order. Whether or not they chose their lifestyle, they have embraced it. On the other hand, he explains, "A homeless person may live in a van, but he isn't there because he hates society's rules. No, he has one goal and that is to get back under the tyranny of those rules, where he feels comfortable and safe."

The idea of choosing one's destiny, as it turned out, was a big deal. I heard this time and time again—no matter how narrow the options one had to pick from, choice was key. Ghost Dancer, who ran the vandweller group on Yahoo, put it to me like this in an interview: "The economy is not getting better. You have a choice—you can be free, or you can be homeless."

Social stigma is only part of the issue. Bad things can happen to those who live nomadically—things that are worse than sticks and stones. In recent years America has put unprecedented pressure on people who don't live in traditional housing. *The New York Times* reported the following in 2016:

> A battery of laws that effectively criminalize homelessness is sweeping the nation, embraced by places like Orlando, Fla.; Santa Cruz, Calif.; and Manchester, N.H. By the end of 2014, 100 cities had made it a crime to sit on a sidewalk, a 43 percent increase over 2011, according to a survey of 187 major American cities by the National Law Center on Homelessness and Poverty. The number of cities that banned sleeping in cars jumped to 81 from 37 during that same period. The crackdown comes amid the gentrification that is transforming cities like New York, San Francisco, Los Angeles, Washington and Honolulu, contributing to higher housing costs and increased homelessness.

Such laws prioritize property over people. They tell nomads "Your car can stay here, but you can't." In communities across the country, whether this might express a dark shift in civic values has been left largely out of the debate.

And it's not just happening in the cities. "Economic profiling" has also been taking place on public land. In Arizona's Coconino National Forest, rangers have been interrogating campers in vans and RVs about their home addresses. Anyone who appears to be a permanent nomad—a sticker indicating a vehicle has boondocked in Quartzsite is considered a giveaway—can be ticketed and evicted for making "residential use" of the forest. Meanwhile, *The Statesman Journal* recently reported that the Forest Service is developing a smartphone app that allows citizens to report the locations of suspected long-term campsites.

Negative attitudes toward rubber tramps are nothing new. In the mid- to late 1930s, as house trailers surged in popularity, the media seized on their inhabitants as a growing threat to middle-class morals. They were a mobile menace. Freeloaders. Mooches. Spreaders of disease. Rootless. Drifters. Idlers. Parasites. Shirkers.

"The gasoline gypsy pays less for social services than any other citizen in these tax-ridden United States," complained the editorial board of *The New York Times* in 1937.

"Who should bear the responsibility for the wandering hosts, living briefly here and there as squatters, rootless as air plants, paying no taxes, creating a new kind of motor slums?" asked *Fortune* magazine in the same year.

One manufacturer, Caravan Trailer, lampooned that sentiment by giving a tongue-in-cheek name to its $425, eleven-foot-long economy model: the "Tax Dodger."

But the trailer fad of the 1930s passed. Most of its adherents settled back down amid a reinvigorated economy. Many of the modern nomads I've interviewed, however, say they're never going back. They have no plans to get reabsorbed into mainstream housing. And that means many will have to live in hiding, on and off, until they die.

LaVonne got "the knock" once that spring while stealth camping in San Diego. It could have ended up worse. Officer Nunez was friendly. He wanted to make sure she was alive, he told her. He needed to know she wasn't running a meth lab. LaVonne knew she was lucky. Her van looked new and clean. Her dog was adorable. She was white. He didn't write her a citation. Officer Nunez did, however, take down her name, her license plate number, and the make and model of LaVanne Two. That meant her cover was blown, and she'd soon be moving on again.

CHAPTER ELEVEN

Homecoming

TWO WEEKS AFTER I left CamperForce in Texas, it was Thanksgiving. I called Linda to check in and wish her a happy holiday.

The news was bad. Her family was getting evicted from the house they were renting in Mission Viejo. Her son-in-law had lost the short-term disability benefits he'd started receiving when vertigo and migraines forced him out of his office job a year earlier. They couldn't pay the rent, so Linda gave them her old motorhome, which had been sitting in storage. (She'd almost sold it over the summer, but the offer had fallen through.) She was glad they could use the twenty-eight-foot El Dorado, but worried about it accommodating two adults, three teenagers, and four dogs. The plan had her daughter Audra and son-in-law Collin sleeping in the bedroom, grandson Julian in the loft over the cab, granddaughters Gabbi and Jordan on the fold-out dinette, the dogs wherever.

The family prepared to sell off their possessions, emptying the two-thousand-square-foot house and its attached garage. "It was like, you know, the hoarders on TV," Linda told me. Audra gave each of the teenagers a Rubbermaid tub. Anything they wanted to keep had to fit inside. Linda helped arrange a massive yard sale. There were boxes of clothes and books, boogie boards and bed frames. Dresses hung neatly along a wall at the edge of the lawn. Julian, a talented musician, parted with most of his gear including a beloved accordion. Jordan, an aspiring make-up artist, let much of her extensive wardrobe go. ("She's still not in love with this idea," Linda said drily.) In two weekends of yard sales they made $1,000. A few shoppers saw the Squeeze Inn parked in the garage and asked for a price. Linda was flattered by their interest but said it wasn't for sale.

While Linda put on a good face, the crisis had worn her down. "I was getting exhausted," she told me. "I am still helping, but I've pulled back." Meanwhile Thanksgiving dinner was still happening in the now-empty home. Costco and Ralph's had run out of turkeys, she said, but the family would do just fine with ham.

In late December Linda and I spoke again. She told me that LaVonne had come to Mission Viejo and helped her get the family settled into the RV. After that Linda was ready to go back on the road. Everyone was sad she wouldn't be around for Christmas. Audra cried.

Linda and LaVonne drove from Mission Viejo to Slab City, the sprawling squatters' encampment by the Salton Sea. They'd been hearing about it for years and wanted to visit. When they arrived, it was too dark to look around, so they pulled over to sleep. In the morning they saw trash strewn everywhere. They drove off in LaVonne's van to hunt for a nicer campsite. LaVonne had a Facebook friend staying at the Slabs. When they found her, she told them matter-of-factly that they'd been sleeping "where the meth heads hang out." Linda's heart sank. The Squeeze Inn and her Jeep were still over there. What if someone broke in? They raced back to find out. Linda's home was fine, but the uneasy feeling remained. She and LaVonne left immediately to reconnect with the Rubber Tramp tribe in Ehrenberg.

After a few weeks of stress, catching up with friends felt good.

Linda and LaVonne planned to stay in the area and rented a mailbox together. (They split the cost on their credit cards, Linda explained, adding that you can't borrow money from LaVonne because she'll never let you pay her back, though she's always glad to share: "When her monthly check comes, if someone needs $50, she'll give it to them.") After a heart-to-heart about the stigma of low-income living, they both posted on Facebook pages a passage from Kurt Vonnegut's novel, *Slaughterhouse Five*:

> America is the wealthiest nation on Earth, but its people are mainly poor, and poor Americans are urged to hate themselves ... Every other nation has folk traditions of men who were poor but extremely wise and virtuous, and therefore more estimable than anyone with power and gold. No such tales are told by the American poor. They mock themselves and glorify their betters.

One night LaVonne misplaced her purse in the van. Losing things in small spaces is surprisingly easy—some of her friends had nicknamed the phenomenon "Vandweller's Black Hole"—so she shrugged it off and went over to the Squeeze Inn to see Linda, who gave her some chocolate. ("I love Linda. She is the friend I've wished for my whole life—no judgment, no agenda, just pure friendship, love, and support. Plus, she feeds me," LaVonne later blogged.) Feeling a sudden pang of worry, LaVonne went back to the van. As she feared, she'd locked herself out. The keys were in the ignition and her dog Scout was still inside. She and Linda tried prying open the doors, to no avail. They went to see Bob, but he had no suggestions. The called AAA, but the dispatcher wouldn't send someone into unpaved backcountry. Since Scout had food and water, they decided to wait and solve the problem by daylight. LaVonne fell asleep on the Squeeze Inn's tiny mattress beside Linda, who recorded her snoring. She played it back to LaVonne in the morning—"it sounds like purring!"—after the fire department extricated Scout from the van. The poor dog had defecated everywhere, so LaVonne spent most of that day at the Laundromat.

On Christmas Eve, a couple dozen people showed up for a potluck. Linda met Swankie Wheels for the first time. Kyndal, who gave haircuts at the Rendezvous, made her friends laugh with an art installation: Rocky the Snowman, a pile of stones with a carrot nose. LaVonne and some friends discussed plans to visit Los Algodones. (Linda wanted to go but had to get a passport, which meant first renewing her driver's license that had expired in June using her new address, the post office box in Ehrenberg.)

On Christmas morning, Kyndal and her husband handed out gifts—packets of handy wipes decorated with holiday bows and candies—while Linda made a special breakfast for LaVonne: pumpkin pancakes with cranberry sauce, a concoction suggested by Swankie.

Linda caught me up on many things during that December phone call. She'd paid $30 for a carbon monoxide detector but had dropped it in her pee bucket. She'd recently finished reading Cyndi Lauper's

LaVonne makes pancakes in her van.

eponymous memoir. Over in Quartzsite, at the Long Term Visitors Area, an RVer and his two cats had barely escaped an electrical fire that incinerated their home and all his possessions.

Linda wanted to know if I was coming to the 2016 Rubber Tramp Rendezvous. It was a couple weeks away. She would be there, returning for the first time since her inaugural experience in 2014 when we'd first met. I told her I wouldn't miss it.

DRIVING IN THE DARK on Mitchell Mine Road, I spotted a pair of red strobing lights in the distance. Linda had set out emergency flashers so I could find the RTR campsite at night. It was already ten o'clock when I pulled up in Halen, but she came out to collect the lights and say hello. We went into the Squeeze Inn and she poured me a glass of water. One of the blindingly bright flashers wouldn't turn off. "Put it in the fridge!" I joked. She did.

By the time I got there in mid-January, the RTR was nearly halfway over. It had started slow due to rain, which hampered socializing and forced the nomads to take shelter in their rigs. But the weather improved. Before long, the population was about four times what it had been during Linda's first visit two years earlier; Bob later estimated 250 people came. A few of the old-timers and hard-core introverts were staying away because it felt so much bigger. Trying to leverage their greater numbers, one nomad had started a pool for an upcoming Powerball drawing. The $1.5 billion jackpot stood to be the largest prize in lottery history.

Many of the old seminars repeated, but there were also new events, including a session on living in small cars, as a cheaper and stealthier alternative to vandwelling. Among the presenters was David Swanson, sixty-six, a former professional potter who'd developed severe arthritis in his hands and now got by on Social Security disability payments. Eighteen months earlier, he'd moved into a 2006 Prius that had been totaled and salvaged before he bought it for $6,000.

"My cooking and sleeping are the two most important things to me, and that's what makes me feel like I'm on a retired-guy adventure," David told his audience. "I'm seeing the world! I'm having a great time! As long as I have a nice bed, as long as I can cook, I don't feel homeless, which I otherwise am."

David showed the group how he'd replaced his front passenger seat with a sturdy counter: a slab of two-inch teak from his former work table, on which he'd made hundreds of thousands of pots. Now he used it as a surface to fix meals with an induction hot plate, which he plugged into a power inverter that ran off the car's battery. At night the counter became a platform for his inflatable camping mattress and sleeping bag. For privacy and blocking light, he'd made a dark curtain with button holes along the edge, which hung on hooks over the windows. To create extra space, he had a custom tent that connected to the back of the vehicle when its rear gate was lifted.

He also described the Prius's most significant advantage as a home—it's essentially a smart power generator on wheels. Even when he's sleeping, he can run the vehicle's heating and cooling systems off the built-in battery, with the engine automatically kicking in once or twice an hour to charge it.

Once he got used to the setup, David said, living in his Prius allowed for many comforts. "If I pull up at Starbucks in the morning and use their WiFi, I can have my coffee ready before I could get it by going in there and standing in line," he explained, chuckling. For evening entertainment, he added, "I'll sit in the driver's seat with my little tablet—I have it Velcroed up to the visor—and put the seat back and there's movie night."

A few days after the small vehicle seminar, the RTR prepared for another first-time event: a community talent show. Linda lit candles inside brown paper bags weighed down with gravel, creating a row of homemade footlights that flickered warmly around the impromptu stage. The action began at sunset. There was music—a nomad pounded out rhythms on her djembe, another played Tibetan singing bowls, and a guitarist crooned a Bottle Rockets' song that went: "A thousand-dollar car, it ain't worth shit. You might as well take your thousand dollars and set fire to it." There was comedy—from a monologue about an octopus trying to make love to a bagpipe to a recitation of one-liners including "Camping is an expensive way to look homeless." A shirtless contortionist clasped his hands behind his back and then dislocated his shoulders to rotate his arms over his head, bringing them to the front of his torso. A karate expert chopped a wooden plank in half with his bare hand. One loud drunk kept interrupting and yelled "Julio! Julio!" at a dog that kept trying to hump a dancer's leg. Audience members gave the man dirty looks, which accomplished nothing, before shushing him and pulling his dog offstage.

The mood was cheerful, but with a darker undercurrent than I'd felt before. At one seminar, Bob had mentioned REAL ID, the program that was tightening security standards for driver's licenses. For years, nomads had been establishing residency by using the addresses of local mail-forwarding services. Now many DMV clerks had started looking up each address online. If it belonged to a business, they demanded an actual residential address. Intended to root out terrorism, this also made things harder for nomads, pushing them to come up with bogus information—to claim they lived at a family or friend's place or borrow the address of a random property they'd seen was for sale.

"The government wants you to live in a house," Bob warned them. "They know what we're doing and they're tightening the grip all the time."

Around this time I found myself wondering: What would become of all these people? In particular, I wondered if Linda was still gung-ho about building an Earthship. A few months earlier, she'd mentioned that her search for land had shifted again—to Vidal, California, near the Colorado River—but at the RTR she hadn't been talking about it much. When I asked, she sounded a bit tepid and told me she'd recently gotten rid of some of her books on Earthships during the purge in Mission Viejo.

Over the years, I'd heard nomads discuss chipping in together on a communal piece of land, but plans never seemed to materialize. I knew a couple people who'd gotten off the road by falling back on their adult children, who'd either taken them in or rented apartments for them. Not everyone had offspring, though. And the next generation had financial woes of its own. Some of the adult children were barely able to support themselves, let alone their parents.

I had heard about an assisted living center in Texas that welcomes RVers who can no longer drive. Called Escapees CARE, it is annexed to Rainbow's End, a larger RV park in the town of Livingston. ("Is it true that CARE is where you go to die?" reads a bleak question on the facility's F.A.Q. page.) Residents stay in their own motorhomes. Renting a spot there, however, costs more than $850 a month. Optional adult daycare services add another $200 each week. That was far out of reach for most folks I'd met.

Some of the stories I heard were scary. Iris, the nomad who lived with a talking parrot, recounted how an acquaintance named Ron drank himself to death while boondocking in a Walmart parking lot thirty-six miles from Quartzsite. No one found his body for a month, she said. An Isaiah 58 Project volunteer, Becky Hill, had mentioned an eighty-year-old who had taken shelter at their church for three months. He turned up dead in his RV in the desert near Ehrenberg. "He had no one to help him along," she lamented.

A CamperForce worker I'd interviewed four years earlier had just died that February. When I first met Patti DiPino, she was fifty-seven and stowing merchandise on the overnight shift at an Amazon warehouse in Coffeyville, Kansas. She invited me to chat in her 1993 Ford Montera motorhome.

Patti told me she'd spent fifteen years as a bookkeeper at a Denver construction company, then got laid off when it shut down in 2009. Around the same time, she lost her house in a messy divorce. So Patti moved into her RV and tried to climb back into the full-time work-force. Certain her three decades in office administration would count for something, she sent out thousands of online applications over the next few years. But the job market wasn't kind to an unemployed woman in her fifties. Nothing turned up.

Patti poured me a cup of black coffee. She talked about Sammy, her beloved five-pound Chihuahua, about spending time in Quartzsite, about her plan to apply for a job at Adventureland. She shared a joke: "Bookkeepers never die, they just get out of balance." She told me about her hobby, knitting lap blankets to comfort wheelchair-bound soldiers who'd lost limbs in Afghanistan. (One of her daughters, a Navy veteran, had offered to distribute them at a base in California.)

Patti was glad for the $10.50 an hour she made at Amazon but didn't want to spend her earnings there. "I tell people, 'You know what? Don't go to Walmart, don't buy on Amazon. Go down the street and buy from a mom and pop, and start hurting the pockets of the big guys,'" Patti said. "I mean, the rich are getting richer while we're sitting here getting poorer."

Patti didn't want to wander for the rest of her life. She dreamed of a permanent community. "What I'd like to find is kind of a school that I can get some county to offer to senior citizens to let us build our own gardens and produce our own methane, our own fuel, and stuff like that," she explained. "And I have a kitchen so what the heck, we can cook. People don't know how resourceful we can be. We've got the garden, so guess what, we'll can food, because some of us know how to can. We learned years ago."

Patti was sixty when she died. From what I gathered, she'd been receiving radiation treatment for cancer. On her Facebook page, one of her friends posted a memorial tribute that moved me nearly to tears:

> You are finally debt free and living in your forever home! No more freezing in the desert or in Kansas! No more cramped spaces. Like I always say when I hang up the phone: I love you Patti. I will miss you dearly.

I had once asked Silvianne, the tarot reader, about her long-term plans. "In my mind, I'm going to be doing this forever," she'd told me. "I don't care if it comes to the *Thelma & Louise* thing and all I can do is drive over a cliff."

I'd asked Iris, too. "Just find me dead in the desert," was her reply. "Put rocks over me and let me go."

Bob had a more practical plan for his declining years: "I'm going to dig a big, long trench and buy a cheap school bus and backfill completely over one side and over the roof, with windows on the south side. You can buy a crap school bus that's not running for $500. It's tough as nails and will last forever." But when that wouldn't work anymore, he planned to wander off into the wilderness and take his life with a bullet. "My long-term healthcare plan is bleached bones in the desert," he said.

That desolate endgame also hinted at something larger: Bob wasn't optimistic about the future of civilization. He believed that impending environmental and economic catastrophes would bring down human society. He anticipated a slump that would "make the Great Depression look like an afternoon in the park."

While Bob weighed the fate of the overcrowded planet, some of his website's readers worried that even vandwelling was getting too popular. They wanted Bob and other nomadic evangelists to stop talking about the lifestyle, concerned that more attention would make it harder to keep a low profile and possibly draw a police crackdown.

ONE AFTERNOON I drove to a taco stand in Quartzsite, owned by a guy who called himself the Grumpy Gringo. He'd been trying to sell the business for more than a year, kept dropping the price, but no one was buying. As I ordered my burrito, he told me he wanted to write a screenplay about old people coming to Quartzsite to die. When I looked startled, he told me the town had seen five or six suicides in the past year. "There's nothing here," he concluded bleakly. I took my food and left.

Back at the RTR, I caught up with Peter Fox, sixty-six, whom I'd met the year before. Then he'd been a vandweller in training, staying at the RTR in a borrowed Westafalia camper. After twenty-eight years in the San Francisco taxi industry as a driver, dispatcher, medallion holder, and manager, he had gotten squeezed out by Uber. "The sharing economy—the step-on-the-backs-of-the-little-people economy—has arrived," he announced glumly. "I was at the point where I could no longer both pay my rent and eat." He had tried to sell his medallion, which he thought would bring in about $140,000 after taxes, to retire on the proceeds. But sales were brokered by the city and demand for medallions was low. Peter was still on the waiting list. In the past half-year he had moved into a white Ford E350 twelve-passenger van he named the Pelican. ("Because they fly low and slow," he explained.) Inside he had a statuette of Ganesh, remover of obstacles.

Peter hoped to find workamping jobs, so we carpooled to the Big Tent. I watched him approach one camp host recruiter—"I was forced

Peter makes coffee in the open-air kitchen he set up near his van.

into retirement and need to make money"—and then left him alone to do interviews. After grabbing a quick dinner in town, we started back to camp. "Around this time every night it hits me that this isn't a vacation or a trip," he told me. "This is *it*."

A couple days later we sat and chatted on a tarp outside his van. "I still feel the oscillation between fear and joy," he said. We talked about the future. "Where do people go when they're too old to camp or live in a van?" he mused. He told me he was grateful to a registered nurse at the RTR who had helped him by lancing an infection on one of his fingers. He thought it would be good if there were roving medical teams or way stations to serve nomads, particularly in state parks and other free places where people gathered. He also thought it would be cool to start a non-profit for aging vandwellers. Maybe someone would fund something like that? He wanted to call it the "Hello in There" Foundation, after a John Prine song by that name. I hadn't heard it, so he pulled out a guitar and some sheet music and started to play. His voice swelled as it reached the chorus: a plea for interpersonal warmth and connection to ease the loneliness of old age.

What was his plan for the future? I asked.

"Don't die. Don't get old," he said. "I don't know." If things got desperate, he added, a niece and nephew had offered to take him in.

―――――

AT THE END OF THE RTR, the nomads fashioned a little van out of a cardboard shipping box from Amazon. Everyone signed it. That night, they tossed the effigy on the bonfire. They called the new ritual "Burning Van" and commemorated it by singing lyrics they'd written to the tune of "Little Boxes," the satirical ode to suburban conformity composed in 1962 by Malvina Reynolds.

Little vans out in the desert
Little vans all made of ticky tacky

Little vans out in the desert
Little vans and none the same

There's a white one and a white one
And a white one and a flowered one
And they're all made out of ticky tacky
And there's none two just the same

And the people are rubber trampers
The nicest people anywhere.
And they won't be put in boxes
And they won't be all the same

We are friendly
We are family
We love to get together,
In the desert, in the desert,
Where the terrain is all the same . . .

And we have no pavilion,
No bathhouse, no central stage
But we do have a fire pit where friendships are made
We're all made out of ticky tacky
And none think all the same

The nomads enjoyed the ceremony and vowed to make it an annual tradition. Maybe next year, someone suggested, they should build the van out of plywood so it would burn a little longer.

LINDA GOT A REPORT FROM HER FAMILY. Her grandchildren were now staying in a tent next to the RV. During a bad storm, the rain fly lifted up, drenching them. Water had been coming in through the bottom of the tent, too. One of her granddaughters had tried vacuuming the floor to keep it tidy, without realizing she was drawing grains of sand through the fabric and creating tiny holes. They patched it up with duct tape. They were doing their best, she said.

Meanwhile Linda had some new challenges, too. She told me she'd started seeing a black spot in the center of her vision while driving at night. The instrument panel on the Jeep wasn't working; she noticed this when we were driving along Scaddan Wash after a trip to town. "I'm screwed without a speedometer. Shit," she said. "It's always something."

She and LaVonne had been trying to find workamping jobs for the spring. Linda thought she'd managed to secure another camp hosting job with California Land Management. When I was getting ready to leave the RTR, Linda got a call: The job, she was told, had been eliminated.

THAT'S WHERE I THOUGHT this story would end—with Linda back at the Rubber Tramp Rendezvous, restarting the seasonal cycle that governed her life as a migrant, among the tribe that had become like a family. Her new relationships grew even stronger in the weeks that followed, when Linda decamped with some of the nomads to Ehrenberg. There she came down with a terrible case of bronchitis. As she lay in the Squeeze Inn, too weak to cook, her off-the-grid neighbors arrived with food: boiled eggs, tomatoes, sausage. I'd seen similar caretaking the year before, when a nomad named Beth fell while stepping out of her van (aka The Beast), breaking her left arm. Two members of her "vanily" set up what they called "Camp Recovery," helping her do many things that are impossible one-handed, from tying her shoes to fastening her bra, until she was well enough to move on.

A couple months after Linda's illness, we were catching up on the phone when she said something that surprised me. She'd found land for her Earthship.

She'd seen an ad on Craigslist for five acres near the border town of Douglas, Arizona, on the western edge of the Chihuahuan desert and nine miles north of the Mexican border. This was an area she'd scouted earlier, after her first Rubber Tramp Rendezvous. Back then she was convinced the region was too remote, too isolated. Now she felt differently. "The clock is ticking," she told me. "How much time do I have to be healthy and strong enough to complete the task? It would be such a waste to never live in a home I built for myself." Did she worry about feeling lonely, I asked? "Plenty of my friends run up and down that road and will come and see me," Linda said, referring to her nomad tribe. "I won't be there all alone."

The parcel was in a rural district. There, homesteaders on four or more acres were exempt from county building codes. In other words, it was one of the zones Earthship inventor Michael Reynolds called "pockets of freedom"—places without red tape, where experimental architecture could flourish. It was also at an elevation of 4,200 feet, which meant summers shouldn't get too sweltering. And if the heat got uncomfortable, there were opportunities for camp hosting in the surrounding mountains.

"Unimproved vacant land with very good legal access, and no electric, well or septic," read the ad on Craigslist, which included photographs of endless raw desert with no other homes in sight. It also admitted some drawbacks. The roads bordering the property were overgrown with mesquite. One ran through a dry gulch, where flash floods were likely during thunderstorms.

Eventually the price won her over. The seller wanted $2,500 for the land, in bite-sized installments: $200 down and $200 a month, with no interest, until the total was met. A year earlier, while camp hosting in the San Bernardino Mountains, Linda had been poring over a self-help book, written by a start-up founder, called *Making Ideas Happen: Overcoming the Obstacles Between Vision and Reality*. I had asked her why she was reading it. She told me she'd given it to her son-in-law, but he hadn't seemed interested, so she'd dug into it herself. "I have a stalled project: my Earthship," she said matter-of-factly. "What's my *obstacle*? Finances. But is that really *an obstacle*?" She

An access road to Linda's property disappears into the desert scrub.

paused, took a thoughtful draw on her cigarette. Later she said she could announce her homesteading project at the RTR. Maybe people would come help her out. "Want to come stay on my land? The price is one tire packed with dirt per day!" she said, laughing. "Of course, I'll make them pack more tires when they get here."

When Linda first spotted the Craigslist ad, she was working as a camp host in the Sequoia National Forest, more than a twelve-hour drive away. (She'd been hired by California Land Management again; after the job she'd been promised earlier got eliminated, another one had opened up elsewhere.) She couldn't go to see the land in person. So she went to the tax assessor's website for Cochise County and entered the parcel number, which brought up the latitude and longitude, coordinates she plugged into MapQuest. In the resulting satellite image the plot was camel-colored and stippled with chaparral. Arroyos ran through it like creases in an outstretched palm.

After making the down payment, Linda posted to Facebook that she'd bought the land.

"YES!!! Making it happen," wrote Ash, one of her vandweller

friends from Amazon CamperForce. "Let us know when you need construction workers!"

"Awesome! Awesome! Awesome! I am jealous! We would love to swing by and help work on the build at some point!" added Wendy, another nomad, who lived with her boyfriend and their dogs in a "tiny house on wheels": a former school bus they'd equipped with a composting toilet and a wood stove.

Linda planned to visit the land after finishing work as a camp host, before reporting to her next job, which was at Amazon. Her fellow camp host partner, a vandweller named Gary from the Rubber Tramp Rendezvous, had become a close friend and wanted to see the land, too. He also planned to work at Amazon. Gary seemed to be sweet on Linda, though she went back and forth on whether she wanted a romantic relationship.

Could I go see the land with them? I asked. Linda agreed and I booked a flight to Phoenix. But just before the trip in mid-July, I learned their plans had changed. Gary had suffered a minor stroke. He and Linda had taken refuge with the RTR tribe in Flagstaff so he could recover. They decided to postpone the visit. Apart from Gary's health, Linda worried about the heat down there. She'd expected temperatures in the eighties. The weather report showed 103 degrees. The Jeep's air conditioning was busted. On top of all that, Amazon had assigned them an early start date of August 1, and they had to report to a warehouse in Campbellsville, Kentucky, to join a Camper-Force contingent that would grow to include more than 500 workers. They were planning a slow trip across the country, without driving during the heat of the day. "I'm just bummed I don't get to go down there," Linda said. She sounded exhausted.

I decided to go anyway. The plane ticket was already booked. Linda's five acres were unfenced, open to anyone who wanted to visit. Besides, I figured a pilgrimage to the land might answer some nagging questions. Could the future Linda had already built in her brain become real on that blank patch of desert? Or was it an impossible dream?

My flight touched down in Phoenix on a mid-July evening during Arizona's monsoon season. As passengers disembarked, a chorus of cell phones—including mine—blared emergency alert tones. Warnings flashed from the National Weather Service that a dust storm was approaching. Such storms are also known as "haboobs," to the chagrin of some Arizonans who, in recent years, have protested the use of a meteorological term with Arabic roots. "I am insulted that local TV news crews are now calling this kind of storm a haboob," wrote one Gilbert, Arizona, man in a letter to *The Arizona Republic*. "How do they think our soldiers feel coming back to Arizona and hearing some Middle Eastern term [for what] is clearly an Arizona phenomenon?"

Outside the terminal, the air was stifling and blow-drier hot. The darkening sky was full of fine silt that diffused the white lights on the tarmac, giving them milky halos.

I adjusted the mirrors on a rented Toyota Corolla. (Halen was now parked back East with family.) Linda began texting. She'd just settled in for the night after reaching El Reno, an Oklahoma City suburb, 350 miles east from her previous stop in Tucumcari, New Mexico. She wanted to make arrangements for us to connect the following day.

Linda was still eager to see her land, but now that she wouldn't be able to travel there until January, after the Amazon job ended, we had come up with another plan. After spending the night in Douglas, I would drive into the desert backcountry, getting as close as possible to her five acres. From there I'd set out on foot with a laptop and a smartphone, using GPS to hunt for the markers at each corner. If cell reception was strong enough, I would live-stream video of the hike directly to Linda's phone. She could watch and give directions, pointing out any features of the land she wanted to explore, like a remote pilot at the controls of a low-tech, human-powered version of the Mars rover.

After puzzling out the time difference—Arizona eschews daylight savings—we agreed to begin the next day at one o'clock my time, three o'clock her time. Linda already sounded excited about the vicarious journey.

"Try to see the Gadsden Hotel while you're in Douglas," she urged. "It has marble pillars and Tiffany stained glass from when the area was booming with copper mines." Then she wrote: "Are you driving right now?"

No, I said. The car was parked—I wasn't texting and driving.

"Good," she continued. "There's a Super Walmart in Douglas, make sure you have lots of water."

Water, sunblock, and a hat, I affirmed.

"If you get stuck out there . . . I could get ahold of the guy I brought the property from," she wrote, then revised her thinking. "Don't get stuck."

If the dirt roads were too soft, I would just park back on the pavement and walk in, I told her. She seemed satisfied with that.

"Okay, get going, talk tomorrow," she wrote. "You are one crazy woman. I can't believe you are doing this!" And finally: "Goodnight."

By nine o'clock the air was clear and still. I drove southeast out of Phoenix on Interstate 10, reaching Douglas after midnight. The next morning I went online to the tax assessor's website for Cochise County and pulled up a satellite view of Linda's rectangular lot. I found the same area on Google Maps and plotted each corner of Linda's land with a virtual pin. When those pins were saved to the map, their icons transformed into tiny gold stars. A rectangular constellation materialized in the desert, eight and a half miles northeast of my current GPS location, which appeared onscreen as a blue dot.

I topped off a water bottle and ventured into the hot midmorning. My first stop was Douglas's main street, G Avenue, home to the magnificent historic hotel Linda had told me about. Around it, however, was an assortment of vacant buildings, peeling paint, fading façades, and plywood-covered windows. The sidewalks were deserted. It was hard to believe that this had once been the largest town in Arizona. Founded in 1901 as a smelting center to process ore from nearby copper mines, Douglas boomed for decades. Prosperity wasn't permanent, though. In the second half of the century Americans grew aware of the health and environmental threats created by air pollution. Legislators funded research on the problem in 1955, leading to the Clean Air Act of 1963 and its extensions. But the local smelter, Douglas Reduction Works owned by the Phelps Dodge Corporation, managed to skirt the new federal standards until the 1980s. By then it had become the biggest emitter of sulfur dioxide in American manufacturing, belching out some 950 tons each day of the pollutant that causes acid rain. The smoke was so dense one doctor stopped encouraging patients to exercise, worried about the effects of heavy breathing. "When it gets really bad, your lungs feel slimy," a coffee shop owner in nearby Bisbee told the Associated Press, while preparing to move his family away from the area.

The Environmental Protection Agency ordered Phelps Dodge to install emissions controls at a cost of half a billion dollars. The company shut down the smelter instead. In mid-January 1987, four workers poured the last batch of copper. Clouds of exhaust stopped billowing from the towering smokestacks. A haze hanging over the valley dissipated. No one missed the thick air, but there were other losses: 347 jobs with $10 million in payroll, an estimated quarter of the local economy. That rankled the citizens of Douglas, even those who still had work. "I wish they'd ship all those S.O.B.s that had anything to do with closing the smelter to Russia and Canada," one Coors beer distributor employee told *The Boston Globe*. "As far as I'm concerned, it's communist-inspired."

Douglas's prospects are still in freefall. The town's only hospital shut down in the summer of 2015, taking another seventy jobs. The metro area encompassing Douglas and Sierra Vista, another former smelter town, was recently named the fourth-fastest-shrinking city in America. Between 2010 and 2015, Douglas saw steeper drops in population than two rust belt capitals: Flint, Michigan, and the Youngstown, Ohio, metro area.

As I walked down G Avenue, the gulf between Douglas's heyday and modern era was visible all around. Across from the Gadsden Hotel stood the century-old Brophy Building, a former commercial hub whose neoclassical good looks with ornamental shields, egg-and-dart molding, and a dentil cornice now lent a strange solemnity to boarded-up storefronts. One block north, a marquee at the long-empty Grand Theatre said "NOW SHO ING." Around the Grand's opening in 1919, boosters called the 1,600-seat movie palace the "finest theatre building between San Antonio and Los Angeles," touting such amenities as a pipe organ to accompany silent films, a tearoom, and a candy shop. Apart from showing films, the Grand hosted entertainers from Ginger Rogers to John Philip Sousa. But the rise of television in the mid-twentieth century marked the end of opulent movie houses, and the Grand closed in 1958. The roof later collapsed. Trees sprouted in the ruins. In the early 1980s, preservationists purchased it for $1, but restoration would require some $9.5 million, so it's still dormant. In the 2000s the derelict theater found at least one role: Halloween haunted house. To raise funds for the building, volunteers made an annual tradition of creating scary scenes inside, including an embalming lab built by a real-life funeral home and a *Pet Sematary* horror scene acted by high school students.

Though Linda was intrigued by Douglas's storied past, the town's decline was no tragedy to her. For an experimental homesteader on a budget, it kept things affordable. The cheap real estate was already attracting a trickle of entrepreneurs and artists, from Robert Uribe, a Manhattan transplant who opened a coffee shop in Douglas and was elected mayor four years later, to Harrod Blank, a Berkeley filmmaker who was building Art Car World, a museum of creatively modified vehicles. The fleet included Carthedral, a hearse with stained glass windows and gothic spires, and the Coltmobile, bedecked with 1,045 plastic horses. The latter was created by an alcoholic Vietnam vet who, during his recovery, glued a horse to the car each time he wanted a drink.

But the town posed challenges, too. While researching her new home, Linda had encountered something ominous. "There's been quite a drug smuggling problem because Douglas is right on the Mexican border," she had told me, not long after making the down payment. That information had come from books about Douglas, Linda added, but she didn't know how long ago they were written. So maybe things had gotten better since then?

While reading about the trafficking problem, Linda had learned about the town's most famous drug bust. It dated back to 1990, when agents found a 300-foot-long tunnel running below the border. Used by the Sinaloa cartel to smuggle cocaine, the concrete-reinforced passageway lay three stories underground and started at a house in Agua Prieta, where the entrance was cleverly hidden. Turning on a water spigot activated a hydraulic lift, which raised a pool table—and the slab it sat upon—to reveal a ladder leading down. Inside, the tunnel was five feet tall and air conditioned, lit with electric lights and protected from flooding by a sump pump. A trolley ran end to end on a pair of metal tracks, terminating in Douglas below a 2,000-square-foot warehouse disguised as a truck-washing station. There a hoist-and-pulley system hauled bundles of cocaine up to the surface, where workers loaded them onto waiting tractor-trailers. Agents marveled that the tunnel, nicknamed "cocaine alley," was like "something out of a James Bond movie." Sinaloa kingpin Joaquin "El Chapo" Guzman was even more effusive, boasting his operatives had "made a fucking cool tunnel."

Linda was intrigued by this, but none of it discouraged her from homesteading in the area. "An ex-border patrolman wrote about people getting killed who have been giving information to the police. Informants," she had explained, matter-of-factly. "Yeah, the drug cartel slaughters informants. And I'm like, 'Well, I'm not associating with any of those people.'" After we hung up, I wondered if Linda was trying to reassure herself. Or me. Or both. In any case, she hadn't been exaggerating when she said Douglas was right on the border. Twelve blocks south of the Grand Theatre, the town—and the nation—comes to a halt against two parallel fences, which flank a cement-lined channel that looks like a dry moat. (Its official name, used by federal contractors, is "Douglas International Ditch.") The first fence, on the U.S. side of the moat, is made of heavy wire mesh painted a self-effacing desert beige. The second fence, which faces Mexico and is the official border barrier, looks like something out of a prison film. A bollard-style structure made of heavy steel, it looms eighteen feet overhead, continuing its work out of sight and underground, where it descends another six to eight feet to deter diggers. Its bars are black and dappled with rust, separated by four-inch gaps that frame glimpses of Mexican sister city Agua Prieta, a sprawling industrial metropolis nearly five times the size of Douglas. Many of its citizens work in the maquiladoras—foreign-owned factories that assemble products for export—making everything from car parts to medical supplies, window blinds, electronics, and clothing.

Linda's books were correct about the smuggling, too. Drug couriers can make more in a single night than maquiladora workers earn in a month. So it's little surprise that Border Patrol agents at the Douglas port of entry often find bundles of marijuana stashed in the quarter panels and spare tires of inbound cars. (On rarer occasions, it's meth, heroin, or cocaine.) In a recent bust, they caught a sixteen-year-old Mexican boy using a seat belt to rappel down from the top of the fence into Douglas. His mission: collecting burlap sacks stuffed with ninety pounds of pot, which had already been tossed over the barrier from Agua Prieta, and hauling them to a nearby getaway car. For his work, he'd been promised $400. Back home, he made vehicle timing belts in a maquiladora for $42 a week, money he used to help feed his mother and nine siblings.

Border agents have reported stranger exploits, including traffickers who built a homemade zip line to shuttle drug bundles high overhead like tiny cable cars. Another creative smuggler tried wading into Douglas through the sewers carrying fifty-five pounds of marijuana. Agents popped a manhole and discovered him equipped with a scuba tank and mask, wearing a black and purple wetsuit. He dropped the dive gear and the weed and hurried back toward Agua

Prieta. From elsewhere along the border come tales of pot flying over the fence on remote-control ultralight aircraft. (One of these drones accidentally dropped a twenty-three-pound bale on a carport in Nogales, Arizona.)

IT WAS ALREADY past noon when I set out to see Linda's land, driving up into the Sulphur Springs Valley. Bordering the Sonoran and Chihuahuan deserts, this arid expanse runs nearly a hundred miles through southeastern Arizona and into northern Mexico. The lower half is cradled by a half-dozen mountain ranges: the Dragoons and Mules to the west, and the Chiricahuas, Swisshelms, Pedregosas, and Porillas to the east. Linda's homesteading site was at the foot of the Porillas. She'd told me there were camp hosting jobs to be had north of her place in the Chiricahuas, which were part of Coronado National Forest.

I traversed what felt like endless scrubland, much of it uninhabited. Ahead the asphalt looked like a shimmering puddle—a heat mirage that vanished when I got close. A rotting billboard on the roadside said "FREE TRADE POLICY: DRUGS IN $$$ BILLIONS OUT." Occasionally low-slung ranch houses rose from the chaparral. Some appeared to have been abandoned for a long time— open sockets gaped where doors and windows had been, and skeletal rafters peeked through gaps in the warping roof boards. On the left side of the road appeared a small white shrine full of silk flowers and then, farther along, a solitary late-model RV, way out in the lonesome distance like an establishing shot from *Breaking Bad.*

After a few wrong turns, I found a rough road heading east that was mentioned in the Craigslist ad for Linda's land. It was already one o'clock, so I texted her to say I was running ten minutes behind. The reply came immediately: "I'm ready."

The road was narrow and uneven but the reddish dirt was packed solid. That was lucky, considering the midsummer rains. I was nervous and excited, probably driving a little too fast. *What if I found something bad out here? What if Linda didn't like what she saw?* The car juddered along, flushing birds from bushes that crowded in on both sides. A black-tailed jackrabbit with cartoonishly large ears shot across the road. Soon an intersection appeared, marked with a pair of official street signs. They were the first ones I'd seen out here, oddly formal in an unpaved wilderness. I turned onto another dirt track and drove half a mile. To the left appeared the ghost of a road, overgrown with mesquite. A strip of sun-bleached pink flagging tape dangled from a bush.

I checked my smartphone map. The blue GPS dot was right next to the constellation marking Linda's land. The cell signal was strong, so I used the phone as a WiFi hotspot to go online with my laptop and then rang Linda for a teleconference. On the first try there was no answer, but when I called again, she picked up. She was smiling, eyes crinkling at the corners behind her rose-colored bifocals. I waited for the familiar, three-syllable salutation.

"Hell-ooo-ooo!" Linda exclaimed. The video feed stuttered through a series of frozen images, like pages in a flip book. "You're cutting out," she said. But the audio was clear and the connection didn't drop, so we decided to give it a try. I pointed the laptop forward and headed west on the path. "I see clouds!" Linda exclaimed. I'd angled the camera too high and it was broadcasting a wheeling view of the sky overhead. Trying to tilt it down, I gave Linda a shot of my nostrils from below. Finally I got it right.

"Oh, look! That's the road?" she said incredulously. Her five acres were supposed to be marked with stakes made of PVC pipe, she added. Did I see anything like that? Not yet, I replied. What I could see: dry, reddish earth, the silhouettes of the Mule Mountains on the far side of the valley. "The views sure are pretty, aren't they?" Linda marveled. Then she hollered to an unseen figure. "Gary, come sit down and look!"

"I can't sit down," came a slightly muffled voice.

"Well lean up against a tree, then," Linda replied.

An older man in black plastic-rimmed glasses appeared. His face hovered over Linda's shoulder, brow furrowed as he peered at the screen. His gray hair was thinned out on top and he wore an expression of benevolent curiosity.

"Cloudy today," he remarked. And then: "Look at all that grass!" When Linda laughed at the joke, Gary broke into a grin. "You might need a riding mower," he deadpanned.

A white pole appeared in the distance, poking out of the ground like a splinter. "See the PVC?" I asked.

"No!" Linda replied. She leaned in and squinted. I kept walking. She reminded me to be careful. "Watch where you're stepping," she warned. "Make suuuuuure you don't see any snakes." Rattlers were common around the campground where Linda and Gary had worked in Sequoia National Forest and she knew they lived here, too.

Finally, we got close. The five-foot PVC pipe was planted beside a small rock pile and a rebar stake. "Oh! I see it," Linda said excitedly. "How does that look on your GPS?" The blue dot—my location in the desert—sat right on top of the star marking the northeastern corner of Linda's land. "It matches!" I said. Linda let out a whoop. "Where do you want to go?" I asked. "We can do whatever you want."

Linda wanted to see the arroyo. A dry riverbed cut across the northwestern corner of her property. Other potential buyers had peered down into that cleft and walked away, the seller had told her. But Linda thought it could be an asset, a way to collect rain during desert storms. "You know, I'm thinking, '*more water*,'" she later explained.

We joked around as I hiked west, holding the laptop pointed ahead of me like a divining rod. "If you see any snakes before I do, say something!" I pleaded. Linda, who'd already pointed out the choppiness of the broadcast, was dismissive. "Oh yeah, with the delay and everything," she said, trailing off. We talked about the weather where they were located, just west of Joplin, Missouri, still en route to Kentucky. It was 93 degrees—same as here, but sunny and humid. "Oh, I am soaking wet!" Linda said. Before our meeting, she'd raced to find a rest stop on Interstate 44 with lots of shade trees, one that would be comfortable in the sticky heat of a Midwest summer. ("Racing" meant driving about sixty-two miles an hour in the Squeeze Inn, she later explained. Anything faster made it shake too hard.)

Stepping around a very active anthill, I pointed the laptop camera down to show Linda. "Ooooh, nice ants!" she remarked. That view got her and Gary asking about the consistency of the ground. Gary wanted to know if there were many rocks. "It's not that rocky, but there are some," I said. Linda wondered aloud if the dirt was sandy and granular or fine and powdery. She wanted to install earth cooling tubes—a natural climate control system that involves burying pipes between five and eight feet underground, where the temperature goes down to 55 degrees—and use them to circulate air through her home and also a greenhouse. Putting them in would take a lot of digging.

"It breaks pretty easy," I said, grabbing a fistful of dry, coarse dirt to show them and then spreading my fingers and watching it sift to the ground. "See it streaming through my hand?"

"That may dig well," Gary replied. "That's a huge plus." Linda agreed. "Digging down for cooling tubes looks like it could be very easy. Oh good. Oh wow."

We continued toward the arroyo and Linda admired the vegetation. The summer rains had made the desert plants appear vivid, almost lush. Delicate yellow blossoms hung between the waxy leaves of the creosote. White-thorn acacias were festooned with tiny, pollen-flecked puffballs. The yuccas had just finished a bloom cycle. A withered stalk jutted from each mop of blade-shaped fronds, bearing a head of dried-out blossoms. We passed one mystery cactus with long, undulating arms that looked like spiky tentacles. It was covered in red, knob-shaped fruits that reminded me of prickly pear. Linda knew it was something else, though. "Prickly pear has flat leaves. That's another kind of cactus," she said, adding "Should be able to eat it, though." (I later learned this was night-blooming cereus—also called Queen of the Night—whose nocturnal blossoms open just once a year.)

After I corrected for a wrong turn, the dry riverbed appeared ahead. "Is it a true arroyo or just a ditch?" Linda asked. "How deep is it?" I set the computer up on the edge, with the camera pointing into the arroyo, and clambered into it so she could see. In some places the edge lined up with my hips; elsewhere it hit my shoulders. I guessed between three and four feet.

"Is it that deep all the way through the property?" she asked. No, I explained. It only sliced off a triangle of land in the northwest, and not a very big one. Like the other corners, this one was marked with a pipe and, after stepping out of the arroyo, I went to find it. This time Linda saw the marker right away. "Oh there it is, look!" she exclaimed. "Yeaaaahh!"

After that I hiked back toward the first marker. "So what do you think?" I asked Linda.

"It's better than what I thought," she said, praising the land's panoramic mountain views and the quality of its dirt. "I was thinking I could end up with all rocks like Ehrenberg, but I don't have that," she added, referring to the gravel terraces where she had camped after the Rubber Tramp Rendezvous. That place had looked like a moonscape, with very little plant life. Linda was also delighted that the land had been properly surveyed and marked. "That is a big deal out there!" she said. "Especially for the price, my goodness!"

For three and a half years—since I had first met Linda—she had been showing me pictures of her favorite Earthship, a model called the Nautilus, whose floor plan was based on a Fibonacci series. I imagined it rising from this piece of land, with sloped adobe walls that echoed the contours of the surrounding mountains. "I'm trying to picture the Earthship here," I told her.

"Yes, it's going to be so beautiful right there, isn't it?" Linda replied happily. She planned to come and camp out when her Amazon job was done and the weather was cooler. Once she got to see the land in person, she figured, she could decide where to build. "I'm just gonna have to sit on it for a while and the spot will appear," she said.

For the past half hour, I'd been walking and talking under overcast skies, which kept things comfortable despite temperatures in the nineties. Now the sun came out and made the desert a griddle. A temperature alert flashed on my laptop—it wouldn't work in this heat. The video froze and then the connection cut out. The tour was over.

I'd spent a lot of time thinking about what this land meant to Linda. Here was tangible progress toward the dream of building something no one could take away, something she owned free and clear, something that could outlast her. But seeing her onscreen with Gary added a new dimension. For all her charisma, Linda had always struck me as a lone wolf. She had family and dear friends, of course, but she kept them close while remaining fiercely independent. Now I started wondering what her future would be like if new people entered the picture. Would Gary end up homesteading with Linda? Would LaVonne and other nomads visit her land in their portable homes? And who exactly were Linda's neighbors? Was there anyone in the backcountry she could rely on?

I hadn't seen another soul. So I drank a lot of water and set out in the car again, seeking signs of human habitation.

The first clue was horses. One mile southwest of Linda's plot, three of them stood behind a green-painted gate, watching suspiciously as the car approached, then ambling off. A sign on the gate read "No Trespassing: Violators Will Be Prosecuted." It was perforated with nine rusty bullet holes and one fresh shotgun blast whose edges hadn't rusted out yet. A yellow casing from a twenty-gauge shell lay crushed in the dirt nearby.

A breeze came up, rustling the chaparral and carrying with it another sound, something between a scrape and a creak. It seemed to be coming from a dilapidated A-frame shack that stood a hundred yards to the west. A loose sheet of corrugated tin on the roof seesawed up and down, groaning. For the first time it occurred to me that some folks might not want to be found. Startling people way out here could be a serious mistake. So I approached slowly, calling "Hellloooo!" like a lost tourist. No answer.

The shack was a collage of plywood, chicken wire and tin. A

shredded blue tarp dangled over a hole in the wall. The inside was empty apart from a small bench on the dirt floor. The desert around it was covered in piles of detritus that suggested lives interrupted. There were a couple of teddy bears, a two-handled cooking pot, one high-heeled shoe, clothes hangers, empty cans, ceramic mugs, and a cassette by the group Chicago. I wondered about the owners of the objects and whether they had left this place in a hurry. (Later I would read about the debris that collects in border deserts, much of it left behind by exhausted migrants. In some cases, those entering the country on foot must pare down their possessions before squeezing into the crowded cars that will spirit them away.)

Resuming the drive, I spotted more evidence of humanity. From a dirt road half a mile north of the shack, I could see a patch with a few flat-topped sheds, a corral made of salvaged pallets, two hoop-style greenhouses—gardens, maybe?—and an ancient sedan with the hood propped open, all behind barbed wire. Circling back east, I found a property I'd missed earlier, this one about two-thirds of a mile southwest of Linda's land. A donkey in a paddock brayed loudly as I pulled up. There was also a travel trailer, bleached bone white, with a Porta Potty strapped to its side. Again I called out. No answer.

Satellite maps showed a ranch farther south. Maybe someone was home? Following the map, I passed black cattle lazing under scraggly mesquite trees. Soon a fence appeared and, far beyond that, a house. But the road turned ugly. After a short upward slope, it dipped into a low spot where puddles reflected the sky. I tried skirting the edge. It was soft. Soon the Corolla's front end was mired up to the wheel wells. Trying to back out just made the tires spin, spattering gobs of mud across the white rental car.

I remembered Linda's warning: *Don't get stuck.*

Cell reception was weak from the car, so I waded out and clambered up a berm. After five dropped calls, an AAA agent explained there's no service on dirt roads. Next try was Nalley's Pit Stop, a father-and-son towing company. Lonnie, the owner, was out on a job. Could I wait for a call back? Of course. Heavy clouds were massing to the southeast. Hiking to the ranch house suddenly seemed like a good idea. When I got close, the silence broke apart in a cacophony of barking—a canine doorbell. A dozen dogs roamed the grounds, some free and others pacing in pens. The smallest, a black and white pup, trotted after me like a self-appointed ambassador. In the front yard were a welding rig, a weed whacker, and a toilet bowl full of large stones. I walked up to the gate and yelled hello. Nothing.

The phone rang as I was heading back to the car. Lonnie said he was close. Soon a flatbed tow truck materialized where the cows had been. I climbed up the berm and waved my arms like a castaway.

Lonnie and his son, Lonnie Jr., had seen the clouds and rushed over. Part of the ranch was on a floodplain. A UPS truck had gotten stuck here once in the rainy season. By the time the driver phoned Lonnie for help, he recalled, water was rushing past the tires. Nothing to do until the land dried out.

Lonnie Jr. connected a hook below the Corolla's rear bumper. I put it in neutral and gave him a thumbs-up. As the car began to roll backward out of the mud, a burgundy four-wheel pickup arrived on the other side of the ditch. A man in a weathered black baseball cap and Wrangler jeans stepped out and watched, hands on hips. I waved sheepishly from the driver's seat.

"That's a treacherous spot," the man observed. He had a ruddy beard and skin that was pink like rare roast beef, with freckles. After the car had been extricated, I paid Lonnie and Lonnie Jr. for the tow—$80 plus a $20 tip—and thanked them profusely. The man in the pickup introduced himself as the ranch manager. "You out here by yourself?" he asked. I felt uncomfortable, but couldn't think of any plausible answer except for the honest one. So I mentioned Linda and asked what life was like out here. The manager told me he ran a herd of fifty Brangus cattle—hybrids of Brahman and Angus, bred for heat and drought—and that he'd been living on this land for twenty-six years. Things were mostly quiet here, he said, but sometimes drug mules came tromping through with heavy backpacks. Best to avoid them. He'd been shot at twice. Now he kept an AR-15 in his pickup.

I drove away in the comically dirty rental car, with an inch of mud in the footwell, my sneaker squelching as it pressed the pedals. When a rainbow materialized above the land I'd just left, it felt cheesy—nature's sarcasm?—but I stopped for a snapshot anyway.

Back in downtown Douglas, I parked outside the Gadsden Hotel and ventured into the lobby. The cavernous, amber-colored room was as opulent as Linda had described, with Italianate columns, a sweeping marble staircase, and leather couches. ("Sitting in it feels like lounging in the den of a pirate who had a classical education," a *Los Angeles Times* reporter once wrote.) The Tiffany glass window she had told me about was a forty-two-foot mural on the mezzanine. Its backlit panes depicted a desert scene in swirls of color—tan dirt, blue sky, purple mountains on the horizon, green yuccas in bloom. It could have been mistaken for an illustration of Linda's own land, rendered in precious jewels. I wandered into Casa Segovia, the nearly empty hotel restaurant, and ordered a $7 plate of enchiladas and a michelada. The Tiffany landscape hung in my brain like an afterimage from a bright flash of light. I wanted to see Linda step into that kind of prettified wilderness: a southwestern Eden. But all afternoon I'd been fending off worries. Now that I was alone with my thoughts, they began creeping in.

Two more days of driving would put Linda and Gary in Campbellsville, Kentucky. There they would spend the next five months working ten-hour night shifts in an Amazon warehouse. For Linda, the job was all about earning money to start building her home. Her heart was set on that. But as I thought about the remoteness of the land—along with the dizzying summer heat, armed drug mules, flash floods, and rattlesnakes—I wondered: Was the plan insane? In three years of mulling over Linda's dream, I'd had doubts before. But mostly I'd shared the mantra of Fox Mulder on *The X-Files*: "I Want to Believe."

Later I sent Linda some notes with what I'd learned about the area—both good and bad, admitting my worries. I also emailed her a map with pictures of her land and its surroundings. She didn't answer the first message but did write back from Amazon to tell me how happy she was about the photos. "I open them often and dream of being there," Linda said. "I hate this fucking job and that helps to keep me going. Fifteen more weeks and I'll be free."

Meanwhile, other concerns gathered in the pit of my stomach. Would Linda's body hold up to the rigors of construction? I thought back to her first tour with Amazon in Fernley, Nevada, and the dizziness that landed her in the emergency room from the repetitive-motion injury she got from wielding a scanner gun. Her wrist had taken three years to heal. What if she got hurt again? Amazon had since switched to lighter barcode scanners—maybe that would help? I also worried that the job might wear her out. Though Linda was initially assigned to work as a stower, shelving merchandise, later in the season she'd tell me managers were considering transferring her and other CamperForce laborers to more strenuous positions as pickers, collecting orders. The year before, one picker had worn a Fitbit to work, she'd tell me. On a single day it logged eighteen miles and forty-four flights of stairs.

Even if Linda made it through her tour at Amazon, would she be able to save up enough money to start building the Earthship? The last time she worked for CamperForce, her base wage had been $11.50, before add-ons for night work and overtime. Now it was $10.75. (Linda had initially worked at the Fernley facility, which offered better wages than some other CamperForce locations, but that warehouse had closed in 2015.)

I also worried about her morale. During Linda's first season working for Amazon, she had seen up close the vast volume of crap Americans were buying and felt disgusted. That experience had planted a seed of disenchantment. After she left the warehouse, it continued to grow. When she had downsized from a large RV to a minuscule trailer, Linda had also been reading about minimalism and the tiny house movement. She had done a lot of thinking about consumer culture and about how much garbage people cram into their short lives. I wondered where all those thoughts would lead.

Linda was still grappling with them. Weeks later, after starting work in Kentucky, she would post the following message on Facebook and also text it directly to me:

Someone asked why do you want a homestead? To be independent, get out of the rat race, support local businesses, buy only American made. Stop buying stuff I don't need to impress people I don't like. Right now I am working in a big warehouse, for a major online supplier. The stuff is crap all made somewhere else in the world where they don't have child labor laws, where the workers labor fourteen- to sixteen-hour days without meals or bathroom breaks. There is one million square feet in this warehouse packed with stuff that won't last a month. It is all going to a landfill. This company has hundreds of warehouses. Our economy is built on the backs of slaves we keep in other countries, like China, India, Mexico, any third world country with a cheap labor force where we don't have to see them but where we can enjoy the fruits of their labor. This American Corp. is probably the biggest slave owner in the world.

After sending that, she continued:

Radical I know, but this is what goes through my head when I'm at work. There is nothing in that warehouse of substance. It enslaved the buyers who use their credit to purchase that shit. Keeps them in jobs they hate to pay their debts. It's really depressing to be there.

Linda added that she was coping with "the moral issue. How to honor the money I'm making to complete my plan. I know the money doesn't know where it came from. In these times is there any other way to get the finances I need in the time I need them? My time on this Earth is short."

She distilled her feelings in one final line: "It's like a bank robber doing his last job in order to retire."

But back in Douglas, Linda hadn't told me any of that yet. I picked at my plate of enchiladas and wondered what would happen next. When I got on the road, the sun was setting. I drove north on Highway 191. The rain that had threatened all day hadn't come, but the clouds had moved west and now sat over the Mule Mountains. In between them and the peaks was a crack of sky. The last rays of daylight flared through it, painting conch shell colors—all pinks and tangerines—before fading to a deep red. In twenty miles I turned left, continuing along the upper edge of the Mules. It was dark now. Jags of lightning flickered above the Dragoon range to the north.

I passed through Tombstone—"the town too tough to die"— and stopped at the Texaco in Benson. Above the fuel pumps an illuminated canopy cast a daylight-bright glare and moths and beetles flew drunken spirals—a bug disco. My phone pinged with a text message from Linda: "Did you make it back to town?" she asked. Yes, I replied. She told me that, after we'd lost contact in the desert, she and Gary had progressed seventy miles on their cross-country journey to Kentucky before stopping for the night in Springfield, Missouri. "We have been driving three hundred miles a day," she added. "Gary is very fatigued and the heat is kicking my ass."

"I'm glad you're getting close!" I wrote back. Then I gave up on texting and called her. Our conversation turned back to the land.

"It was beautiful," Linda said. "When you put your hand in the dirt I was like, 'Damn, that's nice dirt!'" Then she told me more about Gary. "He really likes me," she said. "And he's done about as many jobs as I have!" Gary had run a radiology department, managed a grocery store, and worked in construction, she elaborated. "And he is very intelligent and has a good memory. And beautiful handwriting. And he's very good with numbers, does all kinds of math shit in his head."

Would he want to help build an Earthship? "I don't know if he wants to put down roots," she mused. "But he says that I have a really good plan. I'm not imagining things. It's not just some fantasy. It's something doable." No matter what happened between them, Linda added, she would keep the desert property in her name alone. Homesteading was *her* dream, after all.

What mattered now was reaching Kentucky and making it until Christmas. She could already see the other side of Amazon: getting released with cash and a plan to use it, driving to Arizona to camp on her land. Sifting the dirt between her own fingers, planning a future. That image was getting her through the miles of driving. If anything could, it would push her through nights at Amazon. The gravitational pull of her own piece of the country. She'd spent so many years planning. She was ready to release all that pent-up thinking in action.

"I'm happy, happy, happy," she told me. "I can't wait to get there and *do* it."

After that we hung up. It was getting late and Linda had another long day of driving ahead.

The Octopus in the Coconut

IT'S EARLY WINTER IN AMERICA. Snowstorms ride the jet stream, painting a broad white brushstroke across the continent from west to east.

High in the San Bernardino Mountains of California, snow swirls through the Jeffrey pines and settles onto unoccupied campsites at Hanna Flat. It falls upon the silent drywall factory and empty houses of Empire, Nevada. In North Dakota, it blankets the sleeping sugar beet fields. It flurries around the Amazon warehouse in Campbellsville, Kentucky, and nearby RV parks, where CamperForce workers live.

But in a small town in the Sonoran Desert, the sun shines and afternoon temperatures climb into the seventies. The annual migration to Quartzsite has begun, with tens of thousands of nomads streaming in from all over the country. They reunite around evening campfires, telling stories from the year that's nearly over, making plans for the one about to begin.

Swankie Wheels is back in Quartzsite after camp hosting through early autumn in the Colorado Rockies, where she celebrated her seventy-second birthday and cracked three ribs on the job. After struggling through cold nights in her unheated van, she installs a small pop-up tent within the vehicle, cocooning it around her bed as she sleeps. Looking ahead, she trains for a new challenge: hiking the 800-mile Arizona Trail.

Silvianne Delmars is camped near Swankie. By day she works the register at Gem World, an outlet in town that sells crystals and jewelry-making supplies. One night at a karaoke potluck dinner, she gets up the nerve to sing her anthem, "Queen of the Road," in front of two dozen people, to cheers and applause. And she's preparing to go on her first date in seven years—dinner with a handsome RVer she met at the ranger station.

LaVonne Ellis has returned to Ehrenberg after a two-week stint at Standing Rock, where she joined protesters fighting the North Dakota Access Pipeline. In the quiet of the desert, she pushes through writer's block to finish a short childhood memoir, *The Red-Feather Christmas Tree*, which she publishes on Amazon. ("Linda May never doubted," it says in the acknowledgments.) Later she visits Los Algodones for cheap eyeglasses. For the future she's conceiving a new dream: buying land near Taos, New Mexico, where she can permanently park an old school bus, creating a home base to inhabit between her van trips.

Bob Wells is also in Ehrenberg, getting ready to host the largest-ever Rubber Tramp Rendezvous. Anticipating hundreds of people, he sets new rules for the two-week gathering, banning loud music and unleashed dogs. And he removes traditional group meals from the calendar of events, figuring they'll be too hard to organize with so many mouths to feed. (Little does he know: More than five hundred mobile dwellings will roll into the event this year, many drawn by videos he's been posting on YouTube.)

More nomads will arrive soon. Among them is David Swanson, the former professional potter who lives in a salvaged Prius. David is excited to go back to the Rubber Tramp Rendezvous, where he gave onlookers a tour of his vehicle last year. For now he's parked on Padre Island in Texas. In a Facebook message to me, he describes it as "a nomadic paradise" where both cars and tents are legal for beach camping. Then he asks, "Will you be going to RTR 2017?"

I type my regrets: "I have been to the last three RTRs and it's killing me that I can't make it to this one." I tell David I'm trying to finish the book I've been writing.

"Good luck on the word slinging!" he replies cheerfully. "Stay busy!"

But David's question opens a hollow in my chest. After three years documenting the nomads, missing the RTR feels wrong. I repeat to myself a cardinal rule of nonfiction writing: *The story keeps unfolding into the future, but at some point you step away.*

I'm incorrect about the last part, though, because the story has followed me home. In Brooklyn, tiny houses on wheels are ubiquitous. I cannot stop seeing them.

On a side street with unmetered parking near my apartment in Boerum Hill, there's a silver high-top Ford camper van with a *nazar*—a medallion to ward off the evil eye—dangling from its rearview mirror. The windows are tinted dark, almost black, with drawn blinds behind them.

A short walk from my sister's building in Bed-Stuy, there's an old motorhome stationed across from a commercial truck lot. A privacy curtain in the back of the cab is pulled shut. Heat-trapping foil insulation blocks the glass in the sleeping loft. Near the rear-mounted spare tire, trash bags and duct tape cover an empty socket that once held a window.

More camper vans and an occasional RV dock at the edge of Prospect Park. They cluster near low-slung warehouses in Gowanus and Crown Heights, where there are no neighbors to complain. These mobile shelters are everywhere—an invisible city, hidden in plain sight.

The night after the season's first snowfall, I visit Red Hook, one of the last stretches of industrial waterfront in Brooklyn. The backstreets are dim and lined with a motley assortment of work vehicles—contractors' vans, delivery fleets, food trucks, utility trailers—providing good cover to mix among for urban campers. Before long I start seeing them: An ancient travel trailer shaped like a tinned ham. A Chevy Astro van with the telltale privacy curtain, its cabin windows blocked with plastic sheeting and American flags. A converted transit shuttle with tinted glass, jaunty red hubcaps, and a propane furnace welded above the rear bumper to provide heat when the engine's off. Plenty of late-model camper vans, their blinds drawn.

The most spectacular dwelling of all is a short yellow school bus. Its windows are covered with sheet metal for zero visibility. Glinting at the edge of the roof, barely noticeable from the ground, are the aluminum frames of four perfectly aligned solar panels. A drape hangs behind the windshield, which has condensation on its inner surface—another tell. It is parked looking out on the East River, with an unobstructed view of the Statue of Liberty.

The journalist in me wants to knock on the door. But then memories of stealth parking return—how it feels to hide behind covered windows, your heartbeat quickening at a stranger's approaching footsteps.

I walk away.

Encountering so many nomads around Brooklyn is eye-opening. It's not the first time this project has hit close to home, though. Midway through reporting, I learned that Swankie's younger son, a software engineer from Seattle, is someone I'd met years earlier at Burning Man. Later on, LaVonne and I realized that one of her dear friends is married to a journalist pal of mine in Berkeley. Both times I wondered: *What are the odds of that?*

Maybe not so low. After all, millions of Americans are wrestling with the impossibility of a traditional middle-class existence. In homes across the country, kitchen tables are strewn with unpaid bills. Lights burn late into the night. The same calculations get performed again and again, over and over, through exhaustion and sometimes tears. Wages minus grocery receipts. Minus medical bills. Minus credit card debt. Minus utility fees. Minus student loan and car payments. Minus the biggest expense of all: rent.

In the widening gap between credits and debits hangs a question: *What parts of this life are you willing to give up, so you can keep on living?*

Most who face this dilemma will not end up dwelling in vehicles. Those who do are analogous to what biologists call an "indicator species"—sensitive organisms with the capacity to signal much larger shifts in an ecosystem.

Like the nomads, millions of Americans are being forced to change their lives, even if the transformations are less outwardly radical. There are many ways to parse the challenge of survival. *This month, will you skip meals? Go to the ER instead of your doctor? Postpone the credit card bills, hoping they won't go to collections? Put off paying electric and gas charges, hoping the light and heat will stay on? Let the interest accumulate on student and car loans, hoping someday you'll find a way to catch up?*

These indignities underscore a larger question: *When do impossible choices start to tear people—a society—apart?*

It's already happening. The cause of the unmanageable household math that's keeping people up at night is no secret. The top 1 percent now makes eighty-one times what those in the bottom half do, when you compare average earnings. For American adults on the lower half of the income ladder—some 117 million of them—earnings haven't changed since the 1970s.

This is not a wage gap—it's a chasm. And the cost of that growing divide is paid by everyone.

"I am, somehow, less interested in the weight and convolutions of Einstein's brain than in the near certainty that people of equal talent have lived and died in cotton fields and sweatshops," reflected the late writer Stephen Jay Gould. A deepening class divide makes social mobility all but impossible. The result is a de facto caste system. This is not only morally wrong but also tremendously wasteful. Denying access to opportunity for large segments of the population means throwing away vast reserves of talent and brainpower. It's also been shown to dampen economic growth.

The most widely accepted measure for calculating income inequality is a century-old formula called the Gini coefficient. It's a gold standard for economists around the globe, along with the World Bank, the CIA, and the Paris-based Organization for Economic Cooperation and Development. What it reveals is startling. Today the United States has the most unequal society of all developed nations. America's level of inequality is comparable to that of Russia, China, Argentina, and the war-torn Democratic Republic of the Congo.

And as bad as the situation is now, it's likely to get worse. That makes me wonder: *What further contortions—or even mutations—of the social order will appear in years to come? How many people will get crushed by the system? How many will find a way to escape it?*

A FEW DAYS AFTER WE FIRST MET, Linda noticed an octopus-shaped ring on my right hand. "Have you ever seen an octopus in a laboratory, how smart they are?" she marveled. "They're escape artists!"

Linda described a video she'd seen online: "So there's food in this other tank, and this big octopus is in the first tank all by himself. He squishes himself down into a tube and he gets over to the other tank." More experiments followed. "They kept making it more difficult and more difficult," she added. "Like he had to open a hatch and then get into a tube."

No matter what, the octopus got out.

"Sometimes people can be like that," I suggested.

"Yeah, if you try to keep us in a box," Linda said. She laughed.

I think of that conversation much later, when Linda links to a new video on her Facebook page. The footage shows an octopus traversing the ocean floor. Its gait is an awkward shuffle and a caption points out why—the octopus is carrying a pair of empty coconut halves. Suddenly it jumps inside them. Drawing the shells close to its body, it continues the journey, rolling along like a tentacled bowling ball.

The octopus had created a tool for both transportation and protection—a sort of coconut mobile home. A scuba diver in Indonesia had captured the moment on video. Linda posts a comment calling it "the cutest, smartest octopus ever."

———

LINDA'S ON THE ROAD AGAIN. Released from her seasonal job at the Amazon warehouse in Campbellsville, Kentucky, she begins her westward trek. Gary has stayed behind to work longer, so this time she travels alone, towing the Squeeze Inn behind her Jeep through short winter days and long, dark nights.

Her first destination is Taos, New Mexico. There she plans to visit her favorite Earthship, the Nautilus, and consult an architect about adapting the design to her needs. Then she'll continue to the Rubber Tramp Rendezvous. After that, she'll drive to the desert near Douglas, Arizona, to lay eyes on the land that is her future.

But outside Taos, the "Check Engine" light appears on the instrument panel of her Jeep. She hears snowstorms are rolling into the area. Hoping to avoid a bad-weather breakdown while driving through the mountains, Linda reshuffles her itinerary and heads straight to Douglas.

She arrives without incident. On the first night, she camps in the parking lot of an abandoned Safeway, even as predawn temperatures drop below freezing. The next day, she finds a cut-rate RV park on the fairgrounds north of town. A couple from Montana is staying in the spot next to her. They live in a gutted seventeen-foot Airstream trailer that's seen better days. Linda tells them about her Earthship and shows them the three-ring binder full of plans.

We catch up on the phone a day later. She tells me that, apart from the abandoned plan to visit Taos, her return trip from Kentucky was smooth. "The weather was perfect!" she says. "I ran into three raindrops the whole time." The trip only took three days. She's still at the RV park, which costs just $15 a night. Today she got to shower; during the journey she subsisted on baby wipes. "I've been sitting in my trailer and resting," she says, letting out a contented sigh.

And she has visited her five acres. The patch of desert she first saw in photographs on Craigslist last spring—and then as a video feed on her smartphone over the summer—has become three-dimensional. The land is real, tangible, an environment through which she has walked. She swears she even heard a rattlesnake there. "It's beautiful," she says.

Now the future feels urgently close. "I'm sixty-six," she says matter-of-factly. "I need to speed things up here. I want to be able to relax and enjoy it at some point."

The details come out in a torrent. Linda tells me she just bought a 4,000-watt portable generator for $26—more than half off. "Oh my god, I got electricity!" she crows. It'll run as loud as a vacuum cleaner, but that doesn't bother her. Its output dwarfs the trickle of power she's been getting from a 45-watt solar panel.

Linda describes finding an inexpensive water delivery service near her land that can fill large tanks. (Though Earthships have cisterns to collect rainfall, there may not be enough of it, and she'll need to sustain herself through the building process.) She talks about having the land surveyed—she'll need to know the elevations before cutting berms for permaculture. And tomorrow she will visit the county buildings department to learn about setbacks—how far from the road she must build—and other zoning particulars.

"I already read on their website that you can clear up to an acre without a grading permit," she says. "That's all I wanted to do anyway."

Linda plans to start construction after the Rubber Tramp Rendezvous. Gary has agreed to return to the land with her. LaVonne's going, too. Together, they will start building a greenhouse, which will allow for organic farming and provide protection from the elements during the construction of her home.

Linda can see it now, as if the pictures in her three-ring binder have come to life. The Earthship she has imagined for so many years rises from a barren patch of desert. She builds it with her own determined hands, with help from friends who have become a family. When it's done—and it will be done—the Earthship will shelter them. With renewable systems for food, water, power, heating, and cooling, it will be a home but also a living thing, an organism that exists in harmony with the desert. It will outlive them all.

That future begins in the new year, which is only weeks away. Linda has already planned the first step: breaking ground. She's found an excavator operator who charges $35 an hour, with nothing extra for gas or travel. "His time starts when his butt hits the tractor seat," she says happily. She's spoken with him and reserved a date in late January.

The project should take eight hours, she tells me. This is how it goes:

First the excavator clears the overgrown access road, opening a path to her land. Next it scrapes out a driveway, somewhere the Squeeze Inn can park.

Finally it starts working on the main construction site. The arm extends. The bucket dips. Metal teeth bite into the ground, over and over, as the excavator tears at tough desert scrub. Everything it touches yields: the gnarled brush, the hardy cactus, the heavy stone. These are obstacles standing in the way of Linda's future. One by one, they get lifted away.

Soon the job is done. When the excavator departs, Linda walks into the flat, blank space it left behind. This land is ready for her now—one perfect acre, something to build on.

ACKNOWLEDGMENTS

You meet a lot of people in three years and 15,000 miles. This book exists due to their kindness. I'm thankful to everyone on the road who shared wisdom, bad jokes, campfires, and coffee and to everyone back home whose support made the journey possible.

My deepest gratitude goes to Linda May. Trusting someone to tell your story is no small thing, particularly when the writer hangs around, on and off, for three years, sleeps in a van outside your daughter's house, and jogs after your campground maintenance golf cart while scribbling on a notepad. I hope Linda's resilience—along with her wit and large heart—will move others as they did me.

A couple hundred nomads shared their time and leave traces here. They are too numerous to list, but I'm especially thankful to LaVonne Ellis, Silvianne Delmars, Bob Wells, Charlene Swankie (aka "Swankie Wheels"), Iris Goldberg, Peter Fox, Ghost Dancer, Barb and Chuck Stout, Lois Middleton, Phil and Robin DePeal, Gary Fallon, Lois Middleton, David Roderick, Al Christensen, Lou Brochetti, Jen Derge, Ash Haag, Vincent Mosemann, David Swanson, Mike, Kat, and Alex Valentino and, of course, to Don Wheeler, man of mystery.

Enthusiastic support came from the Columbia School of Journalism, especially my colleagues Ruth Padawer and David Hajdu. The Rockefeller Foundation provided a month at the Bellagio Center, a place made magical by the hard work of Pilar Palaciá and Claudia Juech. My cohorts there (aka "Il Convivio") shared camaraderie, deep insight, and spontaneous dance parties. Extra appreciation goes to photographer Todd Gray, who asked the right questions at the right time (and also took my picture).

James Marcus at *Harper's Magazine* was the first editor who believed in this story and is a model of human decency. Other allies on the *Harper's Magazine* article included Giulia Melucci, Sharon J. Riley, and the talented photographer Max Whittaker, whose images accompanied it. Lizzy Ratner and Sarah Leonard at *The Nation*, Clara Germani at *The Christian Science Monitor*, and Alissa Quart at the Economic Hardship Reporting Project all supported parts of what became the book.

Joy Harris, my fierce nurturer of an agent, "got" this project from the start with profound empathy. Editor Alane Mason at Norton pulled it together with a steady hand. Adam Reed, Ashley Patrick, Kyle Radler, and Laura Goldin also helped a great deal.

Michael Evans, Robert and Karen Kopfstein, Jerry Hirsch, Stella Ru, and Stu Levin gave (literal) shelter to me and Halen. Ann Cusack sent me off with a care package including such sundries as Neosporin and Irish Spring, along with a small American flag. Lonnie and Lonnie Jr. of Nalley's Pit Stop in Douglas, Arizona, hauled my wheels out of the mud. Aaron, Bill, and the crack team of mechanics at Conklin Cars in Hutchinson, Kansas, stayed open after business hours to fix my alternator.

I'm grateful to my family: My father Ron helped co-pilot Halen during much of the journey back East. My mother Susan (the soon-to-be "Dr. Bruder") taught me how to write from early days. My sister Megyn is fierce and fabulous and one of the best things about being back home. Max the dog (aka Mutt-Mutt Wagglebutt) sighed and snuggled beside me through long writing nights.

I'm very lucky for my community, or "logical family," including Douglas Wolk, Rebecca Fitting, Chris Taylor, Jess Taylor Wolfe, Caroline Miller, Josh and Lowen Hunter, Sarah Fan, Chris Hackett, Sarah McMillan, Dorothy Trojanowski, Eleanor Lovinsky, Marlene Kryza, Julia Solis, John Law, Christos Pathiakis, Robert Kutruff, Rob Schmitt, Stacey Cowley, David Dyte, B'Anna Federico, Nate Smith, Raya Dukhan, Michael Evenson, Ellen Taylor, Clark McCasland, Martha Prakelt, Baris Ulku, Shel Kimen, Iva Roze, James Mastrangelo, Niambi Person Jackson, Amelia Klein, Anthony Tranguch, and David Carr, whom I miss terribly. I'm also thankful to my tribes: the Madagascar Institute, the Flaming Lotus Girls, Illumination Village, 29 Hour Music People, and Dark Passage.

Co-conspirator Julia Moburg (aka "Surfer Julia") helped keep me in balance. She is better than marmosets and more than I deserve.

This book is dedicated to my best friend, Dale Maharidge. For the past fourteen years, you've been the voice that answered the phone, no matter the hour.

We are what a modern family looks like.

NOTES

Some of the reporting throughout this book originally appeared in my article "The End of Retirement: When You Can't Afford to Stop Working," *Harper's Magazine*, August 2014.

Sources' ages correspond to the chronology of their stories, rather than the time of publication. All of the people in this book are referred to by their real names, except for Don Wheeler and the people I met while I was working at the sugar beet harvest and CamperForce.

CHAPTER ONE

Much of the reporting in this chapter dates to May 2015, when I traveled with Linda May to Hanna Flat Campground in the San Bernardino National Forest to document her experience working there.

- 3 **United States Geological Survey on San Bernardino Mountains**: https://geomaps.wr.usgs.gov/archive/socal/geology/transverse_ranges/san_bernardino_mtns.
- 3 **San Bernardino Mountains still rising**: Paul W. Bierman-Lytle, "Case Study: San Bernardino Mountains and Urban Communities Interface: Historical, Contemporary and Future," in *Climate Change*

Impacts on High-Altitude Ecosystems, ed. Münir Öztürk et al. Cham, Switzerland: Springer, 2015, pp. 292–93.

4 **Hunter Compact II vintage advertising brochure**: Downloaded from a repository of old RV brochures: http://www.fiberglassrv.com/forums/downloads//ec_tmp/CompactIIBrochure.pdf.

5 **California Land Management brochure and American Land & Leisure banner**: Observed during visits to the annual Quartzsite Sports, Vacation & RV Show in Quartzsite, Arizona, 2014–2016.

7 **Minimum-wage workers' rent shortfall**: Diane Yentel et al., *Out of Reach 2016: No Refuge for Low Income Renters.* Washington, D.C.: The National Low Income Housing Coalition, 2016. http://nlihc.org/sites/default/files/oor/OOR_2016.pdf.

7 **One in six households spends majority of income on housing**: Marcia Fernald, ed., *The State of the Nation's Housing 2016.* Cambridge, MA: Joint Center for Housing Studies of Harvard University, 2016, p. 31. http://www.jchs.harvard.edu/sites/default/files/jchs_2016_state_of_the_nations_housing_lowres_0.pdf.

11 **Ortega Highway hazards**: Dan Weikel, "Driving a Deadly Dinosaur," *The Los Angeles Times*, August 11, 2001, p. A1.

13 **"Grout" didn't stick**: John McKinney, "Grout Bay Trail Leads to History," *The Los Angeles Times*, July 25, 1999, p. 8.

14 **Butler II wildfire consumed more than fourteen thousand acres**: Incident record from Cal Fire, September 21, 2007.

16 **Silvianne's blog**: Silvianne Wanders, The Adventures of a Cosmic Change Agent, https://silviannewanders.wordpress.com.

17 **Lyrics for "Queen of the Road"**: Written by Silvianne K. Delmars and reproduced with her permission.

18 **"A Full Set of Stuff"**: Randy Vining, *Forty Years a Nomad: Poems from the Road*, Kindle ed., self-published, 2015.

18 **Books Linda was reading**: Anne LaBastille, *Woodswoman: Living Alone in the Adirondack Wilderness.* New York: Penguin Books, 1991; Scott Belsky, *Making Ideas Happen: Overcoming the Obstacles between Vision and Reality.* New York: Portfolio, 2012.

23 **Article on workampers Greg and Cathy Villalobos**: Jane Mundy, "California Labor Law Also Applies to Seniors," LawyersAndSettlements.com, July 16, 2014. http://www.lawyersandsettlements.com/articles/california_labor_law/interview-california-labor-law-43-19945.html.

When reached on Facebook, Greg Villalobos confirmed his identity as the man in the article and added via direct message: "The problem is very common but most camp hosts just do the extra work quietly with no compensation. I have worked at two camp host positions and both were handled the same. These were two different companies. I do not do camp hosting anymore. Loved the campers but not the management."

24 **California Land Management's one-star review**: https://www.yelp.com/biz/california-land-management-palo-alto.

25 **Email from California Land Management President Eric Mart**, dated December 26, 2016, also included:

"Working 'off-the-clock' for any reason is a violation of Company policy and employees violating this policy will be subject to disciplinary action up to and including termination of employment. . . .

"In the 36 years we have been in business we have investigated many employee complaints. What we often find is that the facts surrounding the complaint are different than what the employee alleges. When, however, we do find evidence of management abuse we take corrective action against that manager.

"We employ over 450 people during the height of the summer season and we have a very high percentage of our seasonal work force returning from year to year. This would clearly not be happening if our personnel policies were permitting the things alleged in your letter."

CHAPTER TWO

32 **U.S. Postal Service rejected "Casino" as name for a town**: Frank Aleksandrowicz, "Nevada by Day: The Other Attractions Around Las Vegas," *The Elyria Chronicle-Telegram*, June 17, 1990, p. E11.

35 **Dennis Weaver's documentary**: *Dennis Weaver's Earthship*. Directed by Phil Scarpaci. Robert Weaver Enterprises, 1990.

35 **Jokes about Weaver's Earthship by Jay Leno, neighbors**: Associated Press, "Actor Builds Treasure with Other People's Trash," *Colorado Springs Gazette Telegraph*, November 28, 1989, p. B8.

36 **Cost to build Weaver's Earthship**: Patricia Leigh Brown, "Father Earth," *The New York Times*, January 10, 1993, p. A1.

36 **New Zealander Brian Gubb's Earthship**: http://gubbsearthship
.com.

36 **"Earthdinghy" in Seattle**: Sara Bernard, "Earthship!" *Seattle
Weekly*, August 12, 2015, p. 9.

36 **Michael Reynolds on Heaven's Gate**: Martha Mendoza/Associated
Press, "'Earthships' Meld Future with Past," *The Los Angeles Times*,
May 18, 1997, p. 1.

36 **Documentary on Reynolds's struggle**: *Garbage Warrior*. Directed
by Oliver Hodge. Open Eye Media, 2007.

36 **Statements from Reynolds's website**: "monster called the economy": http://earthship.com/a-brief-history-of-earthships; "economy
is a game": http://earthship.com/Designs/earthship-village-ecologies.

38 **Older women and poverty**: Jasmine Tucker and Caitlin Lowell,
National Snapshot: Poverty Among Women & Families, 2015. Washington, D.C.: National Women's Law Center, 2016. http://nwlc.org/wp
-content/uploads/2016/09/Poverty-Snapshot-Factsheet-2016.pdf.

38 **Women earning less Social Security than men**: Joan Entmacher
and Katherine Gallagher Robbins, *Fact Sheet: Women & Social Security*. Washington, D.C.: National Women's Law Center, 2015. http://
nwlc.org/wp-content/uploads/2015/08/socialsecuritykeyfactsfactshe
etfeb2015update.pdf.

38 **Gender pay gap**: Ariane Hegewisch and Asha DuMonthier, *The
Gender Wage Gap: 2015*. Washington, D.C.: Institute for Women's
Policy Research, 2016. http://www.iwpr.org/publications/pubs/the
-gender-wage-gap-2015-annual-earnings-differences-by-gender
-race-and-ethnicity.

38 **Outliving men by five years**: Jiaquan Xu et al., *Mortality in the
United States, 2015*. Hyattsville, MD: Centers for Disease Control
and Prevention National Center for Health Statistics, 2016. https://
www.cdc.gov/nchs/data/databriefs/db267.pdf.

CHAPTER THREE

Most of the reporting about Empire, Nevada, in this chapter originally
appeared in my article "The Last Company Town," *The Christian Science
Monitor*, magazine/print edition, June 13, 2011, p. 33.

42 *The Hills Have Eyes*: The cult classic: *The Hills Have Eyes*. Directed
by Wes Craven. Vanguard, 1977. The remake: *The Hills Have Eyes*.
Directed by Alexandre Aja. Fox Searchlight Pictures, 2006.

44 **Comparing Empire to Chernobyl**: Jenny Kane, "Gypsum Mine, Town of Empire Sold," *The Reno Gazette-Journal*, June 4, 2016, p. A5.

44 **Unfinished coffee and unturned calendars**: Jenny Kane, "Empire Mining Co. Will Only Restore Part of Ghost Town," *The Reno Gazette-Journal*, August 24, 2016, p. A4.

44 **As of this writing, Google Maps** had still not updated its street view and a citizen of Empire could still be seen watering her lawn here: https://www.google.com/maps/@40.572901,-119.34298,3a,75y,340 .84h,74.5t/data=!3m6!1e1!3m4!1sNxqoMbTKOKuCSPqoolMttQ!2e o!7i3328!8i1664.

45 **More than fifteen miles**: "Amazon CamperForce Program," promotional video, published by AmazonFulfillment on July 19, 2013, https://youtu.be/jT1D1RsW1bQ.

47 **"Okies of the Great Recession"**: http://lovable-liberal.blogspot. com/2013/08/grapes-of-workamping.html; "American Refugees": http: //unlawflcombatnt.proboards.com/thread/9293; "Affluent Homeless": http://earlystart.blogs.cnn.com/2012/12/12/workampers-filling -temporary-jobs-for-amazon-com-cnns-casey-wian-reports-on -these-affluent-homeless; "Modern-Day Fruit Tramps": http://union perspectives.blogspot.com/2012/02/workampers-are-new-iww -wobblies.html.

47 **Workamping classifieds**: *Workamper News* http://workamper.com and *Workers on Wheels* http://www.work-for-rvers-and-campers.com.

48 **Preparing for fireworks job**: *Workamper News*, July/August 2013, p. 33.

49 **Story Land recruiting ad**: *Workamper News*, November/December 2015, p. 36.

49 **Georgia farm llamas ad**: *Workamper News*, September/October 2013, p. 20.

49 **Water taxi volunteer ad**: *Workamper News*, September/October 2013, p. 17.

50 **South Dakota residency requirements for "people who travel full time"**: http://dps.sd.gov/licensing/driver_licensing/obtain_a_ license.aspx.

50 **Recreation Resource Management hiring**: Kristyn Martin, "Working into Their 70s: The New Normal for Boomers," *Al-Jazeera America*, October 17, 2014. http://america.aljazeera.com/watch/ shows/real-money-with-alivelshi/2014/10/Workampers-retirement -babyboomers.html.

50 **KOA hiring; Workamper News membership**: Melissa Preddy, "Work Camping: Seasonal Jobs on the Road," *AARP Bulletin*, December 2014.

50 **Fashionable vandwelling**: Eric Spitznagel, "What the Kids Are Doing These Days," *The New York Times Magazine*, November 6, 2011, p. 9.

52 **CamperForce referral bonus $125**: Amazon CamperForce Referral Form, 2015; was $50 in 2012: *Amazon CamperForce Newsletter*, May 2012, p. 5.

52 **CamperForce veterans' tips**: *Amazon CamperForce Newsletter*, July 2012, pp. 2–5.

52 **Hard Times Dance in Fernley, Nevada**: *Amazon CamperForce Newsletter*, April 2012, p. 3.

52 **Pecan-preneurship**: *Amazon CamperForce Newsletter*, March 2013, p. 3.

53 **CamperForce Recruiting handout**: https://www.scribd.com/document/133679509/CamperForce-Recruiting-Handout.

53 **Less touchy-feely incentives**: "Bottom Line at Amazon.com: Money," *Workamper News*, July/August 2014, pp. 31–34.

57 **Busing in workers**: *Amazon CamperForce Newsletter*, July 2013, p. 1.

58 **AmCare**: Unhappy workers later coined the portmanteau "Shamcare" while discussing Amazon's in-house medical service on Facebook.

59 **CamperForce administrator on older workers**: *"Workamper News* Jobinar with Amazon CamperForce," http://www.youtube.com/watch?v=STC3funa1Gg [uploaded March 21, 2013].

59 **Blog comment on Amazon's use of tax credit**: http://talesfromtherampage.com/amazon.

60 **Beet harvest recruiter on older workers**: *"Workamper News* Jobinar with Express Sugar Beet Harvest," https://www.youtube.com/watch?v=cbJtFHJHf_M [uploaded February 26, 2014].

63 **Older Americans' employment**: Bureau of Labor Statistics, U.S. Department of Labor, Labor Force Statistics from the Current Population Survey, Unemployment Level 65 years and over: https://data.bls.gov/timeseries/LNU02000097.

63 **Fear of outliving assets**: "Reclaiming the Future: Challenging Retirement Income Perceptions," Allianz Life Insurance Company of North America, 2010.

63 **Retirement views**: S. Kathi Brown, "Retirement Attitudes Segmentation Survey 2013," AARP Research, Washington, D.C., 2013.

63 **Editorial on William Osler**: "Old Men at Forty," *The New York Times*, February 24, 1905.

64 **Unpopular novel *The Fixed Period***: David Lodge, "Rereading Anthony Trollope," *The Guardian*, December 15, 2012, p. 16.

64 **Pension advocate's dire outlook**: Lee Welling Squier, *Old Age Dependency in the United States: A Complete Survey of the Pension Movement*. New York: The Macmillan Company, 1912, pp. 28–29.

64 **Poorhouses in Colorado and Ohio**: Harry C. Evans, *The American Poorfarm and Its Inmates*, Des Moines, IA: The Loyal Order of the Moose, 1926, pp. 13, 29.

65 **Monopoly poorhouse**: Nancy Altman, "Social Security at 80: Lessons Learned," *The Huffington Post*, August 18, 2015.

65 **Older Americans' self-sufficiency**: U.S. Social Security Administration, "Historical Background and Development of Social Security: Pre–Social Security Period," https://www.ssa.gov/history/briefhistory3.html.

66 **Transferring risk**: Jacob S. Hacker, *The Great Risk Shift: The Assault on American Jobs, Families, Health Care, and Retirement and How You Can Fight Back*. Oxford: Oxford University Press, 2006, pp. x, 5–6.

66 **Social Security as major income source**: "Fact Sheet: Social Security," U.S. Social Security Administration, https://www.ssa.gov/news/press/factsheets/basicfact-alt.pdf.

66 **From three-legged stool to pogo stick**: Emily Brandon, "The Retirement Pogo Stick," *U.S. News & World Report*, February 5, 2009, online only http://money.usnews.com/money/blogs/planning-to-retire/2009/02/05/the-retirement-pogo-stick.

66 **Five-dollars-a-day food budget**: Teresa Ghilarducci, "Our Ridiculous Approach to Retirement," *The New York Times*, July 22, 2012, p. SR5.

67 **Former U.S. Senator Alan Simpson on Social Security**: Jeanne Sahadi, "Co-Chair of Obama Debt Panel under Fire for Remarks," CNNMoney.com, August 25, 2010. http://money.cnn.com/2010/08/25/news/economy/alan_simpson_fiscal_commission.

CHAPTER FOUR

Biographical information on Bob Wells comes from in-person interviews, along with attending his seminars at the Rubber Tramp Rendezvous for three years and reading his website, http://CheapRVLiving.com. (Earlier published versions of the site were accessed via The Wayback Machine, http://archive.org/web/.)

69 **"Maybe you were a gypsy"**: https://web.archive.org/web/20130 114225344/http://cheaprvliving.com.

71 **The Great Alaska Earthquake**: "The Great M9.2 Alaska Earthquake and Tsunami of March 27, 1964," http://earthquake.usgs.gov/ earthquakes/events/alaska1964.

72 **Damage to Denali Elementary School, Anchorage International Airport control tower and J. C. Penney building**: "The Great Alaska Earthquake of 1964: Engineering," National Research Council, 1973, pp. 310, 416–418, 823; Wallace R. Hansen et al., "The Alaska Earthquake: March 27, 1964: Field Investigations and Reconstruction Effort," U.S. Geological Survey, 1966, p. 83.

73 **Bob on getting forced into the van**: "What's Your Vision for Your Life?" https://web.archive.org/web/20120728075840/http://cheaprv livingblog.com/2012/07/whats-your-vision-for-your-life.

73 **Bob on recession popularizing CheapRVLiving.com + fraying social contract**: "Thriving in a Bad Economy," https://web.archive .org/web/20121223110050/http://cheaprvlivingblog.com/2012/09/ thriving-in-a-bad-economy.

74 **Mid-thirties house trailer boom**: David A. Thornburg, *Galloping Bungalows: The Rise and Demise of the American House Trailer*. Hamden, CT: Archon Books, 1991.

74 **Living in house trailers**: "Two Hundred Thousand Trailers," *Fortune*, March 1937, p. 220.

74 **"Escape taxes and rent"**: Philip H. Smith, "House Trailers— Where Do They Go From Here?" *Automotive Industries*, November 14, 1936, p. 680.

75 **Trailer prophesies and Roger Babson**: Clyde R. Miller, "Trailer Life Seen as Good for Nation, Aiding Instead of Displacing Homes," *The New York Times*, December 20, 1936, p. N2.

75 **A new way of life**: Konrad Bercovici, "Gypsy in a Trailer [Part I]," *Harper's Magazine*, May 1937, p. 621.

75 **A million and a half to two million house trailers**: David A. Thornburg, *Galloping Bungalows: The Rise and Demise of the American House Trailer*. Hamden, CT: Archon Books, 1991, p. 181.

75 **Bard of the trailerites**: David A. Thornburg, *Galloping Bungalows: The Rise and Demise of the American House Trailer*. Hamden, CT: Archon Books, 1991, pp. 2, 60–61.

76 **Bob on budgeting**: "Where Does My Money Go?" http://www.cheaprvliving.com/blog/where-does-my-money-go.

77 **Trooper Dan**: http://www.cheaprvliving.com/survivalist-truck-dweller.

77 **Charlene Swankie profiled**: http://www.cheaprvliving.com/inspiring-vandweller-charlenes-story.

80 **Lance5g's introduction**: https://groups.yahoo.com/neo/groups/liveinyourvan/conversations/messages/2.

80 **Ghost Dancer on his jury-rigged internet connection**: https://groups.yahoo.com/neo/groups/vandwellers/conversations/messages/156516.

81 **"Live in Your Van 2" Yahoo group**: https://groups.yahoo.com/neo/groups/VanDwellers.

81 **"Vandwelling's founding father"**: http://swankiewheels.blogspot.com/2012/01/ghost-dance-arrived-at-rtr-today.html.

82 **"Vandwellers: Live in Your Van" Facebook group**: https://www.facebook.com/groups/Vandwellers/files.

83 **Vandwellers subreddit**: https://www.reddit.com/r/vandwellers/.

83 **Walmart parking lot melee**: Jim Walsh, "Family in Walmart Melee Performed," *The Arizona Republic*, March 25, 2015, p. A8; Jon Hutchinson, "Camping Ban Now Enforced at Cottonwood Walmart Store," *The Verde Independent*, March 27, 2015, http://www.verdenews.com/news/2015/mar/27/camping-ban-now-enforced-at-cottonwood-walmart-st.

83 **"Morons" ruining overnight parking**: http://rvdailyreport.com/opinion/opinion-will-walmart-camping-become-thing-of-the-past.

84 **Mobile food pantry founder on Walmart denizens**: Jimmy Maas, "Meet Austin's 'Real People of Walmart,'" KUT 90.5 FM, May 26, 2016, http://kut.org/post/meet-austins-real-people-walmart.

84 **"Walmart Overnight Parking Locator"**: http://www.allstays.com/apps/walmart.htm.

85 **The Adventures of Tioga and George**: http://blog.vagabonders-supreme.net.

85 **Hobo Stripper blog**: https://rvsueandcrew.com.

86 **RV Sue & Her Canine Crew**: older posts: https://rvsueandcrew
.com/; newer posts: http://rvsueandcrew.net.

91 **Jimbo's Journeys blog**: https://jimbosjourneys.com.

CHAPTER FIVE

95 **Amazon Town**: To the best of my knowledge, this phrase for the
ephemeral CamperForce settlements was first coined in the following article's title: Stu Woo, "Welcome to Amazon Town," *The Wall
Street Journal*, December 20, 2011, p. B1.

96 **Climbing anchors**: Shelby Carpenter, "What Happens When
Climbing Bolts Go Bad?" Outside website, November 4, 2015,
https://www.outsideonline.com/2031641/what-happens-when-
climbing-bolts-go-bad.

97 **Hunter charged with starting wildfire**: "Man Charged with Starting Massive California Blaze," The Associated Press, August 8, 2015.

97 **"The Value of Friendship"**: *Amazon CamperForce Newsletter*, June
2013, p. 1.

98 **"Getting Ready to Make History in 2013!"**: *Amazon CamperForce
Newsletter*, March 2013, p. 1.

98 **"What to Expect . . . "**: *Amazon CamperForce Newsletter*, April 2013,
p. 1.

99 **Some of the material about scrutiny of Amazon's warehouses**
originated in my column "With 6,000 Jobs, What Is Amazon Really
Delivering?" Reuters, June 17, 2015, http://blogs.reuters.com/great-
debate/2015/06/17/with-6000-new-warehouse-jobs-what-is-
amazon-really-delivering.

99 **Some of the material about Amazon's employee tracking systems** originated in my article, "We're Watching You Work," *The
Nation* print edition, June 15, 2015, p. 28.

102 **OSHA report**: Nevada Occupational Safety and Health Administration Inspection Report Number 317326056 (October 7, 2013).
This and other reports were provided by Nevada OSHA in response
to a May 2016 request under the Nevada Open Records Act.

103 **Amazon wage case**: Richard Wolf, "Justices Say Security Screening
After Work Isn't Paid Time," *USA Today*, December 9, 2014, http://
www.usatoday.com/story/news/nation/2014/12/09/supreme-court-
amazon-workers-security-screening/20113221.

104 **OSHA inspections dealing with static shocks**: Nevada Occupational Safety and Health Administration Inspection Report Number 315282491 (March 24, 2011) and 316230739 (February 7, 2012).

107 **Chris Farley's vandwelling character**: "Matt Foley, Motivational Speaker," *Saturday Night Live*, NBC, May 8, 1993.

111 **Amazon record holiday sales**: "Record-Setting Holiday Season for Amazon Prime" BusinessWire, December 26, 2013.

CHAPTER SIX

115 **"Garden of Eden on wheels"**: E. B. White, "One Man's Meat," *Harper's Magazine*, May 1941, p. 665.

115 **Year-round population**: 3,626 as per U.S. Census 2015 population estimate, https://factfinder.census.gov/faces/nav/jsf/pages/community _facts.xhtml#.

116 **Itinerant blacksmith's bus visits Quartzsite**: http://www.fulltime .hitchitch.com/dec2010-1.html; Joe Vachon, the blacksmith himself: http://joetheblacksmith.com.

120 **Addicted to Deals is "freaking crazy"**: https://www.yelp.com/biz/ addicted-to-deals-quartzsite.

120 **Architecture of Reader's Oasis**: Bill Graves, "Inside the Desert Bazaar—Quartzsite," *Trailer Life*, November 1999, p. 118.

120 **Preacher quotes**: From a recording I made of the Last Call Tent Ministries service on January 14, 2014.

122 **"Spring Break for Seniors"**: http://obsirius.blogspot.com/2009/01/ like-spring-break-for-seniors.html.

122 **"Poor Man's Palm Springs"**: Mark Shaffer, "Snowbirds Walk on the Wild Side," *The Arizona Republic*, February 22, 2004, p.1.

122 **$180 for up to seven months:** Dennis Godfrey, "Where Friends Are Like Family," *My Public Lands: The Bureau of Land Management Magazine*, Spring 2015, p. 26.

124 **Neighborhood signage in the desert**: http://littleadventures-jg.blogspot.com/2015/01/odds-and-ends-from-quartzsite.htm; http://www.misadventureranch.com/winter07.htm.

124 **Rules for Loners on Wheels**: Henry Wolff Jr., "Loners, But Not Alone!" *The Victoria Advocate*, April 17, 1988, p. 2, and the group's website: http://www.lonersonwheels.com/membership-form.html.

124 **Locals poke fun at nudists**: Comments on Quartzsite Chatter Facebook group, December 8, 2016.

125 **"Bizarre and seriously demented"**: Nicholas Woodsworth, "Flight of the Polyester-Clad Snowbirds," *The Financial Times*, March 8, 1997, p. 19.

125 **Fort Tyson, Quartzsite, Hadji Ali**: Federal Writers' Project, *The WPA Guide to Arizona: The Grand Canyon State*. San Antoinio, TX: Trinity University Press, 2013, p. 361.

125 **Memoirist on Tyson's Wells**: Martha Summerhayes, *Vanished Arizona: Recollections of the Army Life of a New England Woman*. Philadelphia: J. B. Lippincott, 1908, pp. 138–139.

126 **Camel mail from Tucson to Los Angeles**: Kenneth Weisbrode, "The Short Life of the Camel Corps," *The New York Times*, December 27, 2012, http://opinionator.blogs.nytimes.com/2012/12/27/the-short-life-of-the-camel-corps.

126 **Eleven families left**: Peter T. Kilborn, "Where Scorpions Roam and Snowbirds Flock," *The New York Times*, February 10, 2003, p. A1.

126 **Quartzsite flea market origins**: Kate Linthicum, "Keeping It Quirky," *The Los Angeles Times*, April 16, 2011, p. 1.

130 **The Grand Gathering**: http://www.qiaarizona.org/Grand-Gathering.html.

133 **Shooting with Bluebirds**: http://www.wanderlodgeownersgroup.com/forums/showpost.php?p=193151&postcount=126.

CHAPTER SEVEN

135 **The Joads in Needles**: John Steinbeck, *The Grapes of Wrath*. New York: Viking, 1939.

136 **RTR invitation**: http://web.archive.org/web/20140112194330/http://www.cheaprvliving.com/gatherings.

140 **Road warrior-ish future**: http://www.cheaprvliving.com/tribe/report-winter-rtr-january-2014/#comment-10786.

142 **Al Christiansen's Rolling Steel Tent**: http://rollingsteeltent.blogspot.com/2014/01/someone-asked-my-story-fool.html.

142 **Bob's book**: *How to Live in a Car, Van or RV: And Get Out of Debt, Travel & Find True Freedom*, CreateSpace Independent Publishing Platform, 2014, p. 43.

143 **"The knock"**: Charlene Swankie Facebook post, August 13, 2015.

148 **Glenn Morrissette on hearing the Eagles in Los Algodones**: http://tosimplifyold.blogspot.com/2014_01_01_archive.htm.

150 **LaVonne Ellis blogs about her first RTR**: http://completeflake.com/looking-back.

154 **Adventureland Workamper death:** Iowa Occupational Safety and Health Administration Citation and Notification of Penalty (August 16, 2016) following Inspection Number 1154435; Kevin Hardy, "Worker Who Dies Was Just Six Days on His Job," *The Des Moines Register*, June 14, 2016, p. A4.

157 **LaVonne on saying good-bye**: http://completeflake.com/the-down-side-of-vandwelling-is-saying-goodbye.

CHAPTER EIGHT

163 **Chirpy press coverage:** Lynn Neary, "Amazon's Seasonal 'Workampers' Fill Holiday Orders," *All Things Considered*, National Public Radio, December 22, 2011.

164 **No whiners:** Jaimie Hall Bruzenak, "Great Expectations—Do You Need an Attitude Adjustment?" *Workamper News*, September/October 2013, p. 7.

164 **American delusions:** James Rorty, *Where Life Is Better: An Unsentimental American Journey.* New York: Reynal & Hitchcock, 1936, p. 13.

165 **Community in the face of adversity:** Rebecca Solnit, *A Paradise Built in Hell: The Extraordinary Communities That Arise in Disaster.* New York: Viking, 2009.

171 **First night in a van**: Bob Wells, *How to Live in a Car, Van or RV: And Get Out of Debt, Travel, & Find True Freedom*, CreateSpace Independent Publishing Platform, 2014, p. 88.

174 **One in three lack dental coverage**: National Association of Dental Plans, "Who Has Dental Benefits," http://www.nadp.org/Dental_Benefits_Basics/Dental_BB_1.aspx#_ftn1; for further reading, Sarah Smarsh's definitive essay on poverty, stigma, and bad teeth is brilliant: "Poor Teeth," *Aeon*, October 23, 2014, https://aeon.co/essays/there-is-no-shame-worse-than-poor-teeth-in-a-rich-world.

175 **The Wandering Individuals Network**: http://rvsingles.org.

179 **Amazon's official CamperForce page on Facebook**: https://www.facebook.com/amazoncamperforce.

179 **"Roughing it" and privilege:** Christian Lander, "#128 Camping," Stuff White People Like, August 14, 2009, https://stuffwhitepeoplelike .com/2009/08/14/128-camping.

CHAPTER NINE

185 **Truck accidents:** Sarah Volpenhein, "Amid Sugar Beet Truck Accidents, Some Question Minnesota, North Dakota Regulations for Ag Drivers," *The Grand Forks Herald*, October 7, 2015, http://www .grandforksherald.com/news/business/3856308-amid-sugar-beet-truck-accidents-some-question-minnesota-north-dakota.

194 **Definition of "takt":** https://ocw.mit.edu/courses/engineering-systems-division/esd-60-lean-six-sigma-processes-summer-2004/ lecture-notes/8_1assembly_op.pdf.

CHAPTER TEN

202 **LaVonne on feeling homeless:** http://www.completeflake.com/ what-vandwelling-is-really-like.

203 **LaVonne on untouchables:** http://www.completeflake.com/second -chances.

204 **Bob's definition of homeless:** Bob Wells, *How to Live in a Car, Van or RV: And Get Out of Debt, Travel, & Find True Freedom*, CreateSpace Independent Publishing Platform, 2014, pp. 6–7.

205 **NYT on criminalizing homelessness:** Adam Nagourney, "Aloha and Welcome to Paradise. Unless You're Homeless," *The New York Times*, June 3, 2016, https://www.nytimes.com/2016/06/04/us/ hawaii-homeless-criminal-law-sitting-ban.html.

205 **"Residential use" of the forest:** Cyndy Cole, "Some Folks Camping Out for Life," *The Arizona Daily Sun*, August 9, 2011, http:// azdailysun.com/news/local/some-folks-camping-out-for-life/ article_5623148e-2326-5ce2-97c2-2ce18b6cde82.html.

205 **Forest Service developing app:** Zach Urness, "Trashing the Forest: Long-Term Camping Causes Environmental Problems," *The Statesman Journal*, April 19, 2016, p. D3.

206 **"The gasoline gypsy":** Editorial, "Trailer Lessons," *The New York Times*, May 4, 1937, p. 24.

206 **"Motor slums":** "Two Hundred Thousand Trailers," *Fortune*, March 1937, p. 106.

206 **"Tax Dodger"**: "Slants," *Automotive Industries*, October 31, 1936, p. 564.

206 **LaVonne got "the knock"**: http://completeflake.com/the-dreaded-knock.

CHAPTER ELEVEN

209 **"America is the wealthiest nation"**: Kurt Vonnegut, *Slaughterhouse-Five*. New York: Dell Publishing, 1991, pp. 128–129.

209 **LaVonne on Linda**: http://completeflake.com/why-i-spent-the-day -at-the-laundromat-or-shit-happens.

211 **$1.5 billion Powerball**: Charles Riley, Sara Sidner, and Tina Burnside, "We Have Powerball Winners!" CNNMoney, January 14, 2016, http://money.cnn.com/2016/01/13/news/powerball-winner-lottery.

216 **Bob on future slump**: http://www.cheaprvliving.com/budget/poverty-prepping-food-pantry.

224 **Haboobs**: Marc Lacey, "'Haboobs' Stir Critics in Arizona," *The New York Times*, July 22, 2011, p. A11; Don Yonts, "Don't Call Our Dust Storm Haboobs," *The Arizona Republic*, July 16, 2011, p. B4.

225 **Once Arizona's largest town**: Thomas Palmer, "A Town in Search of a Future," *The Boston Globe*, February 8, 1987, p. 73.

226 **Clean Air Act history**: https://www.epa.gov/clean-air-act-overview/evolution-clean-air-act.

226 **Smelter pollution**: Iver Peterson, "Acid Rain Starting to Affect Environment and Politics in West," *The New York Times*, March 30, 1985, p. 6; Scott McCartney, "Country Town's Air Goes up in Smoke of Copper Smelters," *The Los Angeles Times*, July 27, 1986, p. 2.

226 **Smelter closure**: "Last Copper Is Poured at a Polluting Smelter," *The New York Times*, January 15, 1987, p. A14.

226 **Blame the communists**: Thomas Palmer, "A Town in Search of a Future," *The Boston Globe*, February 8, 1987, p. 73.

226 **Hospital closure**: Anthony Brino, "Cochise Regional Hospital in Arizona to Close after Medicare Stops Reimbursements over Safety," *Healthcare Finance News*, July 29, 2015, http://www.healthcare financenews.com/news/cochise-regional-hospital-arizona-close-after-medicare-stops-reimbursements-over-safety.

226 **Fourth-fastest-shrinking city**: Thomas C. Frohlich, "Going, Going, Gone: America's Fastest-Shrinking Cities," *USA Today*, April 8, 2016,

http://www.usatoday.com/story/money/2016/04/08/24-7-wallst-america-shrinking-cities-population-migration/82740600.

227 **Douglas's Grand Theatre**: Bonnie Henry, "Keeping Their Dream Alive," *The Arizona Daily Star*, June 19, 2008, p. E1; Cindy Hayostek, "Haunted Theatre a Success," *The Douglas Dispatch*, November 5, 2002, http://www.douglasdispatch.com/news/haunted-theatre-a-success/article_674369bc-6037-529a-8325-64394a4a8d6a.html; National Registry of Historic Places Nomination Form, Entered July 30, 1976, http://focus.nps.gov/nrhp/GetAsset?assetID=684cabb 7-8870-4872-bffc-b0492928ffb6.

227 **Newcomers to Douglas**: Perla Trevizo and Luis F. Carrasco, "Artists Try to Help Paint New Future for Douglas," *The Arizona Daily Star*, December 19, 2015, p. A1.

228 **El Chapo's tunnel**: "Agents Find Drug Tunnel to U.S.," Associated Press, *The New York Times*, May 19, 1990, p. 7; Monte Reel, "Underworld," *The New Yorker*, August 3, 2015, p. 22; Adam Higginbotham, "The Narco Tunnels of Nogales," *Bloomberg Businessweek*, August 6–12, 2012, p. 56.

229 **Sixteen-year-old smuggler**: Nigel Duara, "Teen Drug Mules Are in for a Shock in Arizona; County Charges Them as Adults Instead of Freeing Them," *The Los Angeles Times*, May 3, 2016, p. A1.

229 **Homemade zip line**: Perla Trevizo, "Beyond the Wall: Shifting Challenges on Rugged Arizona Line," *The Arizona Daily Star*, July 10, 2016, p. F9.

229 **Scuba smuggler**: Devlin Houser, "Man in Sewer System Drops 55 Lbs. of Weed," *The Arizona Daily Star*, February 27, 2010, p. A9; Brenna Goth, "Creative Pot Smugglers Try 'a Little Bit of Everything,'" *The Arizona Daily Star*, September 28, 2011, p. A1.

230 **Drone drops pot**: Elahe Izadi, "What a Marijuana Bundle Dropped from the Sky Can Do to a Doghouse," *The Washington Post*, September 28, 2015, https://www.washingtonpost.com/news/post-nation/wp/2015/09/28/what-a-marijuana-bundle-dropped-from-the-sky-can-do-to-a-dog-house.

238 **Pirate's den**: Lawrence W. Cheek, "Heritage Hotels: Time Stands Still at Four Historic Arizona Hotels Rife with Amusing Quirks and Characters of the Old West," *The Los Angeles Times*, January 5, 1992, p. L1.

CODA

244 **New rules at RTR**: http://www.cheaprvliving.com/blog/rubber-tramp-rendezvous-schedule-2017.

247 **The bottom half's income**: Patricia Cohen, "A Bigger Economic Pie, but a Smaller Slice for Half of the U.S.," *The New York Times*, December 6, 2016, https://www.nytimes.com/2016/12/06/business/economy/a-bigger-economic-pie-but-a-smaller-slice-for-half-of-the-us.html.

247 **Einstein's brain**: Stephen Jay Gould, "Wide Hats and Narrow Minds," *New Scientist*, March 8, 1979, p. 777.

248 **Dampening growth**: Sean McElwee, "Three Ways Inequality Is Making Life Worse for Everyone," *Salon*, Friday, April 3, 2015, http://www.salon.com/2015/04/03/3_ways_inequality_is_making_life_worse_for_everyone.

248 **U.S. most unequal**: "Inequality Update," Organisation for Economic Co-operation and Development, November 2016, https://www.oecd.org/social/OECD2016-Income-Inequality-Update.pdf.

248 **Comparing nations' inequality**: http://www.indexmundi.com/facts/indicators/SI.POV.GINI/rankings.

248 **Octopus in a coconut**: https://www.facebook.com/LADbible/videos/2969897786390725.